COMPUTER SCIENCE

AND CODING

Library of Congress Cataloging-in-Publication Data is available.

ISBN 978-1-5235-0277-6

Author: Grant Smith
Illustrator: Chris Pearce
Vetter: Dawn Dupriest
Designer: Abby Dening
Concept by Raquel Jaramillo

Workman books are available at special discounts when purchased in bulk for premiums and sales promotions, as well as for fund-raising or educational use. Special editions or book excerpts can also be created to specification. For details, contact the Special Sales Director at the address below or send an email to specialmarkets@workman.com.

Workman Publishing Co., Inc.
225 Varick Street
New York, NY 10014-4381
workman.com

Printed in Thailand

First printing March 2020

10 9 8 7 6 5 4 3 2 1

THE **COMPLETE** MIDDLE SCHOOL STUDY GUIDE

EVERYTHING YOU NEED TO ACE COMPUTER SCIENCE

AND CODING

IN ONE BIG FAT NOTEBOOK

WORKMAN PUBLISHING
NEW YORK

EVERYTHING YOU NEED TO ACE

COMPUTER SCIENCE

AND CODING

HI!

In this notebook you'll find everything you'll need to ace computer science and coding: from understanding computer systems to reading and writing with programming languages; from using basic algorithms to writing Boolean expressions; from working with Scratch and Python to exploring web development. This is the really important stuff that you'll need to understand computer science and to build a foundation in coding.

You'll find the notes pretty straightforward, with the following formatting to keep things organized:

- vocabulary words highlighted in **YELLOW**
- definitions set aside in boxes
- important people, places, dates, and terms written in blue
- doodles, graphics, and charts that show the big ideas
- main ideas underlined

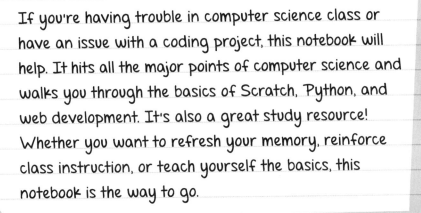

If you're having trouble in computer science class or have an issue with a coding project, this notebook will help. It hits all the major points of computer science and walks you through the basics of Scratch, Python, and web development. It's also a great study resource! Whether you want to refresh your memory, reinforce class instruction, or teach yourself the basics, this notebook is the way to go.

CONTENTS

UNIT 1: COMPUTING SYSTEMS **1**

1. What Is Computer Science? **2**
2. What Is a Computer? **13**
3. How Do We Interact with Computers? **29**

UNIT 2: DATA AND ANALYSIS **39**

4. Storing Information **40**
5. Collecting and Using Information **57**

UNIT 3: SOFTWARE ENGINEERING 67

6. Designing Computer Systems 68
7. Testing 73
8. Documenting 81
9. Incorporating Feedback 89
10. Collaborating 97

UNIT 4: ALGORITHMS AND PROGRAMMING 109

11. Using Algorithms 110
12. Programming Languages 121
13. Computational Thinking 139

UNIT 5: UNIVERSAL PROGRAMMING PRINCIPLES 147

14. Variables 148
15. Conditional Statements 163
16. Loops 179
17. Events 187
18. Procedures 191

I AM A DATA TYPE.

UNIT 6: PROGRAMMING WITH SCRATCH 199

19. Getting Started 200
20. Basic Algorithms 223
21. Data and Operators 247
22. Control Blocks and Event Blocks 273
23. Reusing Scripts 299

UNIT 7: PROGRAMMING IN PYTHON **309**

24. Getting Started with Python **310**
25. Variables in Python **323**
26. Strings **333**
27. Numbers as Variables **351**
28. Lists and Boolean Expressions **365**
29. *For* Loops **381**
30. *While* Loops and Nested Loops **393**
31. Conditional Statements **403**
32. Functions **423**

LET'S GET CODING!

UNIT 8: WEB DEVELOPMENT **443**

33. What Is the Internet? **444**
34. Cybersecurity **463**
35. Creating a Basic Web Page **481**
36. HTML Text Elements **497**
37. Link Elements **511**
38. Styling with CSS **523**
39. Styling Individual Elements with CSS **539**

PASSWORDS

Index **555**

Unit 1

Computing Systems

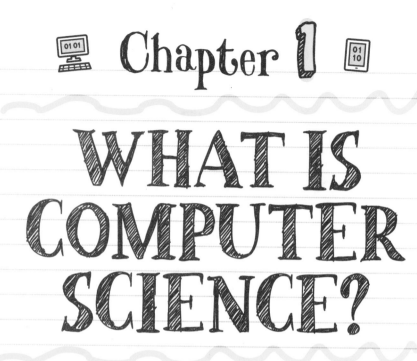

Chapter 1

WHAT IS COMPUTER SCIENCE?

A **COMPUTER** is a device that stores and processes (changes, moves, or rewrites) information. It can perform complicated computations and organize and store huge amounts of information. Computer science is the study of computers and how computer technology can be used to solve problems. It involves studying **COMPUTING SYSTEMS**, programming rules, data and analysis, networking, the internet, and how computers affect our lives. Computers are better than humans at storing and sharing tons

> **COMPUTING SYSTEM**
> All the basic hardware (the parts you can see and touch) and software (the programs) that work together to make a computer run.

of information, solving complex calculations quickly, and learning things. Computer scientists use computers' abilities to help them develop new technologies that make our lives easier.

Computer technology affects the way we live and think. It can help us solve our problems and make our lives seem easier, more fun, and safer.

For example:

* Computers helped navigate spacecraft to the moon and Mars.

* Robots help surgeons perform surgeries with great precision.

* Computers add realistic visual and sound effects to movies and video games.

Computer scientists use and create technology to solve problems. They program computers to both complete tasks better and faster as well as teach them how to do new things. Becoming a computer scientist means shifting from being only a **consumer** (someone who uses something) to being a **creator**.

Computer science is a type of problem solving; it includes the study of computers, their design, and the way they process information.

Examples of what computer science IS and IS NOT:

COMPUTER SCIENCE IS	COMPUTER SCIENCE IS NOT
creating a phone app (application or program) that allows friends to share funny cat videos with each other.	watching videos on the internet of cats riding tricycles.
programming your own video game.	playing your favorite video game.

COMPUTER SCIENCE IS	COMPUTER SCIENCE IS NOT
writing a program that calculates the answers to the math problems in your homework.	doing your math homework on your school's laptop.
writing a program to automatically post nice comments on your friends' pictures.	commenting on the latest picture your friend posted.

All the examples in the **IS NOT** list only use technology, while the examples in the **IS** list create new technology.

DON'T JUST PLAY ON YOUR PHONE. PROGRAM IT!

THE FIVE CONCEPT AREAS OF COMPUTER SCIENCE

Computer science can be divided into five concept areas (main parts) of study:

1. Computing Systems

Computing systems are the machines that run programs and process information. Examples are desktop computers, laptops, and phones. Many electronic devices are run by **PROGRAMS** and have small built-in computers. For example, dishwashers, TVs, smart watches, and even some light bulbs.

2. Algorithms and Programming

ALGORITHMS and programming involve writing the programs (code) that tell computers what to do. Programs can be very complex—like iTunes, Safari, Chrome, or Roblox—following many different instructions. They can also be simple, like a program that only prints out the message "Hello, World!"

PROGRAM

A set of instructions (or an algorithm) that has been translated into commands a computer can understand (**code**).

ALGORITHM

A list of steps or instructions written in human language that tells a person how to complete a task.

Writing a program is sometimes broken up into two steps:

STEP 1: The computer scientist makes a list of step-by-step instructions for what she wants her program to do.

Algorithm

STEP 2: The computer scientist translates her instructions into a language (code) the computer can understand. Now the algorithm is a program.

Programming

Computers are powerful, but they really aren't that smart. They can only do what they're told. Programs give computers the instructions they need to work.

3. Data and Analysis

DATA and **ANALYSIS** refer to collecting, storing, organizing, and studying facts to help us understand what the data means. For example, in a personality test program, we would want to collect answers to questions (such as: "Do you like having lots of friends over to play games?" or "How do you like to spend your free time?"), store the answers, and study them to understand someone's personality. Another simple use of data might be to collect and store the score in a video game so that we can see if a player has won, or who the highest scorer was.

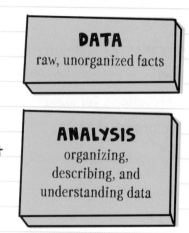

DATA
raw, unorganized facts

ANALYSIS
organizing, describing, and understanding data

Computers are great at storing, sharing, and calculating huge amounts of data. This makes them perfect for analyzing data.

4. Networks and the Internet

NETWORKS are a group of connected devices (like computers, laptops, and servers). They share information, and may also share resources like a printer. The **INTERNET** is the worldwide network that connects millions of computers. Part of studying networks and the internet is figuring out better and more secure ways to share information across devices.

5. Impacts of Computing

Understanding the impacts of computing involve studying how computers influence our lives, culture, safety, laws, and behavior. Just because we can make new technologies doesn't always mean we *should*.

We should ask how these new technologies affect the lives of others.

For example, what if you made a program that could hack anyone's phone and delete all their favorite pictures?

Questions to consider:

- What would the effect be on the victims' lives?

- How would your actions affect your friendships?

- Are there laws against using such programs?

- Would it be wrong to share a program like that even if we didn't use it ourselves?

- Would this new technology make life better or worse for others?

CHECK YOUR KNOWLEDGE

1. What is computer science?

2. Which of these are most likely NOT computing systems?
   A. Cell phones
   B. Newer TVs
   C. Books
   D. Electronic readers

3. What is a program, and why do computers need programs?

4. Computer science is NOT:
   A. Studying interesting questions like how to make deliveries faster using an algorithm
   B. Building a computing system as a solution to a problem
   C. Playing computer games
   D. Understanding how a new computer technology could negatively impact people

5. What is a computing system? Provide examples of computing systems.

6. Computer scientists have created systems that help farmers produce more food for society. This advancement most closely represents which of the five concept areas of computer science?

7. What is the difference between a consumer and a creator?

8. What is a group of connected computers called?

9. Reviewing a collection of student scores from an exam to understand how well the class did is an example of which concept area of computer science?

10. Explain what an algorithm is.

CHECK YOUR ANSWERS

1. Computer science is the study of using computers to solve problems.

2. C

3. A program is a set of instructions that has been coded into a language that a computer can understand. Without programs, computers wouldn't understand what we want them to do.

4. C

5. Computing systems are one or more computing devices. They include laptops, tablets, and other devices that are run by programs.

6. Impacts of computing. While each of the five concept areas of computer science are used to develop better tools for farmers, the emphasis on how it benefits society makes this an example of impacts of computing.

7. Consumers only use programs or content. Creators make the content that consumers use.

8. A network, or computer network

9. Data and analysis

10. An algorithm is a list of instructions on how to do something.

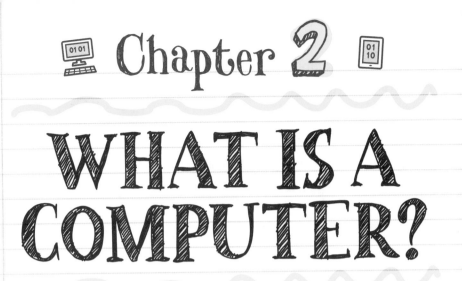

Chapter 2

WHAT IS A COMPUTER?

A **COMPUTER** stores, shares, and analyzes huge amounts of data. It can also perform complex math calculations.

> Although a CD (compact disc) can store information like music, it's not considered a computer because the CD itself can't change information.

COMPUTERS THROUGH TIME

Thousands of years ago, people made devices like the **ABACUS** to help them calculate complex math.

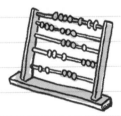

In the 1600s, computing became
a profession and the word "computer"
meant "a person who makes
calculations." Computers (the people)
used a tool called the **SLIDE RULE**
to help them calculate.

In 1944, during World War II,
the first electronic computer
was made.
It was called
COLOSSUS MARK 1
and was used
by the British
government to
crack secret
German codes.

THIS IS
A BIG
COMPUTER.

In 1945, Americans created a faster computer called ENIAC.

ENIAC
Stands for "Electronic Numerical
Integrator and Computer," which
was the first programmable,
general-purpose computer.

Early computers were massive—they took up entire rooms! These computers were used by large businesses, governments, or researchers.

The first mass-produced personal computer, the APPLE II, was introduced in 1977. Owners could use the computer to run simple programs or play games.

Today, computers are tiny and everywhere, including phones. Smartphones are considered computers because:

- they run programs (like messaging, photo editing, and maps).

- they store information (like photos, contact information, and documents).

- they perform calculations (with a calculator, with the clock/stopwatch, with maps).

Smartphones are more powerful computers than the computer used on the rocket that took astronauts to the moon in 1969.

PARTS OF A WHOLE

Computers are made up of two parts:
HARDWARE and **SOFTWARE**.

Hardware

Hardware is the physical parts of a computer, like the keyboard, mouse, and screen. An easy way to determine whether part of a computer system is hardware is to look: If you can see it with your eyes, it's hardware.

Software

Software is the set of programs (instructions) that tell a computer what to do, like phone applications, editing programs, and entertainment services. There are all kinds of software: from games for a gaming system, to the program that runs your microwave, to the web browser on your phone. Software is stored on storage devices (hardware) like hard drives, flash drives, and CDs.

> An **application** (app) is a program designed for the user to perform a task—like take a photo.
>
> All applications are programs, but not all programs are applications. Some programs are for the computer's use only—not the person using the computer.

A CLOSER LOOK AT HARDWARE

Hardware can be separated into different categories:

Input

Input refers to the parts used to send information to a computer, including a keyboard, mouse, game controller, and webcam.

A LITTLE TO THE LEFT!

Storage

Storage refers to the parts that the computer uses to store information, including hard drives, **USB FLASH DRIVES**, CDs, and **RAM**.

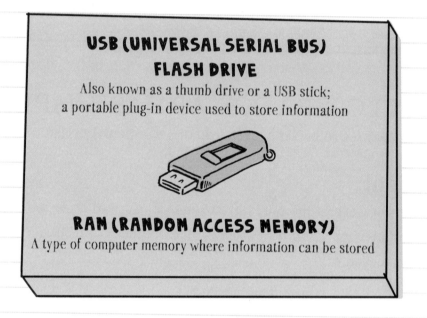

USB (UNIVERSAL SERIAL BUS) FLASH DRIVE

Also known as a thumb drive or a USB stick; a portable plug-in device used to store information

RAM (RANDOM ACCESS MEMORY)

A type of computer memory where information can be stored

Processing

The processing parts of the computer run programs, interpret input, and supply output, including the central processing unit (CPU) and the graphics processing unit (GPU).

CENTRAL PROCESSING UNIT (CPU)

This is the brain of a computer. It receives input information and executes commands from other hardware and software.

It is made up of the main memory, the control unit, and the arithmetic logic unit.

GRAPHICS PROCESSING UNIT (GPU)

This part of the computer focuses on graphics. Graphics are images of all kinds (pictures, animations, videos). The GPU delivers images, animations, and videos that can be viewed on the computer's screen. If you want to get the best picture quality for your favorite computer game, you'll need a high-end GPU to make the graphics look good.

Think of the CPU as a jack-of-all-trades (like a handyman) and the GPU as the master of a trade (like a plumber). The CPU is great for completing a variety of everyday tasks well; the GPU specializes in processing display information quickly. You wouldn't want a handyman to replace all the pipes in your home. Instead, you'd want your plumber to use his or her special skills to perform that task.

Output

Output refers to the parts that the computer uses to send information to you. This includes the projector, the monitor, the printer, speakers, and headphones.

The parts of hardware all work together. Data (information) comes from the user (who may be a person or a computer) and goes through the input device into processing. Data can then be placed in storage (saved) or taken out of storage and then sent to the user.

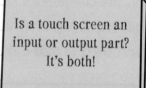

Is a touch screen an input or output part? It's both!

The process is like digestion: We take in food, process it and store it, and then pass it out.

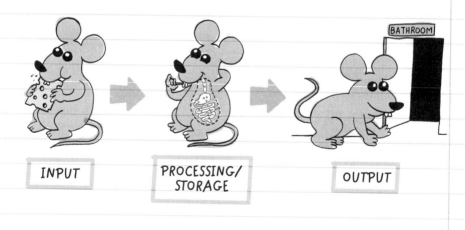

INPUT

PROCESSING/ STORAGE

OUTPUT

A CLOSER LOOK AT SOFTWARE

Application Software (Apps)

Application software (apps) are programs that allow the user to complete tasks.

"App" is short for "application."

Word processors, internet browsers, and games are all examples of application software. Every app in a phone's app store is also application software. There's a wide variety of application software, and programmers can specialize in one of the subcategories.

FOR EXAMPLE

* A WEB DEVELOPER is a programmer who makes application software that runs on websites.

* A MOBILE DEVELOPER is a programmer who writes application software for mobile devices like phones and tablets.

* A GAME DEVELOPER is a programmer who develops application software video games.

System Software

System software are the programs that make sure the individual hardware devices work together and properly with other programs. **OPERATING SYSTEMS** like Windows on a laptop or iOS (the mobile operating system) on an iPhone are examples of system software. Operating systems run in the background; you cannot see what they're doing on-screen. The operating system makes it possible to install games, social media, and other apps on the phone.

Applications cannot work without the system software.

OPERATING SYSTEMS
Programs that communicate with hardware, allowing other programs to run in the background.

Hardware and software are pretty much useless on their own. Only when they are put together in a complete system do they become tools.

For example:

HARDWARE		SOFTWARE		FINAL RESULT
CAMERA	+	PHOTO APP	=	PHONE TO TAKE SELFIES
KEYBOARD + PRINTER	+	WORD PROCESSING PROGRAM	=	PRINTED PARTY INVITATION
CAR + SENSORS + CAMERAS	+	STREET NAVIGATION PROGRAM	=	SELF-DRIVING CAR

CHECK YOUR KNOWLEDGE

1. What is the difference between hardware and software?

2. What is a computer?

3. How have computers changed over time?

4. What kind of hardware is each of these parts? Choose from **input**, **output**, **processing**, or **storage**.
   A. TV screen: _____
   B. CPU: _____
   C. Keyboard: _____
   D. Headphones: _____
   E. USB flash drive: _____

5. How are storage and processing hardware parts different? Are they both necessary for a computer to work?

6. What is the difference between the CPU and the GPU?

7. Why was the Apple II significant?

8. How is a new smartphone similar to the first computers ever made? How is it different?

9. What kinds of tools existed before programmable computers were invented?

10. What is the difference between system software and application software?

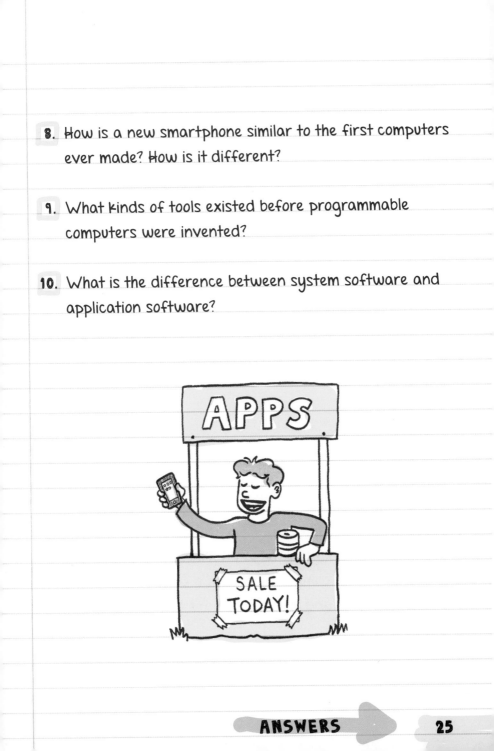

CHECK YOUR ANSWERS

1. Hardware is the physical parts of a computer, and software is the code or programs that the computers run.

2. A computer is a device that stores and processes information.

3. Computers have become smaller and much, much more powerful over time.

4. Hardware:
   A. Output
   B. Processing
   C. Input
   D. Output
   E. Storage

5. A processing unit like a CPU runs programs, and a storage unit like RAM stores information. Both parts are necessary in a computer because a computer is a device that can store and manipulate data (which requires a processor).

6. A CPU is the main brain of a computer and runs most of the programs, while the GPU mainly processes display information for your screen.

7. It was the first mass-produced personal computer.

8. Just like the first computers, smartphones use both software and hardware to run. They also both have input, output, storage, and processing parts. But smartphones are much more powerful and many times smaller than the first computers.

9. Before programmable computers were invented, there were several tools that humans used to help solve math equations, like the abacus and the slide rule.

10. System software makes sure the individual hardware devices properly work together and with other programs. Application software are programs that allow the user to perform specific tasks.

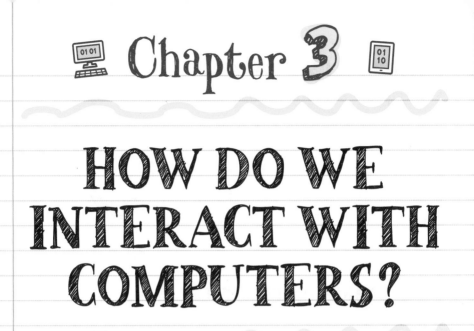

Chapter 3

HOW DO WE INTERACT WITH COMPUTERS?

Over time, computers have become easier to use. However, things can still go wrong. When problems happen, there are things you can do.

HUMAN-COMPUTER INTERACTION

The **USER INTERFACE** (UI) includes all the parts of a computing system that you use to operate the computer. For example, the user interface for playing a video game on a phone includes the touch screen, speakers/headphones, and the game's on-screen menus, buttons, and graphics.

A **GRAPHICAL USER INTERFACE** (GUI, pronounced "GOO-ey," like soft brownies) is a type of user interface that uses icons and symbols on a screen instead of just plain text. A GUI makes it easy for just about anyone to use a computer. Most user interfaces are GUIs.

The **COMMAND-LINE INTERFACE** (command line, or CLI) uses only text to operate a computer. This type of interface is more difficult to use because the user must type in specific commands, or phrases, for it to work. Although most computer users will never need to use a command-line interface, it's a good thing to learn if you're a computer scientist.

Human-computer interaction (HCI) is the part of computer science that studies and improves how the user works with computers. UIs are easy for all people to use, including those who are blind or low vision or are deaf or hard of hearing.

You can try out an example of human-computer interaction by finding the "Accessibility" settings on your computer or phone and turning on the screen reader to listen to it read aloud what's on the display.

TROUBLESHOOTING

Troubleshooting is taking a systematic, or step-by-step, approach to solving errors within a computing system or software. Or, debugging programs in software.

Using a **systematic approach** means following a fixed plan or process, step-by-step. Like instructions for making a PB&J sandwich. If your computer won't turn on, one of the first things you would do is make sure it is plugged into a power source, and then you would check that all the power connectors inside the computer are connected securely. The benefit to a systematic approach is that you can repeat the steps exactly and you can be sure you haven't left anything out.

WHERE'S THE JELLY?

Debugging is finding and correcting "bugs," or errors, within a program. Debugging is a specific form of troubleshooting that is used when programming. Bugs may be caused by typos or by not following the rules or format of the programming language.

WHEE!

Troubleshooting Strategies

Troubleshooters use some of these strategies to help them find and fix problems:

- Swapping in working parts from other computers, such as monitors, keyboards, and even hard drives, motherboards, or power supplies.

- Creating a diagram to trace the problem. For example, creating a diagram of all the components in a computer system and how they connect to each other helps a troubleshooter stay organized as they hunt for the problem.

- Making changes in the software to see if the hardware will work. Sometimes a software update has bugs in it and you may need to go back to the previous version. Or maybe you just need to install a new driver (a program that tells the computer how to interact with a piece of hardware).

- Checking software settings and the compatibility of components. Some software is made for specific hardware. For example, you can't install an iPhone app on an Android phone.

- Getting help from a more knowledgeable troubleshooter. Sometimes an issue is too big for one person to solve on their own. There are many websites dedicated to helping people troubleshoot all sorts of computer issues—they are a great resource to search through.

CHECK YOUR KNOWLEDGE

1. What is troubleshooting?

2. Which of these is NOT a troubleshooting technique:
   A. Using a checklist
   B. Getting help from someone else
   C. Replacing a computer
   D. Swapping out parts one at a time

3. What does taking a systematic approach mean? Why is it useful?

4. If your computer won't turn on, which of these things should you do first?
   A. Try to take it apart.
   B. Make sure the power cable is plugged in.
   C. Assume it's broken and return it to the store.
   D. Press hard on the keys.

5. What is debugging?

6. How is troubleshooting different from debugging?

7. Which area in computer science studies the user interface of computers?

8. When you're playing a game on an iPad, which type of user interface is used?

9. What makes a good user interface?

CHECK YOUR ANSWERS

1. Solving problems by using a systematic, or step-by-step, approach.

2. C

3. It means using a step-by-step process that is repeatable with similar results.

4. B

5. Debugging is finding and fixing errors in a program.

6. Troubleshooting is the general process for fixing problems, but debugging specifically has to do with finding and fixing errors in a program (the code).

7. Human-computer interaction

8. Graphical user interface (GUI)

9. A good user interface is one that makes it easy for all types of users to use.

Unit

2

DATA RULES!

Data and Analysis

Chapter 4

STORING INFORMATION

THE INFORMATION AGE

Our world has moved through the Stone Age, the Dark Ages, and the Industrial Age. Many say that right now we are living in the INFORMATION AGE. That's because we have shifted

PAST

STONE AGE

DARK AGES

from a focus on making stuff with our hands to using information technology to create. We have found new ways to use information to help us create.

Computers are **INFORMATION PROCESSORS**. This means they take information and make it easier for us to use. For example:

- **Map apps** process information from satellites to help us find the quickest route to our destination and even avoid traffic.

- **Social media apps** (such as Snapchat, Twitter, Instagram, or Facebook) process our personal information (likes, posts, etc.) and create profiles

INDUSTRIAL AGE   INFORMATION AGE

FUTURE

of who we are that businesses can use to try to sell us stuff.

Note: You don't pay anything to use social networks, but that doesn't mean they are free. The cost of using them is that you hand over tons of information about yourself. That's why it's always important to get guardians' permission and guidance before giving out ANY personal information online.

- **Self-driving cars** gather and analyze large amounts of information to make predictions and decisions. **RADAR** (using radio frequency to detect the presence of or distance from an object), **LIDAR** (using laser light to

RADAR
Stands for "<u>ra</u>dio <u>d</u>etection and <u>r</u>anging"

LIDAR
Stands for "<u>li</u>ght <u>d</u>etection and <u>r</u>anging"

measure the distance to a target), ultrasonic sound waves, and video recordings from cars' external cameras and sensors are collected, temporarily stored on the cars' hard drives, then sent over the internet to powerful computers that analyze the data using artificial intelligence (AI) programs. The AI programs piece the data together to learn how to drive by analyzing how humans drive safely.

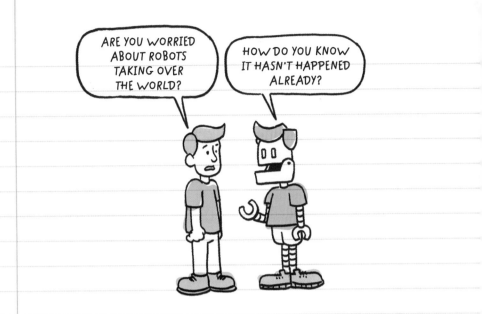

The more information we have and the better tools we have to understand the information, the better decisions we can make. For example, when you try to buy a birthday present for your friend, it is much easier to do than trying to buy a present for a new kid that just moved into town. This is because you have more information about your friend, so you're able to make a better decision about what they would like.

COMPUTERS USE DATA

DATA is a collection of unorganized figures, words, and numbers that have not yet been given meaning. Data has many different forms depending on what kind of information it represents.

INFORMATION is data that has been organized to have meaning. A context is given to the data. For example, all the answers to a survey are data, and the average of the results is information.

Input data is the unorganized information entered into the computer.

Output data is the information after the computer has processed it.

the computer processes

INPUT DATA ➡	OUTPUT DATA
In a video game: pressing keys or buttons on a game console	The character moving around the screen 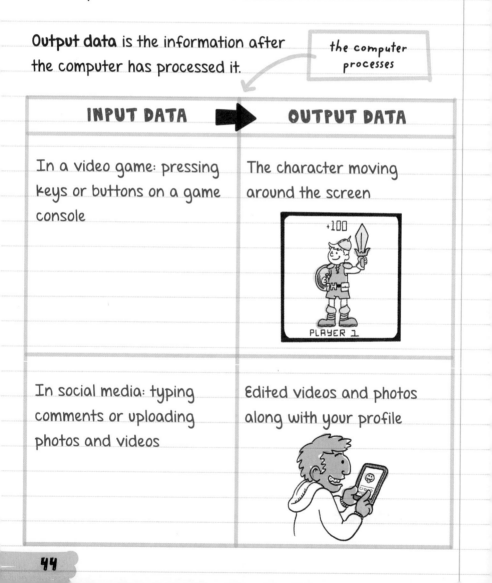
In social media: typing comments or uploading photos and videos	Edited videos and photos along with your profile

INPUT DATA ➡	OUTPUT DATA
On a microwave oven: selecting numbers or buttons on the keypad	The food cooking in the oven for a given amount of time
In a graphing program: entering numbers for different categories	A graph of the numbers

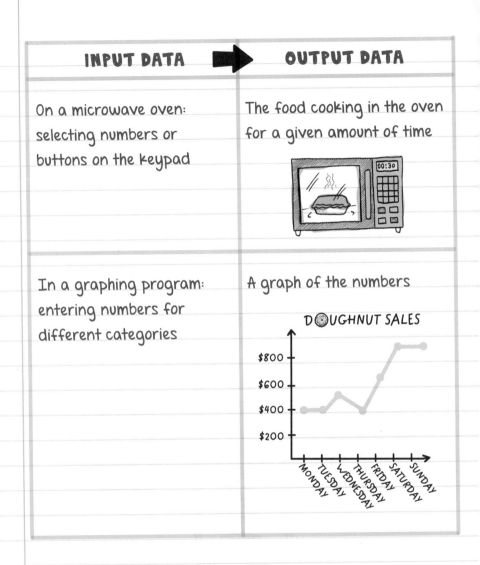

Computers take input data like answers to questions, numbers, and uploaded images and turn the data into a format they can understand and process. For example, pictures are broken up into millions of tiny chunks by a computer, and then the color of each chunk is recorded in a long sequence of code. The computer then processes the code and sends it back to the user as output data. To show the picture, the computer reads

CODE

A system of symbols, letters, and numbers used to represent something else

the long sequence of code and reconstructs the image on your screen by displaying the corresponding color in each tiny chunk, kind of like a super-detailed paint by number.

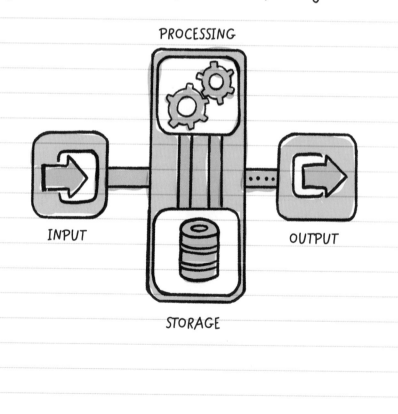

PROCESSING

INPUT

OUTPUT

STORAGE

ENCODING DATA

Data has to be written in a format the computer will understand. This means you have to **ENCODE** the data so that the computer can

process it. When you encode information, you change an image, video, words, etc. into code. For example, MORSE CODE OPERATORS in World War II would encode written messages into dashes and dots that were sent over telegraph wires.

> An outdated communication system that used electrical signals.

When you **DECODE** information, you convert code into an understandable form of communication. For example, when the Morse code operators would receive coded messages in the form of dots and dashes, they would decode the dots and dashes back into English.

Morse code operator

There are several **DATA ENCODING SCHEMES** we can use to help a computer understand input data. Data encoding schemes are ways that we can represent all types of information so that computers can understand it. Computers only understand sequences of the digits 1 and 0.

Any code that uses 1s and 0s is referred to as a **BINARY CODE**. (This will be discussed in detail later.) Encoding schemes were created to help computers understand, interpret, and create data by reducing all data—images, sounds, videos, numbers, colors, symbols, and other types of information—to 1s and 0s.

You could imitate the way computers store an image by making lists of 1s and 0s, where 0 is a white box on the grid and 1 is a green box. Here's how the data would be represented to draw a simple giraffe on a 5 x 5 grid.

ROW 1: 1, 1, 0, 0, 0	
ROW 2: 0, 1, 0, 0, 0	
ROW 3: 0, 1, 0, 0, 0	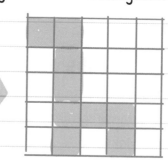
ROW 4: 0, 1, 1, 1, 0	
ROW 5: 0, 1, 0, 1, 0	

Encoding Colors

Different types of data, like colors, numbers, and pictures, can be encoded in different ways. The most common ways colors can be encoded are through the coding schemes **RGB** and **HEXADECIMAL**.

You can use a scanner to encode an old photograph into digital data that a computer can understand. Scanners work by using a sensor that detects colors and encodes the entire photo into a series of number values. The scanner puts all these values in an order that a computer can understand and use to re-create the image on a computer screen.

RGB is color notation that uses three numbers separated by commas, where each number is between 0 and 255 (computers encode each value to binary numbers). Each of the three numbers represents a different shade of **red**, **green**, and **blue**. (That's where the name RGB comes from!) When the different shades of red, green, and blue are combined, they can make many more colors.

There are 16 million ways to combine three numbers between 0 and 255. This means that there are 16 million colors that can be represented in the RGB encoding scheme.

(255, 203, 5)
R   G   B

The **hexadecimal** color notation (or "hex" for short) uses six characters to represent the same 16 million colors as RGB. Hexadecimal is different from RGB because it uses numbers and letters. It uses combinations of the numbers 0-9 and letters A-F. For example, #FF00B4 would make a pink color by using the letters F and B as well as the numbers 0 and 4. Each set of two characters (such as

FF, 00, and B4) represents a different color: The first two characters represent red, the next two green, and the final two blue—and just like with RGB, the different number/letter combinations represent different shades of each individual color.

The computer language CSS uses this symbol to represent hexadecimal colors.

RED   GREEN   BLUE

\# FF 00 B4

Although data such as colors can be represented in different ways, the important part is that each color uses an encoding scheme so that computers can understand the information.

Representing Colors

In the table below, the first two columns are schemes (ways) that computers read colors. Each encoding scheme is translated into binary code. The other three columns are examples of how humans read or identify colors.

COMPUTERS		HUMANS		
HEX CODE	RGB	ENGLISH	SPANISH	VISUALLY
FF0000	255,0,0	Red	Rojo	
0000FF	0,0,255	Blue	Azul	
FFFF00	255,255,0	Yellow	Amarillo	
008000	0,128,0	Green	Verde	
000000	0,0,0	Black	Negro	

Encoding colors into numbers and letters is just one way information is made readable by computers. Sounds, keyboard inputs, touch screen taps, thumbprint readings, GPS locations, and all sorts of data are collected and encoded into a format that computers can understand.

CHECK YOUR KNOWLEDGE

For questions 1-3, complete the sentences.

1. We are currently living in the _____ Age.

2. Converting data into code is called _____.

3. Converting data from code to a readable format is called _____.

4. What is the difference between data and information?

5. Label each option below as an example of encoding or decoding.
A. Green → 008000
B. 000000 → Black
C. Amarillo → 255,255,0
D. FF0000 →

6. How many different colors can be made using hexadecimal or RGB?

7. Label which color each of these pairs represents in this hexadecimal code:

_____   _____   _____

↓   ↓   ↓
∧   ∧   ∧

\# 33   54   A2

8. What is data encoding, and why do computers need it?

9. How do social media companies use the information you share to make money?

10. Name one data encoding scheme.

CHECK YOUR ANSWERS

1. Information

2. Encoding

3. Decoding

4. Data is unprocessed or raw facts, and information is data that has been processed into usable or useful facts.

5. A. Encoding
B. Decoding
C. Encoding
D. Decoding

6. About 16 million

7. Red Green Blue
↓   ↓   ↓
∧   ∧   ∧
33 54   A2

8. Data encoding is converting data into a format that computers can read. Computers can only understand data that is encoded into binary, so images, sounds, text, and other types of data must be encoded so a computer can read it.

9. Every post, picture, video, or other bit of information you share online gives businesses clues about you and what you like to buy. Companies can sell this information to advertisers.

10. There are many data encoding schemes. Acceptable answers are ways to represent information in a form computers can understand. Examples include: binary, hexadecimal, RGB, or similar.

Chapter 5

COLLECTING AND USING INFORMATION

There are many ways to collect information. You can:

- conduct interviews

- hand out surveys

- make observations

Computers can be used to make all these methods more **EFFICIENT**. A survey can also be a type of sensor that takes human input. Computers can collect and analyze data faster and more accurately than humans.

> **EFFICIENT**
> Takes less time or effort

INTERVIEWS

INTERVIEWS gather information through asking questions. They are a great way to gather detailed information from people. When interviewing, we can ask follow-up questions to get more information and to more clearly understand the interviewee. Interviews work great if you only need to collect data from a small group of people.

> The person being interviewed

A downside to interviews is that data from responses is not easily **COMPUTABLE**. This means that we can't use a math formula or computer algorithm to find a pattern in the data. For example, we can't find the average of a page of written answers. But we can find the average of a group of numbers.

SURVEYS

A **SURVEY** is a list of questions. Surveys can be completed and sent digitally through email, websites, or other types of programs. They can also be completed on paper. The responses to a survey can give us general information about a large group of people.

Computers use the information provided in surveys to efficiently compare large amounts of data.

Surveys are great because we can send them out and people can complete them on their own. Surveys are used because they save time.

A downside to surveys is that people may not take the survey seriously, or they may not complete it at all. Another downside is that it's more difficult to gather very detailed information because follow-up questions can't be personalized.

Different types of survey questions provide different types of data:

Open-ended questions allow for more detailed responses, but like interview responses, the data is more difficult for a computer to analyze.

Multiple-choice questions are great for finding trends and patterns. Election ballots use multiple-choice questions, where voters select one candidate for each position. This makes it easy for a computer to analyze: The candidate with the most votes wins! The downside to multiple-choice questions is that the options are limited to the choices given, which means we won't get detailed responses like with open-ended questions.

LINEAR SCALE QUESTIONS allow users to rank their answer. For example, ice-cream taste testers rate how much they like a new flavor on a scale of 1 to 5, where 1 means they don't like it and 5 means they love it.

Computers use multiple-choice questions and linear scale questions to more efficiently compare data. Computers can also use the data provided to calculate and identify trends.

OBSERVATIONS

OBSERVATIONS require looking at an event and making a record of it.

Data is collected at sports games through observation. Points, fouls, penalties, times, and distances are recorded to understand much more than just who won.

HEY, ALL-STAR! WHAT'S THE SCORE?

THIS ISN'T THE TIME TO DO AN INTERVIEW— JUST OBSERVE THE GAME!

Computers can make comparisons and predictions based on observations.

USING DATA

The first computing machines were made to calculate **CENSUS** information. The population in the United States was getting so big that the government needed a way to add up all the survey data. The HOLLERITH TABULATING MACHINE was used to calculate the survey results, which provided useful information to the government. Computers have always been used to help make sense of large amounts of data.

CENSUS
An official count or survey that collects information about a population (for example, where they live, their age, and number of people in the household)

1890—Hollerith Tabulating Machine
A major step toward modern-day computers, this machine read and summarized information stored on punch cards.

Charts and Graphs

Charts and graphs are ways to visualize data. Computer applications use different types of charts to represent different types of information clearly. Charts and graphs are tools that data scientists can use to visualize information in order to analyze it, draw conclusions, and communicate the information.

Line graphs are used to show how something changes over time. For example, a company could use a line graph to show the growth in sales of their ebooks.

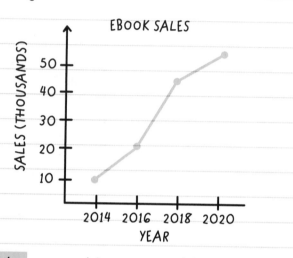

Bar graphs are used to compare different values in a category. For example, they can be used to compare the number of points scored by each player on a volleyball team.

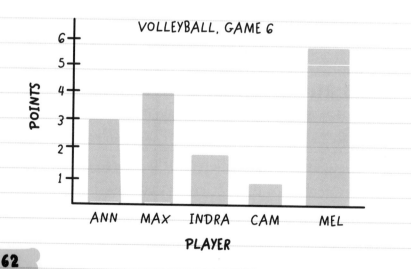

Pie charts are used to show the percentage of parts of a whole. For example, they can be used to show the popularity of different doughnuts sold in a bakery.

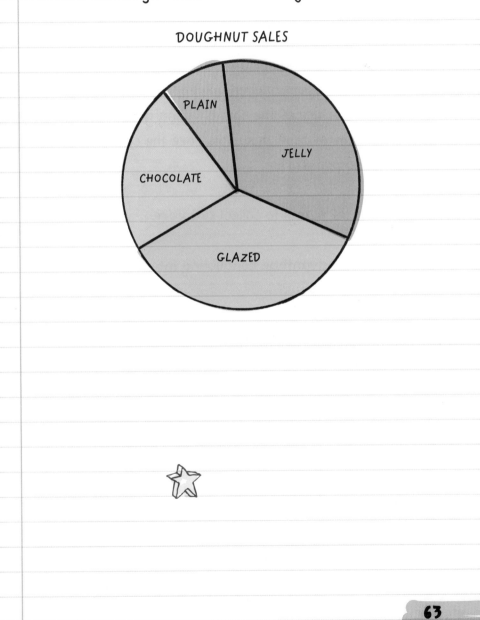

DOUGHNUT SALES

PLAIN

JELLY

CHOCOLATE

GLAZED

CHECK YOUR KNOWLEDGE

1. Which of the following questions would result in easily computable data? (Choose all that apply.)
   A. Do you like eating spicy food?
   B. Does your nose run when you eat really spicy food?
   C. Draw a picture of the spiciest thing you have eaten.
   D. On a scale of 1 to 5, how spicy are the cafeteria's jalapeño poppers?

2. Two ways (of many) to collect data are _____.

3. What is one advantage conducting interviews has over handing out surveys?

4. If you wanted to find out which sports team is the most popular among 100 nearby kids, what kind of data collection tool would you use?

5. If you want to gather easily computable data, which two question types should you avoid?

6. Give one example of when computers are used to collect data.

7. Your friend is running for class president. They want to quickly and easily collect information from all the students to see what kinds of changes they would like the new class president to make. What data collection method would you suggest and why?

8. Which graph or chart would you use to display plant growth measured monthly over a two-year period?

9. Which graph or chart would you use to show how many cats and dogs make up the population of an animal shelter?

ANSWERS

CHECK YOUR ANSWERS

1. **A, B, D**

2. Conduct interviews, hand out surveys, or through observation

3. Conducting interviews gives you more control over the process. You are able to interact with the subject and prod for more relevant answers if you aren't getting the data you need.

4. Interviewing one hundred people would take way too long. So, the best option would be a simple survey.

5. We should avoid open-ended and interview-type questions.

6. Computers are used to collect all sorts of data, for example, about people using social media, maps for navigating in the car, voting, and more.

7. To collect data from a large number of people, surveys are the easiest collection method. Answers to survey questions produce easily computable data.

8. A line graph can be used to show a trend over time.

9. A pie chart can show the percentage of categories in a population.

Unit

3

Software
Engineering

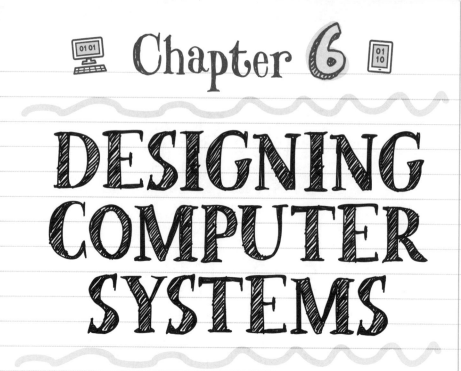

Chapter 6

DESIGNING COMPUTER SYSTEMS

THE ENGINEERING DESIGN PROCESS

When designing computers or programs, computer scientists follow an **ENGINEERING DESIGN PROCESS** to help them understand and improve their designs. Their goal is to make the program as efficient and user-friendly as possible.

ENGINEERING is a branch of science that studies the design, building, and use of machines and structures to solve problems. **Computer engineering** is the application of study of computer science and the practice of engineering to

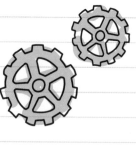

There are many slightly different **engineering design processes**, but a basic version is

1. identify the problem
2. plan a solution
3. build/make the plan
4. test
5. improve

and then the cycle starts again.

computer software and hardware. **Software engineering** is an application of computer science.

Step 1: Identify the Problem

Software engineers identify the problem and what they need to find a solution. They ask themselves:

- What is the problem I want to solve?

  - Example: find the shortest way home from school that includes stopping at the library and grocery store.

- What can be used to help solve the problem?

  - a map showing the locations
  - distances between locations
  - type of transportation used

- What features will I need to solve the problem?

  - be able to calculate
  - be able to draw a map

This stage may include collecting and analyzing data from people who face the same problem. This could include interviewing people, sending out surveys, or observing people. It can also include the use of sensors or GPS tracking.

Step 2: Plan

Software engineers develop plans for a solution to the problem. Planning can include making lists or drawing maps of a proposed solution. Plans should be very detailed.

FROM SCHOOL TO LIBRARY
DISTANCE:____
____ MINUTES WALK

FROM SCHOOL TO GROCERY
DISTANCE:____
____ MINUTES WALK

FROM LIBRARY TO GROCERY
DISTANCE:____
____ MINUTES WALK

FROM GROCERY TO HOME
DISTANCE:____
____ MINUTES WALK

Step 3: Build

The code is written, and other parts of the solution are added to the program. The build step ends when a working product is completed.

Step 4: Test

Identify problems by testing the source code or solution. Software engineers usually ask people to use the product and give feedback. There are different levels of testing. In the early stages, the programmer will run tests on their own; then they will ask peers to test their solution. Later the programmer will ask a group of users to test the solution and give feedback.

Step 5: Improve

Fix problems and improve the solution. In this step, the bugs or other issues identified in the test step are corrected.

EVERYDAY ENGINEERING

Powerful technologies have become smaller, cheaper, and easier to work with, which means anyone can design and build amazing things. With Lego robotics, drones, 3-D printers, desktop laser cutters, micro:bits, Arduinos, and Makey Makeys, you can become an everyday engineer.

micro:bits and **Arduinos** are very small computers on a single chip that can be programmed to do a number of different things, such as keep track of data like a fitness tracker, or behave like a game controller. They are used to teach students coding and programming.

Makey Makeys (a type of microcontroller like a micro:bit or Arduino) are electronic invention kits for kids that allow the user to use alligator clips to connect everyday objects to computer programs. This allows the user to control the objects in a different way.

Chapter 7

TESTING

Testing is an important part of the engineering process. As Step 4 in the engineering design process, this task takes up the most time.

Many things can go wrong with programs. These are ways programmers try to limit the number of problems in their programs so that they run smoothly.

DEFENSIVE PROGRAMMING

DEFENSIVE PROGRAMMING is designing your program so that it keeps working even when things don't go as expected. One way to do this is to intentionally get your program to produce errors to see how you should solve them.

For example, if you write a program where the user should input their email address, you could try to produce an error by entering text that is not an email address.

Then ask:

- Does the program still run correctly if a user inputs their phone number or name in the email address field?

- What can you do to prevent the user from inputting the wrong information?

USE CASES and **TEST CASES** are used in defensive programming to help you see where adjustments may be needed in a program.

Use Cases

Use cases are lists of actions users can take. It describes how users will use your program.

The list could be a very detailed flowchart, or it could be a few ideas you come up with.

It's important that the user is able to run a program without errors. For example, after you complete the programming of a game, you should play the game from beginning to end to make sure it runs the way you want it to.

Test Cases

Use case tests check to see if the user can complete a goal in the program. For every use case, there will be many more test cases. Test cases are specific, more detailed tests. They use conditions that your program may run under. The use case is used to define the functionality required. Use case testing is then testing for that functionality.

Test cases focus on one condition (or variable) at a time to make sure the program works in all situations.

For example, if you were creating a video game, you could create a test case that makes sure your character jumps when you press the spacebar.

If that test passes, you should also test to see what happens if you hold down the spacebar instead of pressing it just once.

Programming defensively would mean making sure that, no matter how long the user held down the spacebar, the character would jump just once.

If you defensively programmed your game, then the character will just jump once.

If you didn't defensively program, or forgot to test what happens when the user holds down the spacebar, the character might do something you don't want them to do.

I CAN FLY!

Another example: If you programmed a calculator app that divides your number by 10, test cases make sure your program works with different types of numbers. Would the program crash if the user tries to enter 1 or 0?

It is important to pick test cases that use many types of input. For example, for a calculator app, instead of testing only with digits 0-9, choose positive and negative integers, rational numbers, and zero.

REMEMBER FROM MATH CLASS

Positive integer: a whole number greater than zero, not a fraction or a decimal.
For example, 2, 5, 9, 50.

Negative integer: a whole number less than zero, not a fraction or a decimal.
For example, -1, -5, -150.

Rational number: any number that can be written as a fraction or a ratio.
For example -5 can be written as $\frac{-5}{1}$ and 2.15 can be written as $\frac{215}{100}$.

CHECK YOUR KNOWLEDGE

1. Explain the difference between a use case and a test case.

2. NASA is testing a program by seeing if an astronaut can use the program to successfully complete all the steps of a mission from rocket launch to orbiting Earth. Is this a use case test or a test case?

3. NASA is testing a small part of the launch program— the part that controls the engines—to see if the program runs correctly even with different inputs. Is this a use case test or a test case?

4. You are a defensive programmer if:
   A. You think testing is a waste of time
   B. Your program will run even if things go wrong
   C. Your program protects against a virus
   D. All of the above

5. For a program that asks users to input the location of graffiti so that volunteers can clean it up, which of the following are test cases? (Choose all that apply.)

A. Can the user create an account and post a location where graffiti is found?

B. What happens if the user types the city name into the zip code text box?

C. What happens if the user types a negative number into the zip code text box?

D. Can a user take a picture of the graffiti, upload it, and add it to a post?

6. Why is testing different kinds of input important in case testing?

7. Use and test cases are used to find _____ in your program.

8. Which of the following would be the best set of numbers to include in a test case for a calculator program?

A. 1, 2, 3, 4

B. -2, -4, -6, -8

C. 0.4, 0.5, 0.2, 0.6

D. -2, 0, 0.4, 16

ANSWERS ➤

CHECK YOUR ANSWERS

1. Use cases are the broad tests that determine if a user is able to complete a general task, while test cases are specific tests that use various types of input.

2. Use case

3. Test case

4. B

5. B, C

6. It's important because you want to make sure your program runs no matter what the user inputs. For example, if your program expects users to type only words in a text box, something may go wrong if the user inputs numbers or hashtags or something else. You would need to make sure that the incorrect input doesn't break the program.

7. Errors (bugs)

8. D

Chapter 8

DOCUMENTING

DOCUMENTATION is information about a program's code. There are two main types of documentation: **comments** and **README** files.

COMMENTS

All programming languages have a way to add comments to the code. Comments are not part of the program; they are skipped when the program is run and can't be seen by the user. Comments are messages written by the programmer about the program's code. They can be explanations about what a chunk of code does, reminders about things to add or change in the code, or questions to other programmers who will look at the code.

> Example:
>
> Add a countdown clock at the top of the screen.

Commenting on code helps you remember what each section does. This is helpful for large programs because you won't remember what every line of code was written to do. Comments also are helpful for short programs because you might want to look at the code long after you finish writing it.

Sometimes you'll want to reuse code from another program, or code you or someone else wrote. Comments help you quickly find the portion of code you want to reuse. For example, if you were making a game, instead of creating the code to move characters around on your own, you could copy a similar chunk of code from another program. You could write a comment so that you know which chunk of code this is in your program.

Comments are also used to help debug a program. Because comments are not read when the program is run, **COMMENTING OUT** a section of code is an easy way to make the computer skip lines of code (that may contain a bug) without deleting them.

COMMENTING OUT
Marking sections of code as a comment so that it will not be run with the rest of the code

Comments can also be helpful in debugging by adding test lines of code that you comment out when you are done testing it.

Comments can also be notes to yourself as you code.

For example, you could leave short notes as reminders to yourself like:

#BUG or **#FIXME**—a known bug that you want to come back to.

#TODO—a note about what code you still need to write but need to come back to later.

README

A README file (usually typed in all caps to get your attention) gives information about a program, including which files are included, how to install it, how to use it, credits and attribution, or known bugs.

PLEASE READ ME.

TXT

A README file can be written for the user, other programmers, or both. Usually only one README file is used per program, and it usually is a **PLAIN TEXT FILE**.

PLAIN TEXT FILE
A text document that has no formatting (like bold type, indents, and paragraph spacing); just words and punctuation

Although README files can include user information, a user guide is a more common way to help users figure out how to use a program. Usually user guides are only created for large, complicated programs like Microsoft Word or Excel.

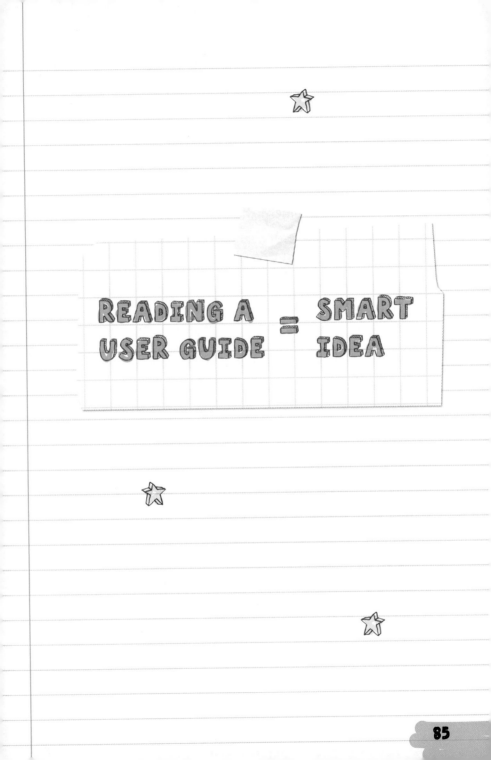

READING A = SMART
USER GUIDE   IDEA

CHECK YOUR KNOWLEDGE

1. What are two types of documentation you can make to help others understand your program?

2. Which type of documentation helps you remember what small chunks of code are supposed to do?

3. Why is commenting out a line of code helpful in debugging?

4. Why are comments useful to you and other programmers?

5. Which of these are reasons to use documentation? (Choose all that apply.)
   A. Makes it easier to find sections of code you want
   B. Makes it easier to collaborate
   C. You can write notes to yourself while programming
   D. Helps you find bugs
   E. Gives credit
   F. Explains how to use a program

6. If you wanted to add a note in your code as a reminder to come back and fix an error, you could add the comment _____.

7. Which of the following would you use to help a user install your program: a README file or a comment in your code?

8. What is a user guide?

CHECK YOUR ANSWERS

1. Comments and README files

2. Comments

3. It helps you prevent small chunks of the program from running without having to delete them from the file.

4. If you are working on a project with others, it's much easier to read a comment explaining a chunk of code than it is to try to read the code and interpret what it does.

5. **A, B, C, D, E, F** (All the reasons are correct.)

6. #BUG or #FIXME

7. README file

8. A user guide is a document that helps the user learn the functionality of a program.

Chapter 9

INCORPORATING FEEDBACK

USER-CENTERED DESIGN

Users decide whether or not a program is good. Their opinions will be based on how easy the program is to use and whether it does what it's supposed to do.

USER-CENTERED DESIGN is a process for creating a program that considers users' wants and needs at every stage of development. To make a program work easily for as many users as possible, you should ask different kinds of users for their opinion on your program.

> **Incorporating feedback** means using the information you gathered from users to revise your design.

When creating a user-centered design, you should focus on several things:

● **USABILITY**— Is it easy to figure out and use?

● **ACCESSIBILITY**—Can people with different abilities use it?

● **CONTENT**—Does your program make sense to the target audience?

people for whom the program is designed

COLLECTING FEEDBACK

Before sharing a program with the world, programmers use **ALPHA** and **BETA** testing to get feedback from users. These users point out bugs or issues in the program.

SERIOUSLY, MORE TESTING?

Alpha testing is the first round of user testing, which is usually done just before the program is finished. Alpha testers are friends or people you trust. At this point your code isn't finished, so you should expect them to find plenty of bugs.
In a coding class, alpha testing can mean asking a classmate to come over and check your program, even if it's only halfway done.

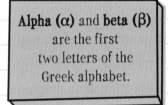

Alpha (α) and beta (β) are the first two letters of the Greek alphabet.

COME CHECK OUT MY GAME SO FAR.

Beta testing is the second round of user testing, which is usually done after the program is finished. Beta testers are a selected group of potential users.

FOR EXAMPLE, if you made a new app to help your friends study for an upcoming math final, the beta testers would be a group of your classmates in math class. Beta testers should find fewer bugs than alpha testers.

Showing your program to potential users helps to identify flaws you might have overlooked before. Fixing these flaws before sharing your program with everyone can help you catch mistakes before the program goes out into the world.

HEY, MRS. ALVAREZ, COULD YOU BETA TEST MY ESSAY BEFORE I TURN IT IN?

CHECK YOUR KNOWLEDGE

1. What is user-centered design?

2. Which of the following is NOT a principle of user-centered design?
   A. Entertainment
   B. Usability
   C. Accessibility
   D. Content

3. What is feedback?

4. How is alpha testing different from beta testing?

5. Will an alpha or a beta tester be likely to find more bugs?

6. What does it mean if a program is accessible, and why does making accessible programs matter?

MORE QUESTIONS

7. You designed an app that tracks the amount of sleep you get and its quality. Who is your target audience?

A. People who shop at Target

B. Tired people

C. Neurosurgeons

D. The programmer

8. What might happen if you share a program with the world before testing it?

CHECK YOUR ANSWERS

1. User-centered design is creating a program based on what *users* want.

2. A

3. Feedback is the information gathered from users testing your program.

4. Alpha testing is the first round of testing, and it's done with a small group of trusted people. Beta testing is the second round of tests, and it's done with a group of users from your target audience.

5. Alpha testers will probably find more bugs because they are the first users to test the program, and the project may not even be complete yet. By the time beta testers see the program, hopefully most of the bugs are fixed.

6. A program is accessible if people with different abilities can use it successfully. As a programmer, you want to make sure that you are not excluding any group of people from using your work, based on their abilities.

7. B

8. While your program might be perfect, it's likely that there are bugs that users will find or adjustments they will suggest.

Chapter 10

COLLABORATING

WORKING ON A TEAM

Collaborating, or working with others, on programming projects is helpful because different people have different strengths. Having several people work together on a large program (instructions that tell a computer what to do) can help the project finish faster. It can also reduce the burden on the programmer.

The Space Shuttle ran on 400,000 lines of code. New high-end cars run on 100 million lines of code. Facebook is made up of around 60 million lines of code. To write millions of lines of code by yourself would take more than a lifetime.

Collaborating on a project by dividing up the work and focusing on your strengths will help you build more efficient programs more quickly.

Tips to help members of a team work well together:

Set clear expectations. Make sure everyone knows exactly what they are supposed to do to contribute to the project. Don't leave out any parts of the project.

Focus on your strengths. Divide up tasks so that each person is assigned a task that they will enjoy doing and will most likely be good at.

Set realistic timelines. Give yourselves time to complete the work, but also push yourselves to work hard and finish the project.

Give equal workloads. Although each team member will be doing different tasks, make sure the work is divided equally so no one feels that they are stuck doing all the work.

Create clear roles. Decide who should be the note taker, the tester, the debugger, or any other role you might need. Clear roles will help you keep on track and focus on your own tasks.

DESIGN FOR THE APP

CODE FOR THE APP

ARTWORK FOR THE APP

PAIR PROGRAMMING

When projects are really small, like those you might do in a class, programming with a large team may be too much. **PAIR PROGRAMMING** is a strategy where two people work at the same computer to complete a project. Programmers use this strategy because it helps them work faster and make fewer errors.

In pair programming, each coder has a specific role. One person is the **DRIVER**, and the other is the **NAVIGATOR**. The driver is in control of the keyboard. They are in charge of typing in the code and double-checking their work. The navigator is in charge of telling the driver what code should be written and for catching bugs while working.

NAVIGATOR   DRIVER

Both the driver and the navigator should communicate with each other while coding. Pairs should rotate roles often so that each person has a chance to drive and navigate.

GETTING HELP FROM THE COMMUNITY

Most programmers spend a lot of their time searching for solutions to their programming problems. When you're making a program you can use many resources to help you finish the project. Even experienced programmers ask other programmers for help.

When you're programming, you should look for opportunities to build on the work of others. This does NOT mean it's <u>okay to copy someone else's code and say that it's your own</u>. Instead, you should use someone else's program for ideas, or copy only a small part of the code.

You should always give **ATTRIBUTION** by making sure that the programmer gets credit for their work. If your program or part of your program was written by you but inspired by someone else, give them credit in a comment or README file. If you want to copy part of someone else's program, first ask the author if it's okay or look for copyright permissions. Then, make it clear which part is their code and which

THIS PART IS MINE.

part is yours. When you're copying code, it's a good idea to include attribution in both a comment and a README file.

Here's an example of what giving attribution looks like:

> I used the example project from @the_coding_master, and I modified it to use more light effects, added a turtle costume to the whole thing, and made it play the music from @music_lover. Credit to @gamer_pro for the game play inspiration!

When you give attribution, you are showing that you are grateful for someone else's hard work and you are helping to create a community of sharing. Also, giving attribution isn't just a nice thing to do—in some cases, it's also the law!

Giving attribution in programming is like CITING quotations or PARAPHRASING other authors when you write a report in English class.

CITE
Referencing the source

PARAPHRASE
Using someone else's idea but saying it in your own words

USING LIBRARIES

LIBRARIES (also known as modules or extensions) give you access to helpful **PREMADE FUNCTIONS**. For example, if you were making a game, you could type hundreds of lines of code to simulate a character jumping around and interacting with another character on the screen. Or, you could use a library that already has all the jumping-and-interacting-with-characters code built in. Some libraries require that you give attribution somewhere in your program, sometimes as a comment in your code.

PREMADE FUNCTIONS
Ready-made lines of code for a specific action

It's always a good idea to look for help or a library that can support your project.

CHECK YOUR KNOWLEDGE

1. Name two benefits of programming as a team.

2. True or false: Most programmers never need to ask for help.

3. It's okay to use someone else's code as long as you do what two things?

4. If you don't copy someone's code exactly, but use it as inspiration, do you still need to give credit? Yes/no.

5. As the driver, how can having a navigator help you?

6. Why would it be important to switch roles often when pair programming?

7. Why would using a physics library (one that has functions that can make your characters and objects look like they are realistically interacting or moving) be helpful to a game maker?

MORE QUESTIONS

8. How would you feel if someone used your code without permission, didn't give attribution, and claimed the code as their own?

9. Giving attribution is:
(Choose all that are true.)
A. A nice thing to do
B. The law
C. A show of gratitude
D. A way to promote a community where people share

CHECK YOUR ANSWERS

1. Any two of the following are good benefits:
   - You can accomplish bigger tasks.
   - You have a variety of strengths to draw from.
   - You have extra sets of eyes to help avoid and catch mistakes.
   - You can learn from others.

2. False

3. Ask or look for permission and give attribution.

4. Yes

5. Having someone who can step back and focus on the big picture can help the driver focus on coding and possibly make fewer errors.

6. Switching roles makes sure both partners have an opportunity to step back and think about the big picture as well as hunt for bugs from different perspectives.

7. Using libraries helps save time and can prevent errors. With a physics library, a game maker can spend less time coding the physics of the characters and more time on the rest of the game.

MORE ANSWERS

Unit 4

Algorithms and Programming

Chapter 11

USING ALGORITHMS

ALGORITHMS

Both humans and computers use algorithms. Algorithms are processes or steps that can be followed. A recipe is an example of an algorithm that both humans and some computers can use.

Algorithms give clear instructions for repeating tasks. Different algorithms could be used to complete the same task. For example, there are different ways to divide two numbers using long division or by doing repeated subtraction. Both ways give you the same result, but one way may be better. In computer science, we are always looking for better algorithms.

Better algorithms are faster, simpler, or more efficient.

Algorithms are useful because they can provide better ways to complete tasks.

Efficient

CLICK!

Inefficient
(the opposite of efficient)

Studying Algorithms

Developing algorithms is its own branch of computer science and is very similar to the study of mathematics. For example, mathematicians and computer scientists have been studying the TRAVELING SALESPERSON PROBLEM for almost 100 years.

> The Traveling Salesperson problem asks, "Given a list of cities and the distances between each pair of cities, what is the shortest possible route that a salesperson can take to visit each city and return home?"

The goal of the Traveling Salesperson problem is to develop the most efficient algorithm that can determine the shortest path that a traveling salesperson should take. The problem can be applied to real life. For example, a delivery truck dispatcher uses a shortest-route algorithm to determine all their deliveries for the day. The algorithm helps the trucking company save time and money.

PROGRAMS

The job of a computer scientist is to come up with a solution to a problem, turn the solution into an algorithm, and then code the algorithm into a program so that it can be read by a computer. A program is an algorithm that has been translated (coded) into instructions for a computer.

Algorithms are often written out in a way that most people can understand. It's less likely that most people can read a computer program and understand it, because it uses a combination of numbers, letters, and symbols in an arrangement we are not used to—but a computer would know just what it says.

Programmers give very specific instructions to computers using **PROGRAMMING LANGUAGES**. Programming languages use combinations of numbers, words, symbols, and formatting to tell a computer what to do in a way that it can understand.

FOR EXAMPLE: Suppose you wanted to find out if today is your friend's birthday. You could write this algorithm or program.

ALGORITHM	PROGRAM (PYTHON)
1. Look up today's date.	#Import datetime library from datetime import *

2. Ask a friend when their birthday is.	#Get Today's Date
	today = date.today()

3. Determine if today is your friend's birthday.	#Get User's Birthday
	dob_str = input("What is your Date of Birth? dd/mm/yyyy")

ALGORITHM	PROGRAM (PYTHON)
| 4. If today is your friend's birthday, say "Happy Birthday!" Otherwise, tell them, "Today is not your birthday." | ```python
#Convert user input into a date
dob_data = dob_str.split("/")
dobDay = int(dob_data[0])
dobMonth = int(dob_data[1])
dobYear = int(dob_data[2])
dob = date(dobYear,dobMonth,dobDay)
#Determine if today is the
user's birthday
thisYear = today.year
nextBirthday =
date(thisYear,dobMonth,dobDay)

if today == nextBirthday:
    print("Happy Birthday!")
else:
    print("Today is not your birthday.")
``` |

When you start learning to program, it's traditional to begin by writing a simple program that makes a computer display, "Hello, World!"

HEY
```

EARLY DAYS OF PROGRAMMING

Programming a computer is also called coding. Coding can be traced back to the nineteenth century.

Ada Lovelace is considered one of THE FIRST PROGRAMMERS. In 1843, Lovelace wrote an algorithm for a machine called the ANALYTICAL ENGINE, which was a mechanical computer.

Augusta Ada King, Countess of Lovelace

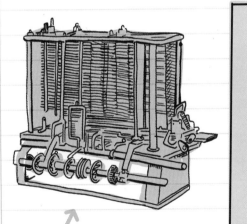

The Analytical Engine

The Analytical Engine was designed by CHARLES BABBAGE. Instead of running on electricity like modern computers, this computer used gears and a steam engine. It was used to count and solve simple mathematical problems.

The Analytical Engine was designed to run simple programs made using punch cards. Each punch card would have holes in it that the machine would read as instructions. The punch cards would be used to program the computer.

punch cards

Lovelace believed that the machine could be given instructions to carry out other tasks. She understood that it could be programmed. Lovelace was the first person to recognize the potential of the Analytical Engine beyond calculating.

CHECK YOUR KNOWLEDGE

1. Explain the difference between an algorithm and a program.

2. Which of the following is NOT an algorithm?
   A. Steps to make a burrito
   B. Instructions on how to French braid
   C. A how-to guide on building a model airplane
   D. An anonymous love note to your crush

3. Why are the best algorithms efficient? Why are computer scientists always looking for more efficient algorithms?

4. Choose the algorithms below that are also programs.
   A. Instructions on how to play an instrument
   B. Microsoft Word
   C. Snapchat
   D. A list of steps for building a drone

5. True or false: Different algorithms can be made to complete the same task in different ways.

6. What kind of languages do computers understand?

MORE QUESTIONS

7. Why do algorithms need to be written in a different way for computers to understand them?

8. True or false: Ada Lovelace wrote the first computer program on an Apple computer.

9. Who designed the Analytical Engine?

10. What kind of work was the Analytical Engine designed to do?

11. Why was Ada Lovelace's work ahead of her time?

CHECK YOUR ANSWERS

1. An algorithm is a set of instructions to complete a task, and a program is a set of instructions that can be understood by a computer.

2. D

3. Efficient algorithms run faster and take up less storage space.

4. B, C

5. True

6. Programming languages

MORE ANSWERS

7. Computers need specific instructions and only understand programming languages.

8. False. Ada Lovelace wrote the first program, but it was for the Analytical Engine.

9. Charles Babbage

10. The Analytical Engine was designed to perform math functions, like a calculator.

11. She saw potential that no one else saw to program machines for multiple purposes beyond mathematical calculations.

Chapter 12

PROGRAMMING LANGUAGES

There are *hundreds* of programming languages, and programmers use different languages for different types of tasks. Languages like JavaScript, PHP, and Python are used to make **WEB PAGES** —documents that can be displayed in a web browser (like Chrome, Safari, or Firefox). A collection of web pages is called a **WEBSITE**.

MOBILE APPLICATIONS are made with the programming languages Swift, Java, C, and others.

> **MOBILE APPLICATIONS**
> Types of software designed to run on mobile devices like cell phones and tablets

USING PROGRAMMING LANGUAGES

Since each programming language has different strengths (for example, some are faster, others are easier to write, or some show graphics better), programmers may use several languages for large projects. For example:

■ Facebook uses Python, JavaScript, PHP, and others.

■ YouTube uses Python, JavaScript, C++, and others.

■ Twitter uses JavaScript, C++, Ruby, and others.

All three websites use JavaScript. That's because JavaScript (along with HTML and CSS) is primarily a FRONT-END LANGUAGE, which means it is used to make the part of a website that can be viewed on a screen.

Websites like Facebook, YouTube, and Twitter also store tons of information (posts, comments, profile pictures, videos, etc.). This means they need another type of programming language (a BACK-END type) to organize and connect all the extra information to the front end.

THIS TIME **YOU** GET TO BE THE BACK HALF.

Different back-end languages are used for different reasons. For example, C++ runs (follows instructions) faster than other programming languages but is harder to write. So a company might start by writing their product in an easier language like Python and then go back and replace parts of the product with C++ to increase the speed at which it processes information.

No computer programmer knows every programming language, just like no one knows every spoken language.

However, it is useful to know a few programming languages so that, for example, you can combine a language that is great for graphics with a language that is great for processing large amounts of code.

HOW COMPUTERS READ CODE

CODE = LANGUAGE A COMPUTER UNDERSTANDS

Binary

Computers process information using **electrical circuits** that can turn on and off. Computer scientists use the digits 1 and 0 to stand for on and off. The 1s and 0s are a type of encoding called

A path or collection of paths through which electricity is carried

BINARY, or **MACHINE CODE**.

A binary digit can be either 0 or 1.

In binary, 1s and 0s are often used, but you can also represent binary with "On" and "Off" or "True" and "False." All words, numbers, letters, symbols, images, videos, programs, emojis, and music can be represented in binary.

BINARY
Binary is how computers talk and represent information.

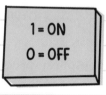

1 = ON
0 = OFF

MACHINE CODE
The most basic language that all programming languages are turned into before a computer runs them

The CPU of a computer can only read instructions written in machine code. So, after a human enters a program into a computer, a computer program then turns it into binary machine code. The process of translating (changing) a program into machine code is called **COMPILING**.

COMPILING
Translating a programming language into machine code

No matter how many different programming languages are used to write the phrase "Hello, World!", the machine code for each version looks the same.

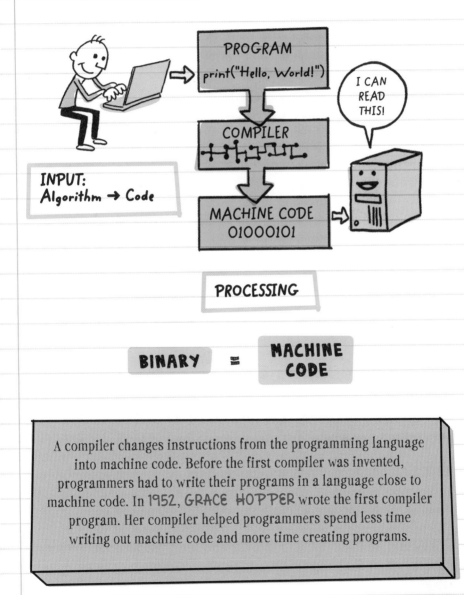

PROGRAM
print("Hello, World!")

I CAN READ THIS!

COMPILER

INPUT:
Algorithm → Code

MACHINE CODE
01000101

PROCESSING

BINARY = MACHINE CODE

A compiler changes instructions from the programming language into machine code. Before the first compiler was invented, programmers had to write their programs in a language close to machine code. In 1952, GRACE HOPPER wrote the first compiler program. Her compiler helped programmers spend less time writing out machine code and more time creating programs.

Representing Numbers Using Binary

Binary is another way of using numbers to count or to represent numbers. Binary is sometimes referred to as BASE 2 because it uses two digits (0 and 1), while our usual way of counting is called BASE 10 because it uses ten digits.

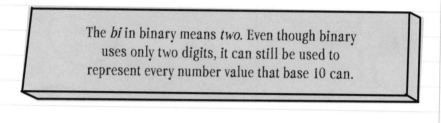

The *bi* in binary means *two*. Even though binary uses only two digits, it can still be used to represent every number value that base 10 can.

In base 10, each place is ten times the value of the place to its right. As numbers get larger, we add digits to the next place value to the left.

binary = 2

In binary, numbers increase in value 2 times as we double (multiply by 2) the value of each new place. From right to left, digits in base 2 (binary) have the place values of 1, 2, 4, 8, 16, 32, 64, and so on, doubling each time.

Binary place values: From right to left, each place is double the value of the previous one.

To represent the number 1 in binary, write "1" in the ones place.

128s place	64s place	32s place	16s place	8s place	4s place	2s place	1s place
							1

There is no "2" digit in binary. To write the number 2, put a 0 in the ones placeholder, then move to the left and put a 1 in the twos place.

128s place	64s place	32s place	16s place	8s place	4s place	2s place	1s place
						1	0

ON ↑   ↑ OFF

0 is in the ones place, so its value is 0 × 1, or 0.

1 is in the twos place, so its value is 1 × 2, or 2.

When you add together the two values (0 + 2), you get 2.

You can use basic addition to figure out binary values.

VALUE	128s place	64s place	32s place	16s place	8s place	4s place	2s place	1s place	
3							1	1	2 + 1
4						1	0	0	4 + 0
5						1	0	1	4 + 1
6						1	1	0	4 + 2

Another way to think of binary digits is how computers do: as "on" or "off."

FOR EXAMPLE, if we had 8 light bulbs lined up in a row (to represent 8 place values in base 2), we could use them to represent a number in binary by turning each light bulb on or off.

You can represent 237 using a row of 8 light bulbs. Each light bulb that is on represents 1, and each light bulb that is off represents 0 value in the placeholder.

1	1	1	0	1	1	0	1

The sum of the place values for the light bulbs that are on is 237.

128 + 64 + 32 + 8 + 4 + 1

Representing Letters in Binary

At first, computers were used just to make mathematical calculations. Later, a way to represent letters and symbols in binary was developed.

The AMERICAN STANDARD CODE FOR INFORMATION INTERCHANGE (ASCII) assigned each letter of the alphabet and symbol its own binary code. Each letter was assigned a number, which was then encoded into binary.

For example, the capital letter A is assigned the number 65, which in binary is written 01000001.

Although the number 65 and the letter A share the exact same binary code, the program tells the computer if it should interpret the binary as letters or numbers.

Bits and Bytes

Terms like "16 gigabytes of memory" or "1 terabyte hard drive" are used when talking about computer storage. These terms represent quantities of binary digits.

A **BIT** is the smallest unit of storage. It represents one digit (1 or 0).

WHAT A CUTE LITTLE BIT!

The next greater measurement is a **BYTE**, which represents 8 bits. For example, 01010101 is 1 byte. (There are 8 digits.)

A BYTE-SIZED FAMILY

b = bit
B = byte

The largest number you can represent with 1 byte is 11111111, which in base 10 is 255.

That's why RGB (color) values run from 0 to 255: because those are the numbers you can represent with 1 byte.

Larger quantities of bytes can be represented using a prefix:

- **Kilobyte (KB)**—about one thousand bytes (A 5-page Word document is around 100 KB.)

- **Megabyte (MB)**—about one million bytes (Audio files are several MB.)

- **Gigabyte (GB)**—about one billion bytes (HD movies are a few GB.)

- **Terabyte (TB)**—about one trillion bytes (Some new hard drives hold around 1-3 TB. The Hubble Space Telescope sends 10 TB of data to Earth every year.)

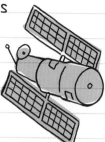

The Hubble Space Telescope was the first major telescope to be placed in space. Launched into Earth's orbit in 1990, it is one of the largest telescopes ever made. Its purpose is to allow scientists to observe distant stars and planets.

CREATING ALGORITHMS

Before typing out a program, programmers first come up with the algorithm, or list of steps, that will be used in the code. They often use **PSEUDOCODE** (pronounced "SOO-doe") and **FLOWCHARTS** to design or plan algorithms before they begin programming.

> **FLOWCHART**
> A diagram that outlines the steps in a process

Pseudocode

Pseudocode is written in a style or format that's similar to the programming language a programmer is going to use. There are no rules on how to write pseudocode, but it's meant to be read by humans, not a computer.

Most programmers format their pseudocode so that each line represents a line of real code in their final program. The pseudocode doesn't have to be perfect; it should just give an idea of what the final program may look like.

> Coding without a plan is like building a house without a blueprint.

Flowcharts

Flowcharts help programmers visualize the steps in an algorithm. Just like making an outline before writing an essay, flowcharts help organize ideas, and they use specific symbols to represent different parts of an algorithm.

Each symbol in a flowchart has a meaning.

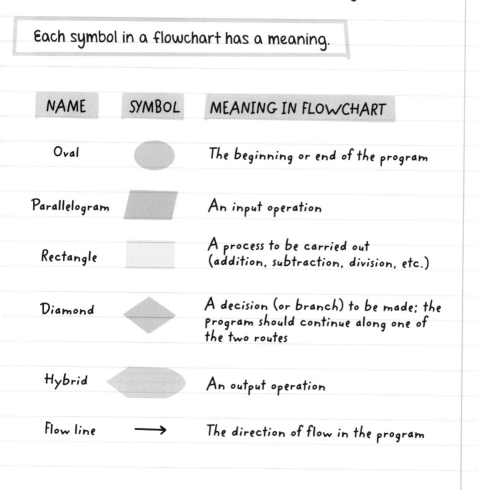

NAME	SYMBOL	MEANING IN FLOWCHART
Oval		The beginning or end of the program
Parallelogram		An input operation
Rectangle		A process to be carried out (addition, subtraction, division, etc.)
Diamond		A decision (or branch) to be made; the program should continue along one of the two routes
Hybrid		An output operation
Flow line	→	The direction of flow in the program

If you wanted to write an algorithm to check if today is your friend's birthday, the flowchart might look like this:

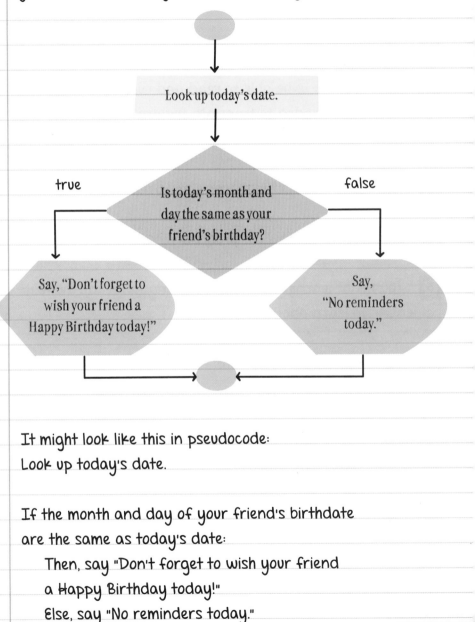

It might look like this in pseudocode:
Look up today's date.

If the month and day of your friend's birthdate
are the same as today's date:
    Then, say "Don't forget to wish your friend
    a Happy Birthday today!"
    Else, say "No reminders today."

CHECK YOUR KNOWLEDGE

1. What is a programming language?

2. For computers to be able to read and run a program, a _____ is needed to translate the program into machine code.

3. What do the 0 and 1 in machine code represent?

4. Why are there different programming languages?

5. Why might learning one programming language make it easier to learn another?

6. How many bits are in a byte?

7. If a computer compiled two programs that both wrote "Hello, World!", would the machine code for "Hello, World!" look different?

8. Which is bigger: a kilobyte or a gigabyte?

9. How do you write the number 2 in binary? What number does 101 represent in binary?

10. Name two good ways to plan out a program before you code it.

ANSWERS 137

CHECK YOUR ANSWERS

1. A programming language is a language used to give specific instructions to computers.

2. Compiler

3. Off and on

4. Each language has different strengths and can be used to create different kinds of programs.

5. Most programming languages use a lot of similar structures.

6. 8

7. No, they would look the same.

8. Gigabyte

9. 10, 5

10. Pseudocode or flowcharts

Chapter 13

COMPUTATIONAL THINKING

Computer science focuses on using computers to create solutions to problems.

COMPUTATIONAL THINKING is the thought process for creating solutions that can be carried out by a computer.

PROCESSING

FOR EXAMPLE, if your problem is that you need to write a book report, a common solution is to read the book, plan out the essay, then write about what you read.

A way you might solve the same problem using computational thinking might be to collect data on the number of times each character talks to another and plot the information on a graph. You might even develop a program that analyzes the data for you. The graph would give you data-driven evidence of the relationships between the characters in the story. The output of your program and data could be used to tell you what to write in your essay.

An extreme example may be to program an artificial intelligence (AI) program that can understand **natural language**, analyze the book, and write the essay for you. While this example might not help you meet your goal of learning about the book, it shows how far computational thinking can go.

> The way people speak to each other

In computer science, artificial intelligence (AI) is a powerful way of programming machines and computers so they can learn from large amounts of data to improve the way they work. This type of computing allows computer programs to make predictions and decisions beyond those that they are directly programmed to make.

There are four major ideas in computational thinking:

1. **Decomposition:** Breaking a problem down into simple parts

2. **Pattern Recognition:** Identifying what different problems have in common

3. **Abstraction:** Separating details that matter from details that are not important

4. **Algorithm Design:** Creating a solution with simple steps that anyone can follow

DECOMPOSITION

Before beginning work on a solution, you need to understand all the parts of the problem. Once you understand each part, you can break the problem into smaller tasks. Decomposition makes problems more manageable to solve.

FOR EXAMPLE, when writing a book report, you would break the assignment down into smaller, simpler tasks:

1. Read the book.

2. Identify the main characters.

3. Identify the theme.

4. Analyze tone, plot, and character relationships.

5. Write about the tone, plot, and characters in the book.

Decomposition helps to identify where to start and the tasks that need to be completed.

PATTERN RECOGNITION

Patterns are events that are repeated. Recognizing where you have created solutions to similar problems before will help you create solutions that can be used to complete different tasks.

FOR EXAMPLE, if you've used a format or a template for writing book report outlines in the past, you can include that same process in your program. A book report outline may be different, but the process of writing the report is the same.

ABSTRACTION

Abstraction is focusing on the important ideas of a problem and ignoring details that will not help you find a solution.

FOR EXAMPLE, focusing on the important parts of the book (like the relationships between major characters, the setting, or the theme), and not on less important information (like conversations between minor characters or daily events), helps you create a program that is not specific to one book. The program would work with books that have different plots, but include major characters, settings, and themes.

ALGORITHM DESIGN

Algorithm design means writing out the steps you need to follow so that you can get the same solution every time. When a solution is carried out by an algorithm, the solution becomes reusable.

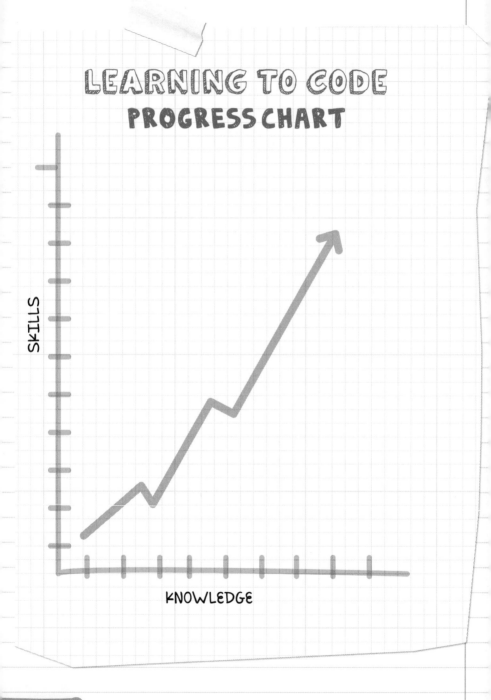

LEARNING TO CODE
PROGRESS CHART

SKILLS

KNOWLEDGE

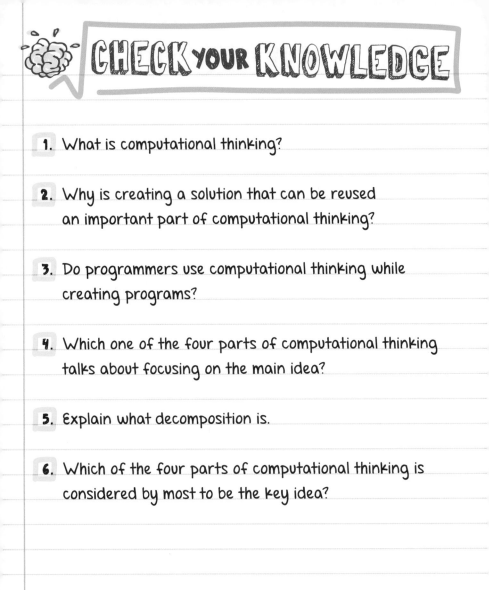

CHECK YOUR KNOWLEDGE

1. What is computational thinking?

2. Why is creating a solution that can be reused an important part of computational thinking?

3. Do programmers use computational thinking while creating programs?

4. Which one of the four parts of computational thinking talks about focusing on the main idea?

5. Explain what decomposition is.

6. Which of the four parts of computational thinking is considered by most to be the key idea?

ANSWERS

CHECK YOUR ANSWERS

1. A way to problem solve by developing algorithms for a solution that can be programmed into a computer language

2. It makes the computer more efficient. The computer can reuse information/solutions it already has.

3. Yes. From planning through testing, computational thinking is used.

4. Abstraction

5. Decomposition is breaking down a large task into smaller tasks.

6. Algorithm design

Unit 5

I'M A FREE SPIRIT KIND OF PROGRAMMER.

Universal Programming Principles

Chapter 14

VARIABLES

In math, a **VARIABLE** is a letter or symbol used in place of a quantity we don't know yet. The variable is a placeholder for a number in a mathematical expression or equation. In computer programming, a variable is a container for storing a value. The variable is stored in the computer's memory and can be used or changed throughout the program. Variables act as stand-ins or placeholders for values that are stored in the computer.

The name of the variable is the **IDENTIFIER**. The information that the variable contains is the **VALUE**. Variable values can be text, numbers, or other types of data.

For example, the score in a computer game is the variable. If the game starts out at zero and the player earns one point, here's how the variable would work:

SCORE

12

Value

Identifier

Variable

The program finds where the variable value for "score" is stored, then replaces the previous value of 0 with the new value: 1.

ASSIGNING AND NAMING VARIABLES

To create a variable within a program, you have to **DECLARE** it. When you declare a variable, you're telling the computer to create a space for information

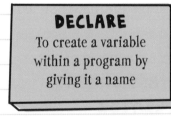

DECLARE
To create a variable within a program by giving it a name

and to assign that space a name. It's like organizing a bunch of toys using boxes on a shelf. For each type of toy, you pick a box, label it, and put the toys inside the box.

To assign a value to a variable, use the equal sign (=). The identifier goes on the left of the equal sign, and the value goes on the right. You can assign a new value to your variable anytime you want.

The = symbol is called an **ASSIGNMENT OPERATOR** in programming because it's used to assign a value to a variable.

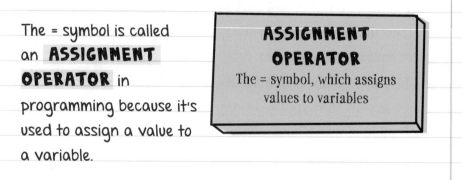

ASSIGNMENT OPERATOR
The = symbol, which assigns values to variables

In programming, the = sign doesn't mean "equals"; it means "is assigned."

name = "Jason" means that the variable *name* is assigned the value *Jason*.

There are specific rules for how you can identify or name variables. Different programming languages may have different rules, but the common rules are:

- Variable names should be short and should clearly describe what the variable represents.

  This works: score

  This doesn't work: this_variable_represents_player_1_score

  > Too long!

- Variables must begin with a letter of the alphabet.

  This works: firstPlayer

  This doesn't work: 1stPlayer

- Variables can contain letters, numbers, and some characters like an underscore. No reserved characters (like #, @, &, %) or spaces are allowed. When you want to use more than one word to name a variable, you can use the underscore (_) symbol instead of a space or use uppercase letters to start each word with no space between words.

These work: first_player or firstPlayer or FirstPlayer

These don't work: first player or first#player or first@player

Some words already have special meanings within a program and cannot be used as identifiers. These words depend on which programming language you are using.

FOR EXAMPLE, Python uses the word "return" to produce a value of an expression or function. Here are some reserved words (words you can't use for naming) in Python:

PYTHON RESERVED WORDS

true	for	false	import	and
not	if	or	else	return
none	while	elif		

TYPES OF INFORMATION VARIABLES CAN STORE

Variables can store many different types of information (called data types).

String Values

STRING variables can store any kind of character (including letters, numbers, symbols, and special characters). For example, in a quiz program, we could use string variables to store questions and answers in the program.

I CAN STORE ANYTHING.

A string is always placed inside quotation marks.

EXAMPLES:

String

name = "Alan Turing"
fruit_salad = "Yummy yummy"

Variable name (Identifier)

Numeric Values

Variables can also store **numeric values**, including integers (positive and negative whole numbers) or floating point numbers (numbers with a decimal point). For example, we can use a variable to store the amount of time it takes a player to complete a level in a game.

Do not use quotation marks with numeric values.

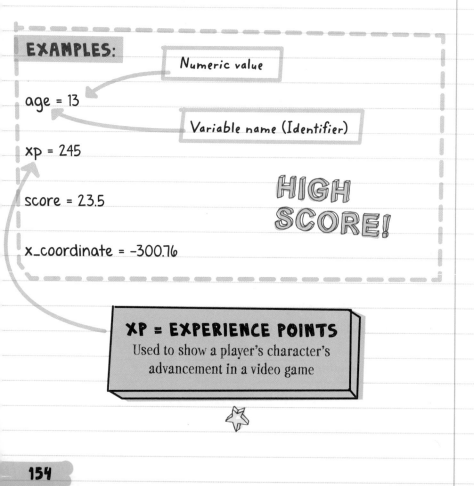

EXAMPLES:

Numeric value

age = 13

Variable name (Identifier)

xp = 245

score = 23.5

HIGH SCORE!

x_coordinate = -300.76

XP = EXPERIENCE POINTS
Used to show a player's character's advancement in a video game

You can use algebraic expressions when assigning values to variables. For example, we can use a variable to store the experience points a player has and add 5 points to the value every time they reach a goal (score = x + 5).

We could also use math to add points to a score variable.

FOR EXAMPLE, to add 2 points to a value we can use:

score = 5 + 2

Because "score" is an integer variable, it has the value of 7, the sum of the integer values.

But if you made "score" store a string by putting 5 + 2 inside quotation marks like this:

score = "5 + 2"

Then "score" is storing the string value of "5 + 2", the actual content within the quotes.

Boolean Values

Sometimes programmers need to know if something is true or false. For example, in a game they want to know if the game is over or if it is still going. Or, did the user get a quiz question right or wrong? When the information we want to store is true or false (can also be "yes" or "no"), then we can use another data type called **BOOLEAN** (pronounced "BOO-lee-un"). Boolean variables can only have two possible values: **true** or **false**.

Boolean variables are named after the English mathematician George Boolean.

TRUE!

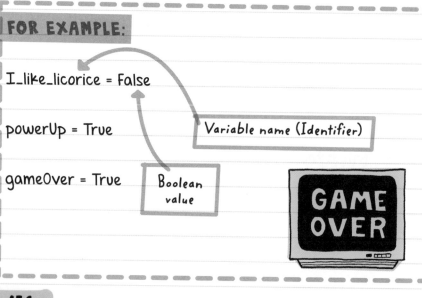

FOR EXAMPLE:

I_like_licorice = False

powerUp = True

gameOver = True

Variable name (Identifier)

Boolean value

GAME OVER

Lists

An **ARRAY** variable stores an entire list of information. This is useful when you have multiple pieces of information that you want to store in one place. For example, in a Hangman game program you could use a list (array) to store all the letters the player guesses. Each time the player guesses a new letter, it would be added to the end of the list.

CHECK YOUR KNOWLEDGE

1. In computer science, variables:
   A. are numbers like pi
   B. represent parts of an experiment that are measured or tested
   C. are placeholders for storing information
   D. are unchangeable

2. What is the difference between a variable's identifier and its value?

3. Explain what it means to declare a variable.

4. Which of the following variables are string types? (There may be more than one.)
   A. character = "Dr."
   B. vehicle = "Ambulance"
   C. speed = 37
   D. lives = "3"

5. Assuming a player's score starts at 0 and increases by 1 whenever they reach a goal, what data type would be best used to store this value in a variable with the identifier "score"?

A. Numeric

B. Array

C. Boolean

D. String

6. What would be the value of "var_x" after this statement runs: var_x = 6 – 4

A. 10

B. 2

C. "6 – 4"

D. undefined

7. What would be the value of "var_x" after this statement runs: var_x = "6 – 4"

A. 10

B. 2

C. "6 – 4"

D. undefined

MORE QUESTIONS

8. What is the assignment operator? What does it do?

9. Label each kind of variable:

    A. adaLovelace = "First programmer"

    B. Hotel_Floor = "13"

    C. Jersey = 18

    D. QueenOf = "Sheba"

    E. I_love_Mom = True

10. Choose the variable names that do not follow the naming rules. Explain why they are incorrect:

    A. "teacherNames"

    B. RangersScore

    C. School Assignment

    D. My_Absolute_Best_Ever_Summer_Vacation_Do_You_ Want_To_Hear_About_It

    E. 6ofSpades

CHECK YOUR ANSWERS

1. C

2. The identifier is the name of the variable and doesn't change, but the value is the data stored in the location designated by the variable and can change often.

3. When you declare a variable, you are telling the computer to create a space for information and to assign that space a name.

4. A, B, D

5. A

6. B

7. C

MORE ANSWERS

8. The assignment operator is the = symbol. It is used to assign values to variables.

9. **A.** String
   B. String
   C. Integer
   D. String
   E. Boolean

10. **A.** Starts and ends with a quotation mark
    C. Has a space in the name
    D. Is too long
    E. Starts with a number

Chapter 15

CONDITIONAL STATEMENTS

Conditional statements run a chunk of code only when a certain condition is met. Conditional statements follow the **IF... THEN FORMAT** (*if* this, *then* that), and they allow programs to be more flexible and powerful because they can change depending on different conditions.

For example:

- If you touch the enemy, **then** your character dies.

- If you cross the finish line first, **then** you win.

- If you score a goal, **then** your score increases by one point.

Here's what a basic conditional statement looks like:

If a specific thing happens
   Then this other thing will happen

Here's what a conditional statement could look like in a quiz game:

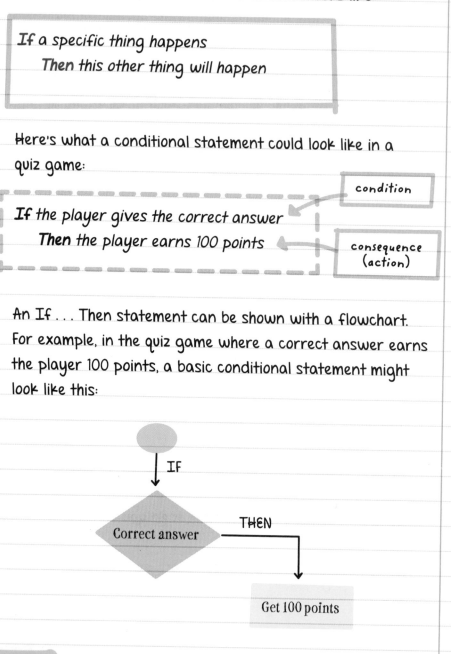

condition

If the player gives the correct answer
   Then the player earns 100 points

consequence
(action)

An If . . . Then statement can be shown with a flowchart. For example, in the quiz game where a correct answer earns the player 100 points, a basic conditional statement might look like this:

IF

Correct answer   THEN

Get 100 points

You can have a different action happen if your condition is false. To do that, use **ELSE** and then describe the different action.

If a specific thing happens
   Then this other thing will happen
Else
   A different thing will happen

Here's what a conditional statement with an "else" consequence could look like in the quiz game:

If the player gives the correct answer
   Then the player earns 100 points
Else
   The player loses 50 points

An If ... Then ... Else statement can also be shown with a flowchart. For example:

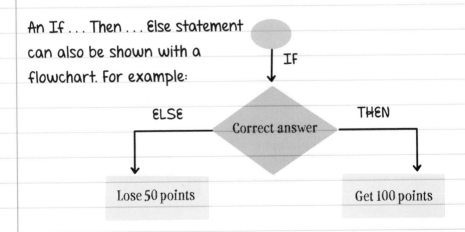

IF

ELSE

THEN

Correct answer

Lose 50 points

Get 100 points

You can combine multiple conditional statements to create even more consequences. To do that, use **ELSE IF** in an "if" statement.

Every "else if" added within a statement adds another action, or consequence, that could happen. For example, here's how you can use an "else if" to get three consequences (three different actions) to happen in a conditional statement:

If a specific thing happens
    this other thing will happen
Else if another thing happens
    A different thing will happen
Else
    Yet another thing will happen

Here's what an if statement with an else if consequence and an else consequence looks like when calculating the number of points a player should get depending on the number of quiz questions they get correct:

If a player answers 10 questions correctly
  Player is awarded 100 points
Else if player answers 5 or more questions correctly
  Player is awarded 50 points
Else
  Player is awarded 10 points

The flowchart would look like this:

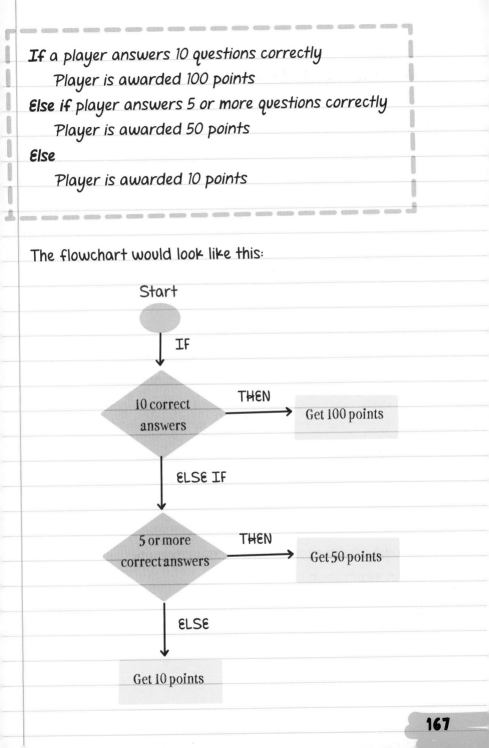

Start

IF

10 correct answers

THEN

Get 100 points

ELSE IF

5 or more correct answers

THEN

Get 50 points

ELSE

Get 10 points

COMPARISON OPERATORS

COMPARISON OPERATORS (symbols used when comparing values) are used in programming to form Boolean expressions.

OPERATOR	DESCRIPTION
>	is greater than
<	is less than
>=	is greater than or equal to
<=	is less than or equal to
==	is equal to
!=	is not equal to

Put a value on either side of a comparison operator to make a Boolean expression.

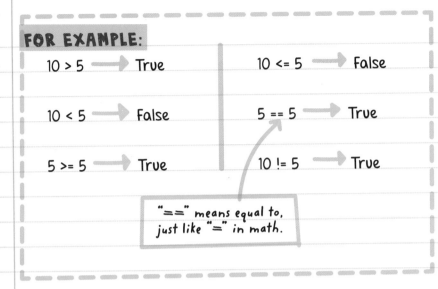

10 > 5 → True	10 <= 5 → False
10 < 5 → False	5 == 5 → True
5 >= 5 → True	10 != 5 → True

"==" means equal to, just like "=" in math.

Comparison operators can be used in flowcharts. This flowchart shows that if 10 is greater than 5, you'll say "yay," else you'll say "boo." You'll say "yay" because 10 > 5 is True.

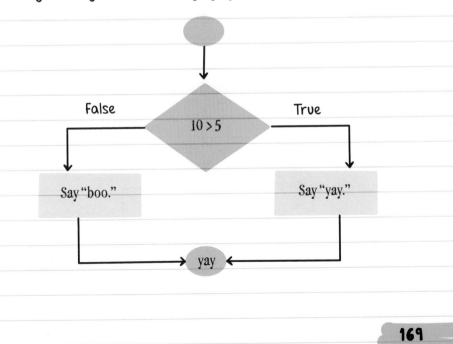

You can use the == operator to compare two values. For example, you could see if a game is over or not based on the player reaching a score of 10 like this:

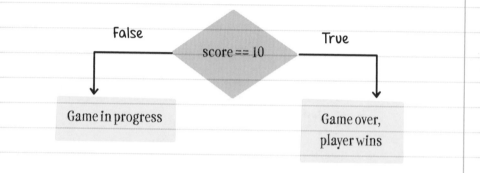

You could also use a Boolean variable by itself.

For example, in a race game, you could have a variable called "boost." The value of the variable is set to True if the player earns a speed boost. The program uses a conditional statement to check if boost is true (the player has earned a boost). If so, then the program should increase the player's speed:

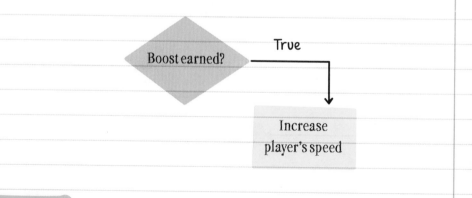

COMPOUND CONDITIONALS

To check if multiple conditions are true in one conditional statement, you can combine Boolean expressions within a single conditional statement.

COMPOUND CONDITIONALS are conditionals that combine two or more Boolean expressions.

LOGICAL OPERATORS are used to combine the expressions. The most common logical operators are AND, OR, and NOT.

AND statements are true when both conditions are true.

True AND True → True

For example, if a player finishes a race and if they finished faster than anyone else, they are the first-place winner.

But if one or both of the conditions is false, then the AND statement is false.

True AND False → False

False AND False → False

FOR EXAMPLE, a game player sets a new speed run record only if they beat the game **AND** finish in less time than the current record.

If the player just finishes the game but doesn't do it in less time, or doesn't finish the game at all (if both conditions are not met), then the player does not set a new record.

Beat game
AND
time < 9.58 minutes

True

Player set new speed record

The OR statement is true if at least one of the conditions is true.

False OR True → True

True OR True → True

False OR False → False

FOR EXAMPLE, in a ball game, if the player hits the right wall **OR** if they hit the left wall, then they lose and the game ends.

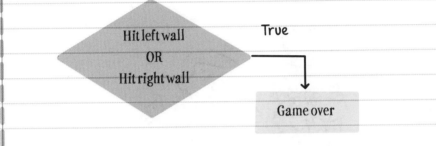

If either condition of hitting either wall is met, then the consequence (losing) becomes true.

The NOT statement doesn't compare two conditions; instead, it reverses the value from True to False and False to True.

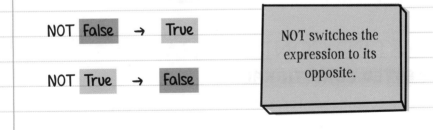

NOT switches the expression to its opposite.

IT'S OPPOSITE DAY.

NESTED CONDITIONALS

A **NESTED CONDITIONAL** is one conditional inside of another conditional. For example, in a virtual pet game you could nest conditionals to determine the mood of the pet based on different conditions like hunger and tiredness. If the virtual pet is not awake, show the mood as asleep.

If the pet is awake, and if the pet's hunger is below 50 percent, then show a happy mood, else show a hungry mood.

So, if the pet is awake and its hunger level is at 75 percent, then its mood will be hungry.

The flowchart looks like this:

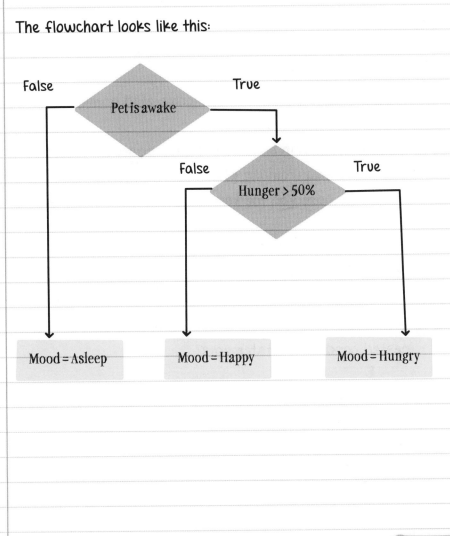

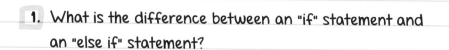

CHECK YOUR KNOWLEDGE

1. What is the difference between an "if" statement and an "else if" statement?

2. Assume a player scored 15 points by the time they completed a game. Does the following evaluate to true or false?

   Player score > 20 AND Player completed game

3. Assume an alien in a game has been aggravated and is 200 feet away from the player. Would the alien attack the player based on the following conditional statement?

   If alien is aggravated OR if alien is within 100 feet
      Then attack player

4. When would you use an "else if" statement versus nested conditional statements?

5. Circle the part of the pseudocode below that is the conditional part of the statement:

   If it is summer
      Then display "Swimming Pool Open!"

6. Assuming a player answered seven quiz questions correctly, how many coins would they earn:

If player answers 10 questions correctly
    Give player 10 coins
Else if player answers 8 or more answers correctly
    Give player 4 coins
Else if player answers 5 or more answers correctly
    Give player 1 coin
Else
    Give player 0 coins

7. Assume it is winter when an electronic display runs the code below. What will the display say?

If it is summer
    Then display "Swimming Pool Open!"
Else
    Display "Swimming Pool Closed"

CHECK YOUR ANSWERS

1. An "else if" statement is always nested within an "if" statement and doesn't exist on its own. An "if" statement can exist without an "else if" statement.

2. False

3. Yes, the alien would attack the player.

4. If the conditions are dependent on each other, then an "else if" statement should be used; otherwise a nested conditional is appropriate.

5. Circle the part of the pseudocode below that is the condition part of the statement:

(If it is summer)
   Then display "Swimming Pool Open!"

6. The player earns 1 coin.

7. The display will say "Swimming Pool Closed."

Chapter 16

LOOPS

LOOP STATEMENTS allow you to easily repeat a chunk of code many times. For example, in a game with a bouncing ball, it would be too much work to type out the code to make the ball bounce up and down a thousand times (move up, then fall down; move up, then fall down; move up, then fall down . . .). Instead, you can put the repeated code in a loop:

Repeat 1,000 times
    move up, then fall down

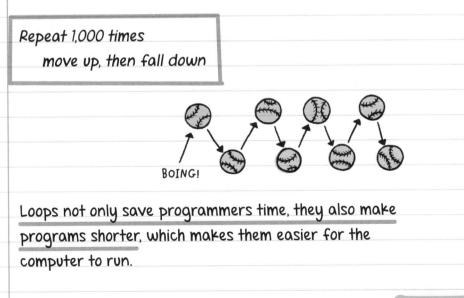

BOING!

Loops not only save programmers time, they also make programs shorter, which makes them easier for the computer to run.

When creating a loop, you should answer these questions:

* What do I want to repeat?
* When do I want the loop to stop repeating?

There are different types of loops:

A **FOR LOOP** is a type of loop that repeats itself a set number of times. *For* loops are used when you know the number of times you want to repeat something. *For* loops and arrays are often used together.

FOR EXAMPLE, we could use a *for* loop to list all the top-ten players of a game whose names are stored in an array.

> an array containing the names of the top-ten players

Top10 = ["player1", "player2", "player3", "player4", "player5", "player6", "player7", "player8", "player9", "player10"]

> begin the *for* loop, repeat the code in the loop for each item in the Top10 list

for item in Top10:

> the code that's repeated—print out each name in the Top10 list

    print(item)

A **WHILE LOOP** will run a chunk of code until a condition is met. This is used when you don't know the exact number of times you want the loop to repeat and it depends on another factor.

FOR EXAMPLE, in a quiz game you can repeatedly ask a question until the user gets the correct answer:

while answer is not correct:
    Ask the user, "What is the name of the current
    Vice President of the United States?"
print "you are right!"

The quiz game would continue to ask the question until the user got the right answer, even if it took 100 attempts!

A **NESTED LOOP** is when one loop is put inside another loop. Nested loops help create more complex repeating code.

FOR EXAMPLE, you could program background music for a game using nested loops.

A nested loop can repeat a beat until the game is over. An inner loop can repeat a bass drum sound 7 times before a snare sound is played:

OUTER LOOP

Repeat until the game is over:

INNER LOOP

Repeat 7 times:
    Play bass drum sound

Play snare sound

In pseudocode, use indenting to show code that is inside or dependent on other code.

Be careful when using nested loops, because it's easy to get confused about which chunks of code should be repeated.

The inner loop always has to run through all its sequences before the outer loop code is run again.

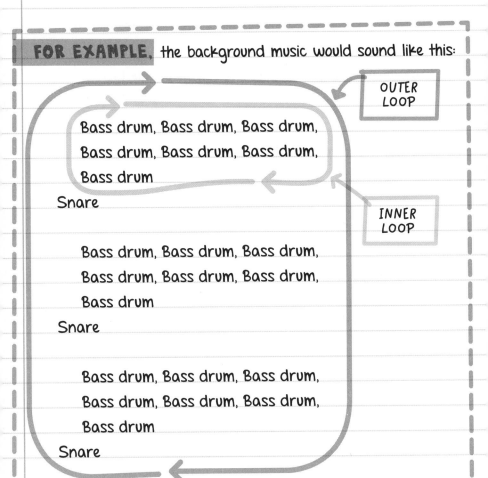

FOR EXAMPLE, the background music would sound like this:

OUTER LOOP

Bass drum, Bass drum, Bass drum, Bass drum, Bass drum, Bass drum, Bass drum

Snare

INNER LOOP

Bass drum, Bass drum, Bass drum, Bass drum, Bass drum, Bass drum, Bass drum

Snare

Bass drum, Bass drum, Bass drum, Bass drum, Bass drum, Bass drum, Bass drum

Snare

The bass sound is played 7 times (running through all versions of its loop) before moving on to the next line of code, playing the snare sound. Then the entire outer loop is repeated until the game is over.

1. How are *While* loops different from *For* loops?

2. When you put a loop inside a loop, it's called a _____ loop.

3. If you want to repeat a chunk of code 6 times, you should use a _____ loop.

4. What will the following print?

Repeat 3 times:
    Print "Jump"
    Repeat 2 times:
        "Duck"
Print "Slide"

5. When will the outer loop in the following pseudocode stop repeating?

While number of ice cream cones > 0:
    Get a cone
    Repeat 3 times:
        Add scoop of ice cream

6. Why is indenting nested loops helpful when writing pseudocode?

7. If you want to loop through the contents of an array, which type of loop should you use?

CHECK YOUR ANSWERS

1. *While* loops will repeat as long as a condition is true, but a *For* loop will repeat a set number of times.

2. Nested

3. *For*

4. Jump, Duck, Duck, Jump, Duck, Duck, Jump, Duck, Duck, Slide

5. The loop will stop running when there are zero ice cream cones.

6. Indenting is a great way to show where loops begin and end, making the code easier to read and understand.

7. *For* loop

Chapter 17

EVENTS

EVENTS are actions that cause something to happen within a program. They make programs interactive because the user is in control. For example:

- clicking a mouse
- pressing a key
- tapping a touch screen

Events can also be things that happen within the program—like when a character dies and the message "Game Over" appears.

Events can be external actions from a user, like a mouse click. They can also be internal actions that happen within a program, like a web browser completely loading a web page.

An **EVENT HANDLER** is the code that is run when an event happens. Pressing the spacebar in a game is an event, but the event handler is the code in the game that tells a character to jump when the spacebar is pressed.

FOR EXAMPLE, in a fruit-chopping game, you could add code like the pseudocode below that swings a chef's knife every time the spacebar is pressed.

```
on press_spacebar:
    swing chef's knife
```

CHECK YOUR KNOWLEDGE

1. Give an example of an event from a keyboard.

2. How is the event handler different from an event?

3. What would your favorite app be like without events?

4. What is the event in the following pseudocode?

on-screen tap:
    If player tapped balloon:
        Pop balloon

5. What is the event handler in the following pseudocode?

on-screen tap:
    If player tapped balloon:
        Pop balloon

CHECK YOUR ANSWERS

1. Pressing any key on a computer's keyboard could be programmed to be an event that can be used to trigger something to happen in a program.

2. The event handler is the code that runs when an event happens. Events are actions.

3. Apps and all interactive programs wouldn't be useful without events. You wouldn't be able to interact with it. Programs would effectively become pictures or movies that you can look at but not interact with.

4. The event is the player physically tapping the device's screen that this program is running on.

5. The event handler is the code that tests if the balloon was touched and pops the balloon.

Chapter 18

PROCEDURES

REUSING CODE

A **PROCEDURE** is a piece of code that you can easily use over and over. Loops are great when you want to repeat an action multiple times in a row. But when you want to use the same chunk of code in different parts of a program, you will need a procedure.

For example, in a four-person game we could program each character individually to jump when each player presses their jump button. But a better way is to create a single jump procedure for each character to use when each player presses their jump button.

> **PROCEDURE**
> A piece of code that has a name and completes a specific task

Declaring a Procedure

Instead of copying and pasting the same chunk of code throughout a program, a programmer can save that chunk of code and name it. When the name of the code (the procedure) is used in a program, the computer understands that it should use that chunk of code.

To create a procedure, you must declare it by giving it a name and adding the code you want to use as a procedure. (It's like declaring a variable, where you give a variable a name and a value).

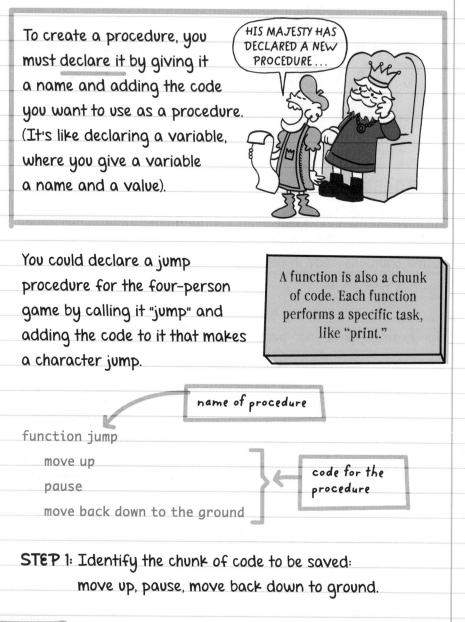

HIS MAJESTY HAS DECLARED A NEW PROCEDURE...

You could declare a jump procedure for the four-person game by calling it "jump" and adding the code to it that makes a character jump.

A function is also a chunk of code. Each function performs a specific task, like "print."

name of procedure

```
function jump
    move up
    pause
    move back down to the ground
```

code for the procedure

STEP 1: Identify the chunk of code to be saved: move up, pause, move back down to ground.

STEP 2: Name the chunk of code and save:

Jump = move up, pause, move back down to ground.

Calling a Procedure

Declaring a procedure just gives it a name; it won't run the code. The procedure will not do anything if you don't tell it to. When you're ready to use the procedure in your program, you have to **CALL** it.

CALL
When you use the name of a procedure in a program so that it can run the code

For example, a procedure can be called as many times as you want.

When Player 1 hits the spacebar
    Jump ← name of procedure

When Player 2 hits the up arrow
    Jump

When Player 3 hits the W key
    Jump

When Player 4 hits the I key
    Jump

The same procedure—jump—is called when four different events happen. When the computer reads "jump," it will look up the jump function and run the code found there.

Parameters and Returns

PARAMETERS are variables whose value is passed into a procedure. It can give limits or ranges to the procedure, like "jump 3 times." The only difference between a parameter and a variable is that a parameter value can only be used within a procedure, but a variable can be used throughout the entire program.

A parameter's input can change how a function acts.

FOR EXAMPLE, in a space battle game we can use a function to animate a laser shooting out of a spaceship's gun. Because we want the laser to shoot at whatever the user is aiming at and not the same spot every time, we need to input (to the laser function) the location that the user is aiming at. The laser function can then change where it shoots each time the user fires the spaceship's gun.

> x and y parameters can give the x- and y-coordinates to the function so the laser shoots in the direction the player is aiming.

Function Shoot_Laser (x,y):
    Display laser graphic next to
    spaceship gun
    While on the screen:
        Move toward (x,y)

Some procedures or functions can **RETURN A VALUE**. The return value is the procedure output. Depending on the procedure, you could get a different return value every time you ran it.

Parameters and return values are often used in the same function.

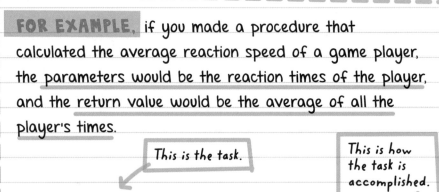

FOR EXAMPLE, if you made a procedure that calculated the average reaction speed of a game player, the parameters would be the reaction times of the player, and the return value would be the average of all the player's times.

This is the task.

This is how the task is accomplished.

Function Average_Time (Player_Times_array):
    Average = Sum all times in Player_Times_array
        divided by number of items in array
    Return Average

This is the result of the task.

After calling the Function Average_Time, the function would return a value that is the player's average time.

CHECK YOUR KNOWLEDGE

1. A piece of code that you can easily use over and over again is called a _____.

2. What's the advantage of using parameters with a procedure?

3. The output of a procedure is called the _____ value.

4. If you want to use the same chunk of code multiple times in your program, you should make the code a _____.

5. What is the return value for the following function?

```
Score = 5
    Function Score_Bonus (score):
        Return Score + 10
```

ANSWERS

CHECK YOUR ANSWERS

1. Procedure

2. It allows you to reuse the same code many times, even with different data.

3. Return

4. Procedure or function

5. 15

Unit 6

Programming with Scratch

Chapter 19

GETTING STARTED

GETTING TO KNOW SCRATCH

Scratch is a free graphical programming language.

- It is a programming language that is simple to use because you don't have to type in commands.

- It works by snapping precoded **BLOCKS** together to create scripts (programs).

- Scratch is useful for making games and interactive stories.

> **BLOCK**
> A block in Scratch is a graphic that represents a chunk of code. Blocks snap together depending on their shape (like puzzle pieces).

BLOCKS

Instead of programming by typing out commands, in Scratch programs are made by connecting blocks together vertically. All a user has to do is snap blocks together and their code will run in order from the first block (at the top) to the last block (at the bottom).

Blocks look like this ➜

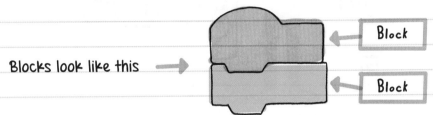

Block

Block

Blocks fit together like puzzle pieces and come in several categories that organize blocks into similar actions. There are six types of blocks that snap together in different ways depending on their shape (like puzzle pieces that only fit in a specific way). The shape of the block doesn't control what it does; it only controls how other blocks connect to it.

You can stack a couple of blocks together to make a short and simple program that will move a character across the screen. Or you can make a long and complicated program that uses hundreds of blocks, like for a game with multiple levels.

SOME SAY HE'S BEEN CODING FOR OVER A HUNDRED YEARS AND HIS PROJECT USES A MILLION BLOCKS!

The **Blocks menu** organizes all the blocks into nine categories, each represented by a colored dot and a category title.

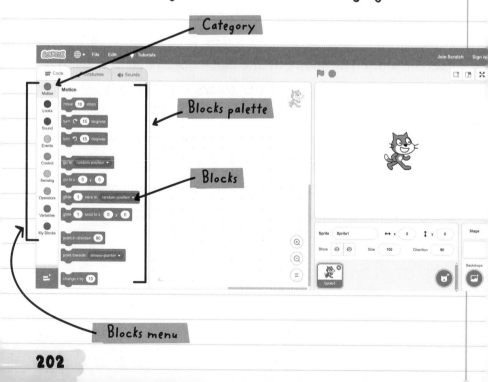

Category

Blocks palette

Blocks

Blocks menu

Each category is a grouping of blocks that does similar things:

- **Motion**, **Looks**, and **Sound** blocks control objects in the program and what they do.

- **Variables** and **Operators** blocks store and manage information.

- **Events** and **Sensing** blocks make specific actions happen.

- **Control** blocks direct the program, script.

- **My Blocks** allow you to make and store your own custom blocks.

Scripts

A single group of blocks that are all connected is called a **SCRIPT**. A script can be a very basic program that is two blocks long, or a million (or more) blocks long. Any number of scripts can be used together to make a single project. Large projects such as a multilevel game can use dozens of long scripts.

When making a script, you can stack blocks together or place one block inside the other.

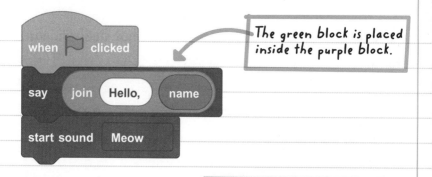

The green block is placed inside the purple block.

Scripts are created in the **SCRIPTS AREA**.

Blocks are used by dragging them over from the Blocks palette to the Scripts Area.

SCRIPTS AREA
The space on the screen where blocks are combined to make scripts

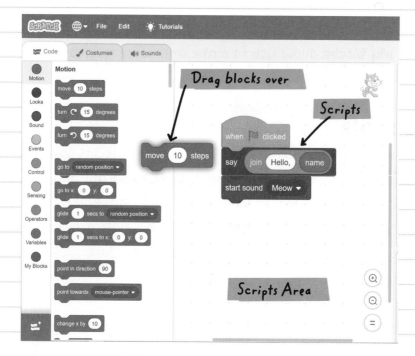

You can add COMMENTS by right-clicking (or ctrl-clicking for Macs) directly on a block or on the Scripts Area and selecting "Add Comment." Comments help programmers keep track of what specific chunks of code do and make it easier to share code with others.

I'M WRITING A SCRIPT.

ME TOO!

Comments are not run as part of the code.

FOR EXAMPLE, if you wrote a chunk of code that slowly subtracted health points from a player in a game, you could comment on it as a reminder to yourself that "this code is for the poison effect; it decreases player health by 5 points every 10 seconds."

This is what a Scratch comment looks like.

this code is for the poison effect; it decreases player health by 5 points every 10 seconds.

If you're using the online version of Scratch, you can store your scripts in the backpack area.

Storing scripts is helpful because you can save time and effort by using the same script in more than one project.

FOR EXAMPLE, you might want to make a game that has a kangaroo that jumps. If you've already made a game that has a rabbit jumping, you could open the rabbit game, drop the jump script from the rabbit game into the backpack, open the new game, and drag the jump script from the backpack to your new kangaroo game.

I'M GOING TO SAVE THIS RABBIT SCRIPT FOR LATER.

SWEET CODING TIP!

SPRITES

SPRITES are the characters and objects used in programs. You can control sprites with blocks.

Programs can use one or many sprites. Scratch has a library of sprites. You can also draw or upload your own sprite.

The SPRITE LIST displays all the sprites used in a project. Each sprite is represented by a **THUMBNAIL IMAGE**.

THUMBNAIL IMAGE
A smaller version of the original image

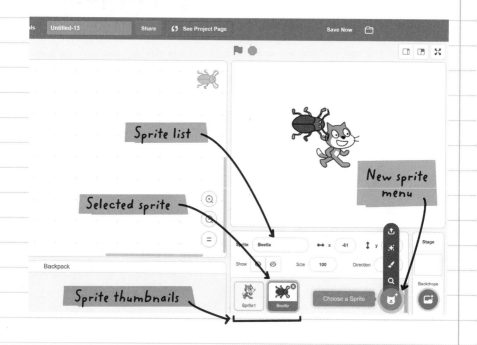

Sprite list

Selected sprite

New sprite menu

Sprite thumbnails

When you have multiple sprites in your program, click on the thumbnail to select the sprite you want to write a script for, change the appearance of, or add a sound to.

New sprites can be added to the Sprite list using the New Sprite menu, where you can Choose a Sprite, Paint, Surprise (a random sprite from the library is chosen for you), or Upload Sprite.

Costumes

Each sprite can have multiple **COSTUMES**. Costumes let you change how a sprite looks, like the position of its limbs, what it's wearing, or its size. Costumes can be used to animate sprites, like the pages in a flip-book cartoon.

> **COSTUMES**
> Different images used to change the appearance of a single sprite

FOR EXAMPLE, here are four costumes that can be used to make it look like the sprite is moving:

Costumes are edited in the Costumes tab.

Costume list

The **COSTUME LIST** shows a thumbnail for each of the sprite's costumes. In the New Costume menu, you can:

- choose a costume from the library
- draw or upload a file
- take a picture

You can view the costumes of other sprites by selecting the sprite in the Sprite list.

The **IMAGE EDITOR** has tools to draw new costumes or edit the costumes of existing sprites. Costumes can be created in either **BITMAP** or **VECTOR** mode. Both modes will allow you to create the same artwork, but they are different in how the image is made.

Bitmap mode: Tools are more recognizable (paintbrush, line, circle, text, fill, erase, and others) as editing tools, but images can look grainy when enlarged.

Vector mode: Add, resize, and reshape shapes by pulling at the corners. Vector mode creates graphics that are more smoothly enlarged, making it better to use for projects that are viewed in full-screen mode.

Sounds

You can program your sprites to play sounds using blocks in the Sound category.

The **Sound list** shows all the sounds available for the selected sprite. You can also add sounds from Scratch's sound library or from uploaded music. Or you can record your own sound.

The **Sound Editor** allows you to edit sounds.

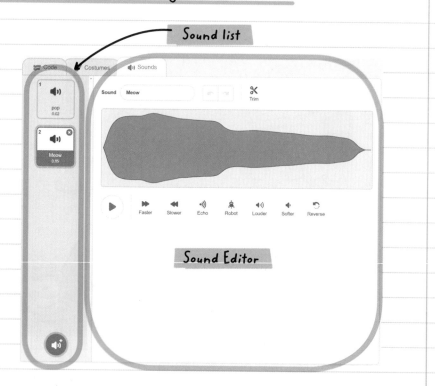

The shape on the screen represents the sound. It changes as the sound is changed.

Setting the Stage

The **STAGE** is the place where you can see the output of running your script. The green flag and the stop sign start and stop the program respectively.

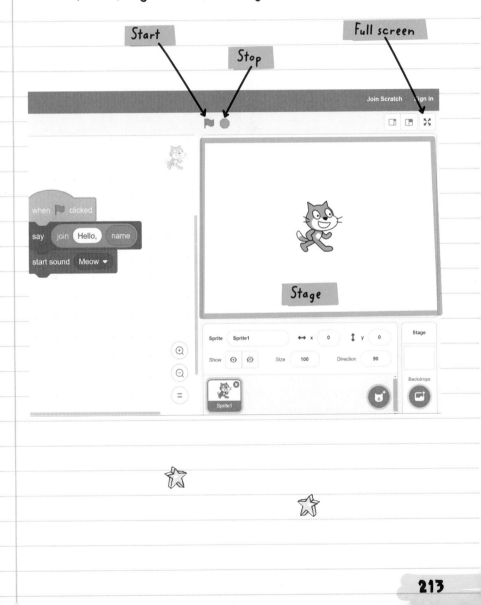

Sprites move around the stage using a **grid system** like the coordinate system used in math. The x- and y-coordinates are used to identify locations.

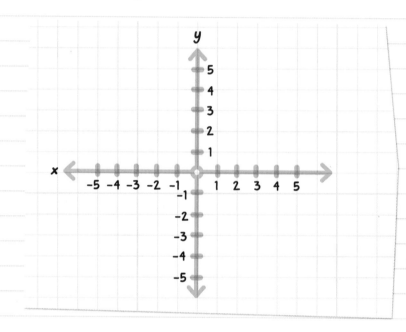

The x- and y-coordinates at the center of the stage are (0, 0). The stage is 360 steps tall and 480 steps wide.

MOTION BLOCKS move sprites around. They allow you to change the x- and y-coordinate positions.

FOR EXAMPLE, the 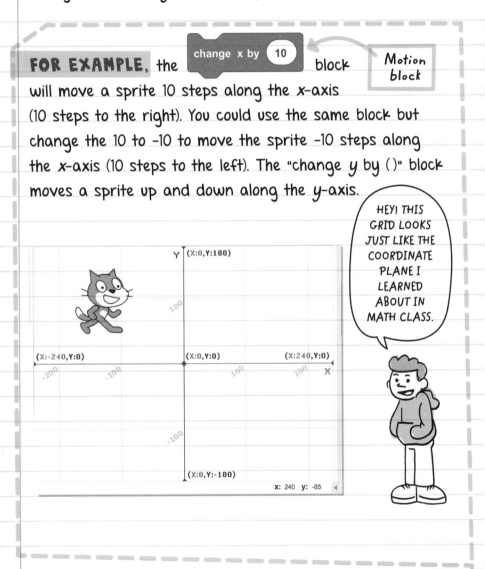 block will move a sprite 10 steps along the x-axis (10 steps to the right). You could use the same block but change the 10 to -10 to move the sprite -10 steps along the x-axis (10 steps to the left). The "change y by ( )" block moves a sprite up and down along the y-axis.

HEY! THIS GRID LOOKS JUST LIKE THE COORDINATE PLANE I LEARNED ABOUT IN MATH CLASS.

The background image (scenery) on the stage is called the **BACKDROP**. Select the stage thumbnail to create scripts for your backdrop and bring up the

> Tip: Add background theme music to a backdrop to play music while users play your game!

backdrop tab. You can edit backdrops with the backdrop tools in the backdrop tab. You can add scripts, additional backdrops, and sounds to the backdrop.

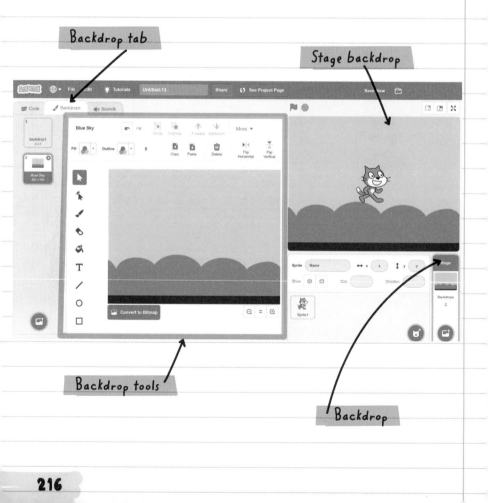

Backdrop tab

Stage backdrop

Backdrop tools

Backdrop

Sharing Projects

The online version of Scratch allows users to publish and share projects with the community. Once a project is shared, anyone in the world who goes to the Scratch website can see it.

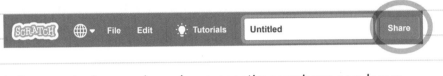

When projects are shared, community members can leave comments (questions, positive feedback) on the project pages. Each project has its own project page where the owner adds instructions, notes, and credits.

Extensions

EXTENSIONS can be used to add more blocks to the palette.

> **EXTENSIONS**
> Additional sets of new blocks that can add more functions

Extensions include:

* Music blocks that can play notes like musical instruments.

* Pen blocks that can be used to draw on the stage.

* Blocks that add interactive capabilities, like video sensing, text to speech, and translate.

* Blocks that allow Scratch to program other devices like micro:bit, LEGO Mindstorms EV3, and LEGO WeDo 2.0.

FOR EXAMPLE, you could build a Lego robot with a Mindstorm EV3 kit, connect it to your computer, and then use Scratch to program it to move around.

CHECK YOUR KNOWLEDGE

1. Describe what a script in Scratch is.

2. What are blocks in Scratch used for?

3. What is the Scripts Area used for and how is it used?

4. If you want to save a chunk of code to use in another project, which Scratch feature should you use?

5. Which of the following comments would not be appropriate to post on a project?
   A. The project rocks!
   B. How did you make the cat sit on the cactus?
   C. Great project. FYI I found a bug on level 2 in the game.
   D. What a waste of time, you should quit coding now.

6. Explain how a sprite would move on the stage with each of the following blocks:

A.

```
change y by 100
```

B.

```
go to x: 0 y: 0
```

C.

```
change x by: 100
```

7. A stack of blocks that will run as part of a program is called _____.

8. Describe what a costume is.

9. What is the stage used for?

10. What do you call the background image on the stage?

11. How can you participate in the Scratch community?

CHECK YOUR ANSWERS

1. A script is a collection of blocks that have been stacked together. Scripts can be a couple of blocks or many dozens of blocks long. They can be combined to create a program.

2. Each block represents a chunk of code. Instead of typing out words, Scratch uses these blocks as the instructions found in a program.

3. The Scripts Area is where the program is created. Blocks are dragged from the Blocks palette to the Scripts Area and snapped together to create scripts.

4. The backpack

5. D

MORE ANSWERS

6. A. The sprite would move up 100 steps.

B. The sprite would move to the center of the screen.

C. The sprite would move to the right 100 steps.

7. A script

8. A costume is a different version of what the sprite looks like.

9. It's where you can see your code run.

10. The backdrop

11. You can share your scripts and post comments on other members' scripts.

WAIT! LET ME CHANGE MY COSTUME FIRST!

BASIC ALGORITHMS

When you run a program in Scratch, each block completes its task before moving on to the next one in the script. Scripts run starting with the top block and working down to the last block.

> An algorithm is a list of steps to complete a task.

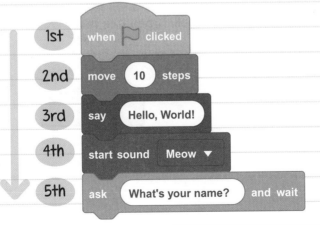

1st — when ⚑ clicked

2nd — move 10 steps

3rd — say Hello, World!

4th — start sound Meow ▼

5th — ask What's your name? and wait

There are two ways to make a script run:

- Click on any of the blocks in the script. (This runs the entire script starting at the top.)

- Use an event block.

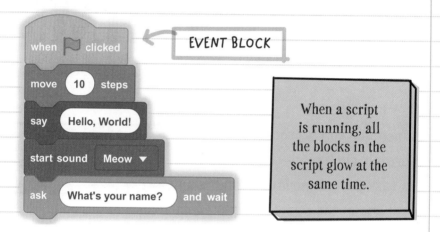

EVENT BLOCK

When a script is running, all the blocks in the script glow at the same time.

TYPES OF BLOCKS

The most commonly used block types are **hat** blocks and **stack** blocks.

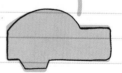

A **HAT BLOCK** starts the script it is attached to. It does not have a notch on its top and cannot fit under other blocks. Hat blocks are **event handlers** in Scratch—they listen for events and run when the event happens. For example, when green flag clicked is one of nine event blocks; it runs the code attached to it when the user clicks the green flag.

WE'RE ALWAYS ON TOP OF THINGS!

ME TOO!

Examples of events are when a user presses a key on the keyboard or when a sprite is clicked on.

A **STACK BLOCK** is a rectangular block that connects to other blocks.

ANIMATING A CAT

The default sprite for every new project is the **SCRATCH CAT**. Sprites can be programmed to move around the stage using blocks in the Motion category.

Walk

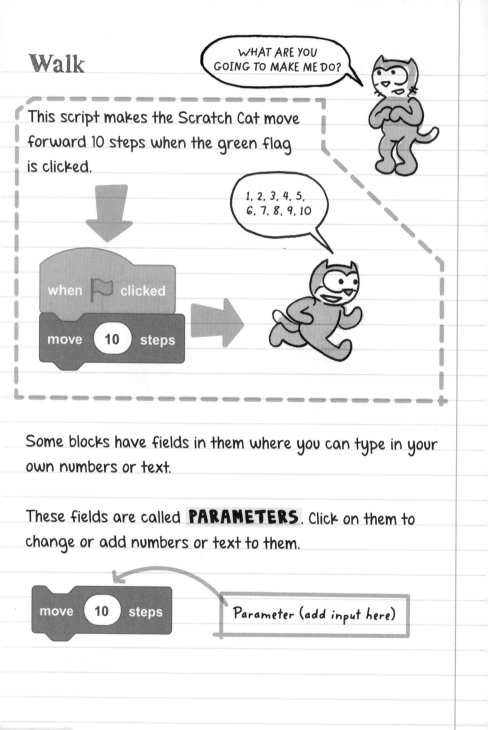

WHAT ARE YOU GOING TO MAKE ME DO?

This script makes the Scratch Cat move forward 10 steps when the green flag is clicked.

1, 2, 3, 4, 5, 6, 7, 8, 9, 10

when [flag] clicked

move 10 steps

Some blocks have fields in them where you can type in your own numbers or text.

These fields are called **PARAMETERS**. Click on them to change or add numbers or text to them.

move 10 steps

Parameter (add input here)

Parameters give the blocks more information and allow you to customize their actions. For example, you can use the say () block to make a sprite say what you want it to.

> say   I'm the coolest person in the world.

WELL, THEN, I GUESS IT MUST BE TRUE!

Parentheses ( ) are used to show a parameter, or input field, when writing out Scratch code. For example, this block:

> move **10** steps

would be written like this: **move () steps**.

Not all blocks have parameters—some are just labeled with the command they perform.

This script makes the Scratch Cat move forward 10 steps then switch to its next costume every time the green flag is clicked.

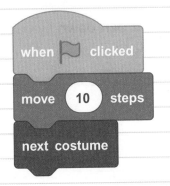

when ⚑ clicked

move **10** steps

next costume

If a script was made up of the event block and a move (1) step block, when you click the green flag a bunch of times, the Scratch Cat will walk across the stage. Clicking the green flag 3 times makes the cat take 3 steps, like this:

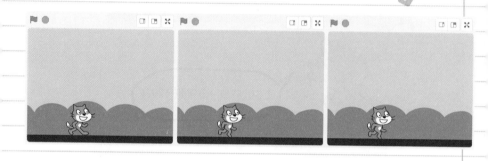

Sprites don't have to walk in straight lines. To make the Scratch Cat walk in a circle, add the turn clockwise (15) degrees block to the end of the script. Then press the green flag 24 times to make the Scratch Cat walk in a complete circle. Use the pen down block to draw the circle.

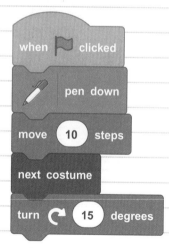

You press the green flag 24 times because 360 (the number of degrees in a circle) divided by 15 (the number of degrees turned each time) equals 24.

To make the Scratch Cat move in a bigger or smaller circle, the parameters in the **move ( ) steps** and **turn clockwise ( ) degrees** blocks can be changed. For example, to make the circle bigger, you can change the **turn clockwise ( ) degrees** input field from 15 to 5. Click the green flag 72 times, and it will make a bigger circle.

The blocks in the **Pen** category can be used to draw shapes on the stage. The **pen down** block is used to trace a line wherever the sprite moves.

To add pen blocks, open the Add Extension menu (bottom-left corner) and select the Pen category. After the Pen category is added, you'll see the Pen category blocks at the end of the Blocks menu.

Blocks can be inserted into the middle of scripts, not just added to the end. Scripts are run block by block from the first one at the top to the last one at the bottom. In order to trace a line wherever the sprite moves, the "pen down" block must run before the Scratch Cat starts to move. Insert the block toward the top of the script instead of at the end.

To insert a block within a script:

1. Hold the block between two other blocks to get a gap and shadow to appear.

2. Let go of the mouse.

The block will be inserted here.

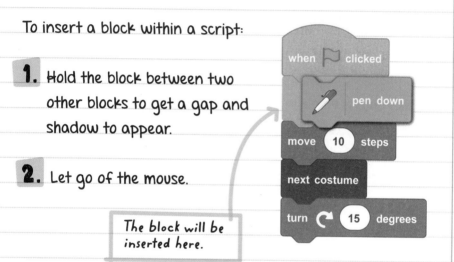

Glide

Another way to make sprites move around the stage is the glide () secs to x: () y: () block found in the Motion category. Instead of making the sprite walk or move instantly the way the move () steps block does, the glide () secs to x: () y: () block assigns a specific amount of time to move the sprite to a new location. The first parameter tells the sprite how long to take (in seconds), and the other two parameters tell it exactly where to go on the stage.

HEY, MAN, WHAT'S THE RUSH? I'M JUST GONNA GLIDE MY WAY OVER.

GOTTA MOVE, MOVE, MOVE!

glide **1** secs to x: **-50** y: **50** = glide for 1 second to coordinates (-50, 50)

Another movement block, the **go to x: () y: ()** block, can instantly move the sprite to a specific point on the screen every time the script runs. By entering 50 in the x parameter field and 50 in the y parameter field, the Scratch Cat will automatically jump to the location (50, 50).

Glide on over to the next page

FOR EXAMPLE: The following script makes the Scratch Cat glide around in a square.

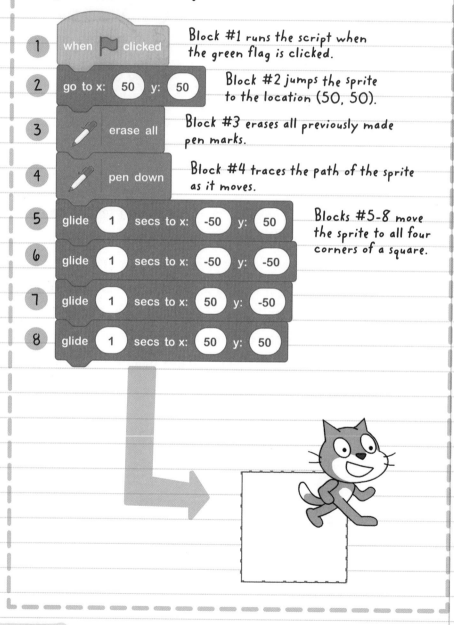

1. when 🏴 clicked

Block #1 runs the script when the green flag is clicked.

2. go to x: 50 y: 50

Block #2 jumps the sprite to the location (50, 50).

3. 🖊 erase all

Block #3 erases all previously made pen marks.

4. 🖊 pen down

Block #4 traces the path of the sprite as it moves.

5. glide 1 secs to x: -50 y: 50

6. glide 1 secs to x: -50 y: -50

7. glide 1 secs to x: 50 y: -50

8. glide 1 secs to x: 50 y: 50

Blocks #5-8 move the sprite to all four corners of a square.

DEBUGGING STRATEGIES

Programs don't always run as the programmer intended. There are strategies to debug (fix problems):

- Review scripts one block at a time. Read each block out loud and think about what each block actually does.

- Work with small chunks of code. Break up scripts and run only small chunks at a time. After running a chunk with no problems, add another set of blocks and continue to check for errors.

- Comment on scripts explaining what they do and review the blocks to make sure they do what you are expecting.

- Ask a classmate to help by using one of the above strategies together.

BLOCKS AND THEIR FUNCTIONS

Motion

The Motion blocks are used to move a sprite around.

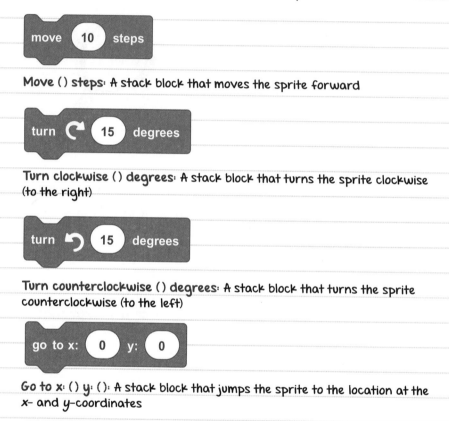

Move () steps: A stack block that moves the sprite forward

Turn clockwise () degrees: A stack block that turns the sprite clockwise (to the right)

Turn counterclockwise () degrees: A stack block that turns the sprite counterclockwise (to the left)

Go to x: () y: (): A stack block that jumps the sprite to the location at the x- and y-coordinates

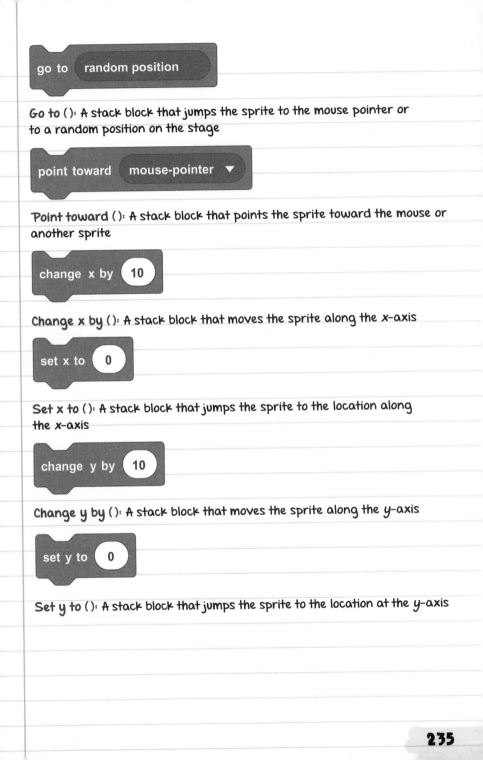

go to (random position)

Go to (): A stack block that jumps the sprite to the mouse pointer or to a random position on the stage

point toward (mouse-pointer ▼)

Point toward (): A stack block that points the sprite toward the mouse or another sprite

change x by (10)

Change x by (): A stack block that moves the sprite along the x-axis

set x to (0)

Set x to (): A stack block that jumps the sprite to the location along the x-axis

change y by (10)

Change y by (): A stack block that moves the sprite along the y-axis

set y to (0)

Set y to (): A stack block that jumps the sprite to the location at the y-axis

> **if on edge, bounce**

If on edge, bounce: A stack block that turns the sprite around when it hits the edge of the stage

> **set rotation style** (left-right ▼)

Set rotation style (): A stack block that sets the rotation style

> **x position**

X position: A reporter block that holds the x value of the sprite's location

> **y position**

Y position: A reporter block that holds the y value of the sprite's location

> **direction**

Direction: A reporter block that holds the direction value of the sprite

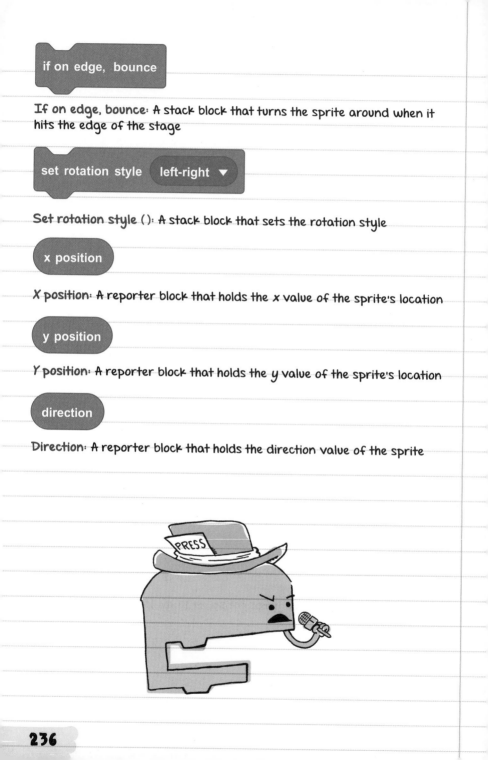

Looks

The Looks blocks are used to change how a sprite looks.

say Hello! for 2 seconds

Say () for () seconds: A stack block that makes a speech bubble appear above the sprite for a set number of seconds

think Hmm... for 2 seconds

Think () for () seconds: A stack block that makes a thought bubble appear above the sprite for a set number of seconds

think Hmm...

Think (): A stack block that makes a permanent thought bubble appear above the sprite

switch costume to costume1

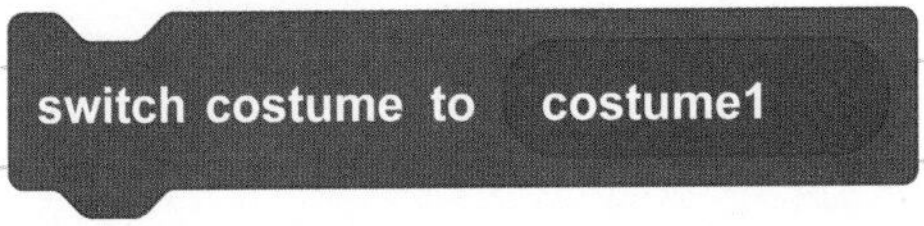

Switch costume to (): A stack block that switches to the named costume

Next costume: A stack block that changes the sprite's costume to the next one in the costume list

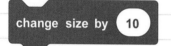

Switch backdrop to (): A stack block that switches to the backdrop that is named

next backdrop

Next backdrop: A stack block that changes the backdrop to the next one in the backdrop list

change size by 10

Change size by (): A stack block that changes the size of the sprite by the number specified

set size to 100 %

Set size to ()%: A stack block that sets the size of the sprite to a set percentage

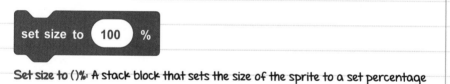

Change () effect by (): A stack block that changes an appearance on the sprite by a set amount

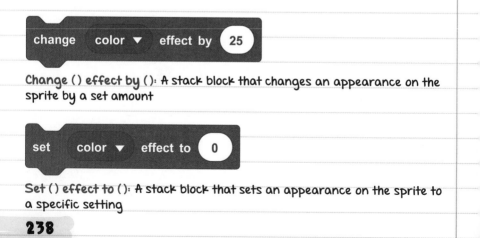

Set () effect to (): A stack block that sets an appearance on the sprite to a specific setting

238

clear graphic effects

Clear graphic effects: A stack block that resets the graphic effects to 0

show

Show: A stack block that shows the sprite

hide

Hide: A stack block that hides the sprite

go to front ▼ layer

Go to () layer: A stack block that brings the sprite in front of or behind all other sprites

go forward ▼   1 layers

Go () () layers: A stack block that sends the sprite in front of or back behind other sprites

backdrop number ▼

Backdrop (): A reporter block that holds the number of the backdrop being shown

size

Size: A reporter block that holds the value of the size of the sprite

Sound

Sound blocks are used to make and modify sounds.

Play sound () until done: A stack block that plays the selected sound and waits to continue the rest of the script until the sound is done playing

Start sound (): A stack block that plays the selected sound

Stop all sounds: A stack block that stops all sounds in the program from playing

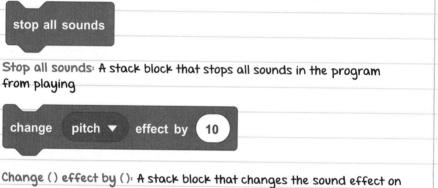

Change () effect by (): A stack block that changes the sound effect on sounds being played by the set amount

Set () effect to (): A stack block that sets the effect on sounds being played to a set number

Clear sound effects: A stack block that removes all sound effects

change volume by -10

Change volume by (): A stack block that changes the volume by the set amount

set volume to 100 %

Set volume to (): A stack block that changes the volume to the set percentage

volume

Volume: A reporter block that holds the value of current volume level

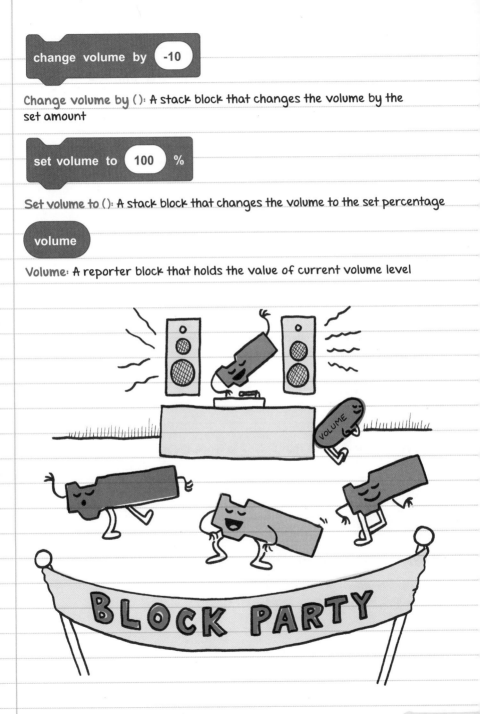

Pen

Blocks in the Pen category are used to draw on the stage. The Pen category is added as an extension and is not one of the default categories.

Erase all: A stack block that removes all pen marks and stamps from the stage

Stamp: A stack block that stamps the image of the sprite to the stage. Stamps cannot be controlled with blocks. Stamps are copies of images of the sprite printed onto the stage.

Pen down: A stack block that begins to trace the movements of a sprite with lines

Pen up: A stack block that stops tracing the movements of a sprite

Set pen color to (): A stack block that sets the pen color to the selected color

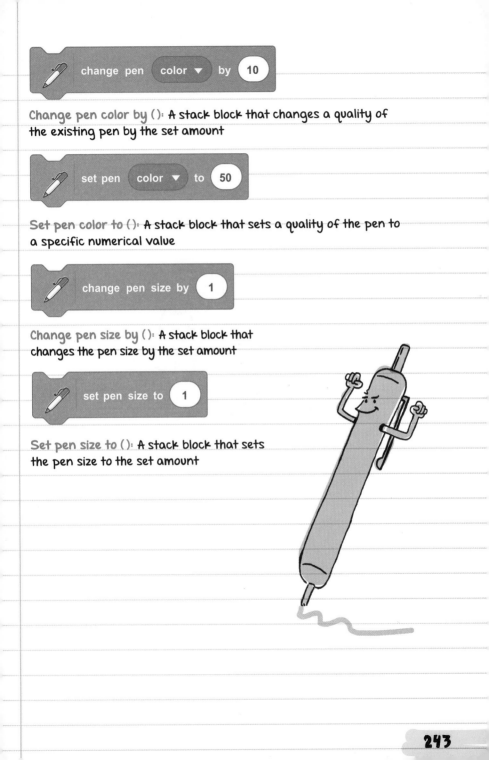

change pen color by 10

Change pen color by (): A stack block that changes a quality of the existing pen by the set amount

set pen color to 50

Set pen color to (): A stack block that sets a quality of the pen to a specific numerical value

change pen size by 1

Change pen size by (): A stack block that changes the pen size by the set amount

set pen size to 1

Set pen size to (): A stack block that sets the pen size to the set amount

CHECK YOUR KNOWLEDGE

1. What do all hat blocks have in common?

2. What does the pen down block do?

3. What does the following block make a sprite do?

   `glide ( 1 ) secs to x: ( -50 ) y: ( 50 )`

4. How can you tell if a script is running?

5. Select all that are true. Hat blocks can be placed:
   A. above other blocks
   B. below other blocks
   C. inside other blocks

6. Select all that are true. Stack blocks can be placed:
   A. above other blocks
   B. below other blocks
   C. inside other blocks

7. How do you insert a block between two other blocks?

8. Which block should you use to erase all the pen markings on the stage?

ANSWERS ➤ 245

CHECK YOUR ANSWERS

1. Hat blocks always go on top of scripts, and they make scripts run.

2. The pen down block makes it so that the sprite draws a line along the path as it moves.

3. Take 1 second to move to the location (−50, 50).

4. The blocks glow in the Scripts Area.

5. **A**

6. **A, B**

7. Drag it between the blocks where you want to place it, wait for the highlight to show up, then let go of the mouse button to drop it in.

8. Erase all

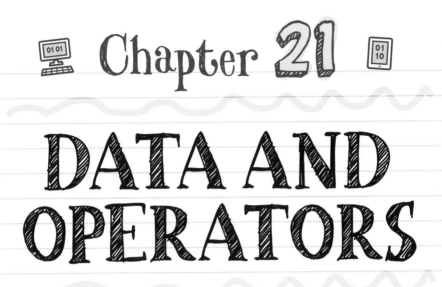
DATA AND OPERATORS

VARIABLES

Storing information is useful when you want to reuse it while running a program. Information can be stored using variables:

> **Reminder:** Boolean values can only be either true or false.

> A VARIABLE IS WHERE A PROGRAM STORES DATA. THE DATA IS CALLED ITS VALUE.

- **Variables:** hold one type of value— a number, string (text), Boolean, or list

REPORTER BLOCKS report out, or deliver, the current value of the variable they represent. They can store numbers and words as variable values.

A reporter block is placed inside the parameter area of any other block.

> There are reporter blocks in every blocks category except Events and Control.

A reporter block is shaped like this:

Variables

You can create a new variable by clicking on "Make a Variable" in the Variable category of the Blocks menu. After you make a new variable, a new reporter block with the variable name appears in the Blocks palette.

There are two ways to change the value of a variable:

1. set () to () block: used to replace the current value with a new value

2. change () by () block: used to add to or subtract from the current value of the variable

FOR EXAMPLE, in a game we can create a variable called "score" and use the set (score) to (0) stack block to set the score variable to 0 when the game begins. We can also use the change (score) by (1) stack block to increase the score by one point every time the user scores a point during the game. We can access the value of the score variable with the score reporter block. The reporter block could be used to display the score on the stage or tell when a player has won the game based on points scored.

Built-In Variables

Some reporter blocks have built-in variables that store data. The values of the variables can be used in programs.

For example, the built-in variables called mouse x and mouse y name the

position on the x-axis and y-axis of the user's mouse cursor on the stage. These values can be inserted into the parameters of the **go to x: () y: ()** stack block to make a sprite go to the user's mouse location on the stage.

USER INPUT

the things users type in

Some built-in variables store **USER INPUT**. We can ask for users to enter words or numbers by using the ask () and wait stack-type block found in the Sensing category. Their answer is stored in the answer reporter block. We can ask a user to enter their name, then use the say () block to have the sprite tell the user hello with their name:

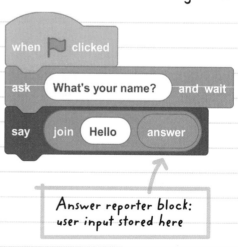

Answer reporter block: user input stored here

The **ask ( ) and wait** block makes a speech bubble appear above the sprite and a text box appear at the bottom of the stage. The script pauses until the user types an answer in the text box and presses enter on the keyboard.

Lists

In Scratch you can store multiple values in a single place with LISTS.

List blocks are used to set values and to use the data they store later in the program.

FOR EXAMPLE, we could make a high-score list called "high_score" and use the add ( ) to ( ) stack block to add the names "Indira," "Leo," and "Kemi":

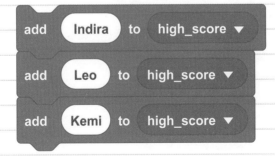

Create a new list by clicking on the Make a List button in the Variable category of the Blocks menu. After creating a new list, these blocks will appear in the Blocks palette:

✓ my list

add thing to my list ▼

delete 1 of my list ▼

delete all of my list ▼

insert thing at 1 of my list ▼

replace item 1 of my list ▼ with thing

item 1 of my list ▼

item # of thing in my list ▼

length of my list ▼

my list ▼ contains things ?

show list my list ▼

hide list my list ▼

Lists start out empty. Use the add () to () blocks to add the names to the high_score list. The list display (shown on the stage) will show that the three names have been added to the high_score list:

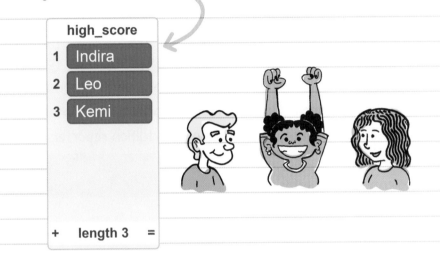

The replace item () of () with () stack block is used to replace items on the list. In the first parameter, type the number of the index for the item to be replaced. To replace Kemi with Margaret, type "3" because Kemi is third in the list. In the last parameter, type "Margaret" because that's the new value.

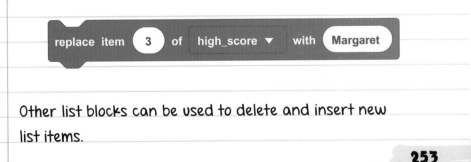

Other list blocks can be used to delete and insert new list items.

OPERATORS

OPERATORS are used to perform calculations on values. There are two types of operators blocks:

REPORTER and **BOOLEAN**

The **reporter blocks** are used to perform mathematical functions on values (such as add, subtract, multiply, divide, round, and others). For example, we could make a sprite go to a location 50 steps above the user's cursor using an addition reporter block:

Boolean-type operators blocks are used to evaluate statements as true or false.

For example, we can use the () > () block to determine if a player's score is greater than 50:

Math Blocks

In the Operators category, there are reporter blocks with math operators built into them:

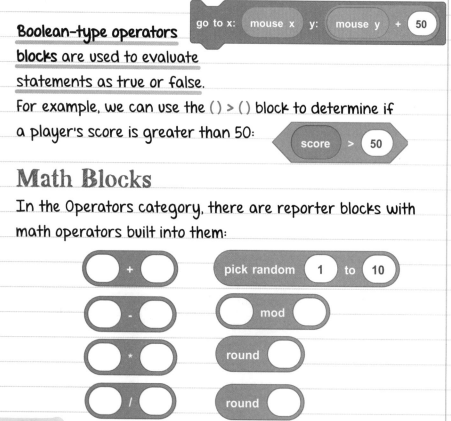

Each block has one or two input fields where you can insert numbers or variables. The value for each block is the solution to the math equation shown in the block.

FOR EXAMPLE, if you wanted to subtract 6 – 2, you would use the () – () block:

6 – 2

The value of this block is 4.

You can use math with variables by inserting the reporter variables block into the input field of a math block.

WHAT? YOU MEAN I CAN GET SCRATCH TO DO MY MATH HOMEWORK FOR ME?!

FOR EXAMPLE, to find out someone's age, you could set a variable, "birth_year," to the year someone was born (for example, 2005), and subtract that from the current year:

2020 – birth_year

Name of variable: birth_year
Value: 2005

Boolean Blocks

BOOLEAN BLOCKS evaluate information to be true or false. They have statements or math equations inside them that are either true or false.

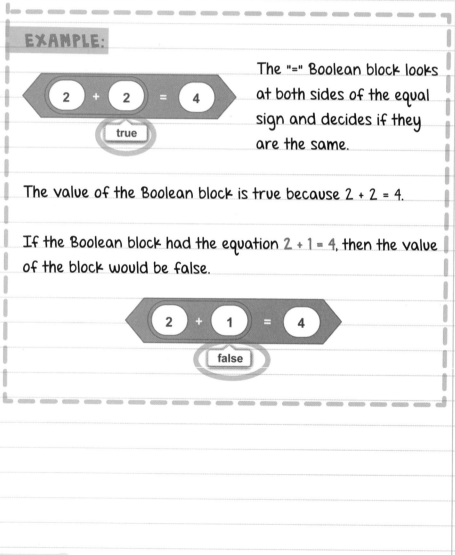

The "=" Boolean block looks at both sides of the equal sign and decides if they are the same.

The value of the Boolean block is true because 2 + 2 = 4.

If the Boolean block had the equation 2 + 1 = 4, then the value of the block would be false.

Boolean blocks can also be used to compare words. For example, Marcos = Marcos is true. Marcos = Greg is false.

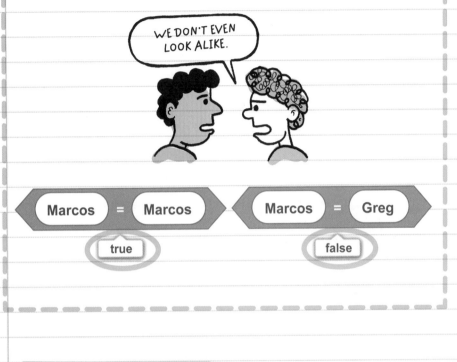

Be careful with spaces! Spaces before or after each word compared must match.

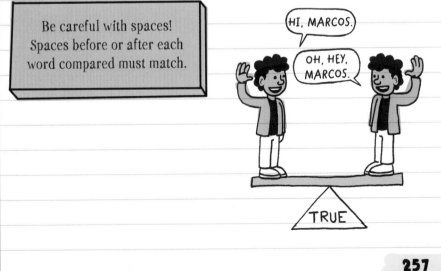

In the Operators category, there are Boolean blocks for comparison (<, =, >) and logical operations (and, or, not). These blocks can be combined by **nesting** them within each other.

FOR EXAMPLE, you could use the () > () , () < () , and () and () Boolean blocks to see if a variable, score, is greater than 10 and the timer is less than 200. To do this, insert the () > () and () < () blocks inside the left and right input fields of a () and () block:

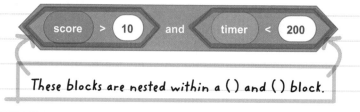

These blocks are nested within a ( ) and ( ) block.

Nesting blocks means putting one or more blocks inside another block.

In the Sensing category, there are Boolean blocks that check for specific conditions. If the condition is met, the block's value is true; otherwise the value is false.

HEY, LET ME KNOW
WHEN THE SPRITE IS
TOUCHING GREEN.
THEN I CAN START
MY HOMEWORK.

BLOCKS AND THEIR FUNCTIONS

Variables

The blocks in the Variables category are used to store and change data as single-value variables or multiple-value lists.

> my variable

variable name: A reporter block that holds the value of the named variable

> set (my variable ▼) to (0)

Set () to (): A stack block that sets the value of the selected variable to a set number, string, or Boolean

> change (my variable ▼) by (1)

Change () by (): A stack block that changes the value of the selected variable by the set amount

> show variable (my variable ▼)

Show variable (): A stack block that will show the variable value in a little display window on the stage

> hide variable (my variable ▼)

Hide variable (): A stack block that will hide the variable value display window on the stage

These blocks give the user the ability to change a list of values.

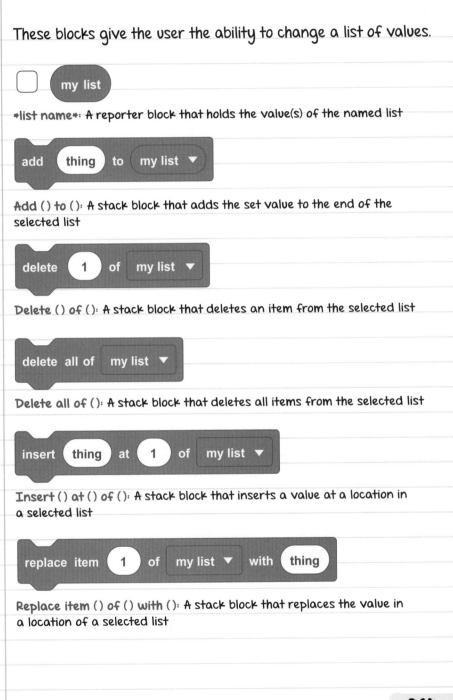

list name: A reporter block that holds the value(s) of the named list

Add () to (): A stack block that adds the set value to the end of the selected list

Delete () of (): A stack block that deletes an item from the selected list

Delete all of (): A stack block that deletes all items from the selected list

Insert () at () of (): A stack block that inserts a value at a location in a selected list

Replace item () of () with (): A stack block that replaces the value in a location of a selected list

Item () of (): A reporter block that holds the value of an item in the selected list

Item # of () in (): A reporter block that holds the index number value of the set value in a list

Length of (): A reporter block that holds the number of items in a selected list

() contains ()?: A Boolean block asking if a selected list has the set value in it (Is "thing" an item in the list? It's true if it is, and false if it is not.)

Show list (): A stack block that will show all the list values in a display window on the stage

Hide list (): A stack block that will hide the list values display window on the stage

The previous blocks give the user the ability to change more than one value in a selected list.

Operators

Blocks in the Operators category are used to control data. Many of the reporter blocks are mathematical functions (like addition, subtraction, multiplication, and more). Other blocks are used to change **STRING VALUES**.

> **STRING VALUES**
> Several symbols or values that are set in a row

() + (): A reporter block that holds the value of the addition equation

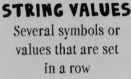

() - (): A reporter block that holds the value of the subtraction equation

() * (): A reporter block that holds the value of the multiplication equation

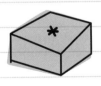

() / (): A reporter block that holds the value of the division equation

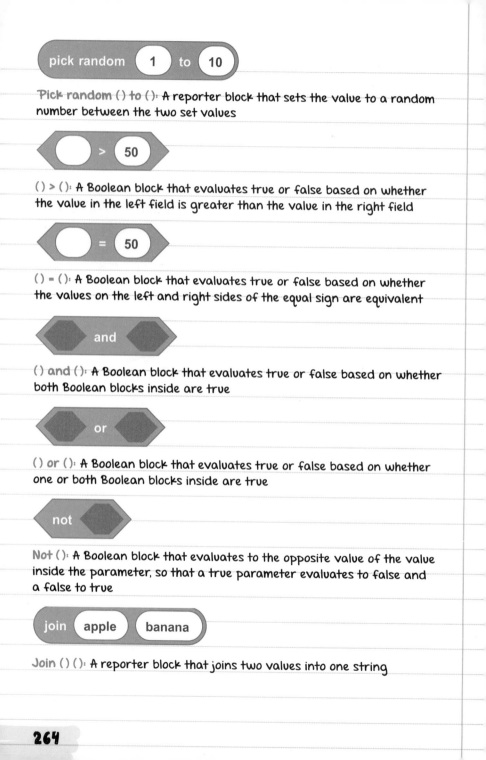

Pick random () to (): A reporter block that sets the value to a random number between the two set values

() > (): A Boolean block that evaluates true or false based on whether the value in the left field is greater than the value in the right field

() = (): A Boolean block that evaluates true or false based on whether the values on the left and right sides of the equal sign are equivalent

() and (): A Boolean block that evaluates true or false based on whether both Boolean blocks inside are true

() or (): A Boolean block that evaluates true or false based on whether one or both Boolean blocks inside are true

Not (): A Boolean block that evaluates to the opposite value of the value inside the parameter, so that a true parameter evaluates to false and a false to true

Join () (): A reporter block that joins two values into one string

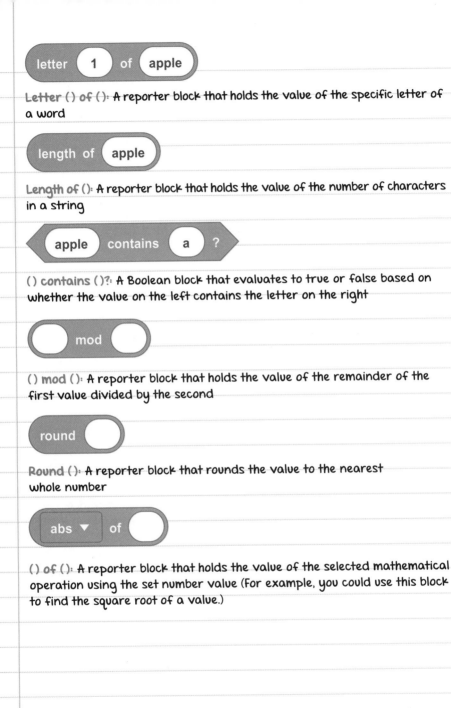

Letter () of (): A reporter block that holds the value of the specific letter of a word

Length of (): A reporter block that holds the value of the number of characters in a string

() contains ()?: A Boolean block that evaluates to true or false based on whether the value on the left contains the letter on the right

() mod (): A reporter block that holds the value of the remainder of the first value divided by the second

Round (): A reporter block that rounds the value to the nearest whole number

() of (): A reporter block that holds the value of the selected mathematical operation using the set number value (For example, you could use this block to find the square root of a value.)

Sensing

Blocks in the Sensing category are used to understand and store information about how the user interacts with the program.

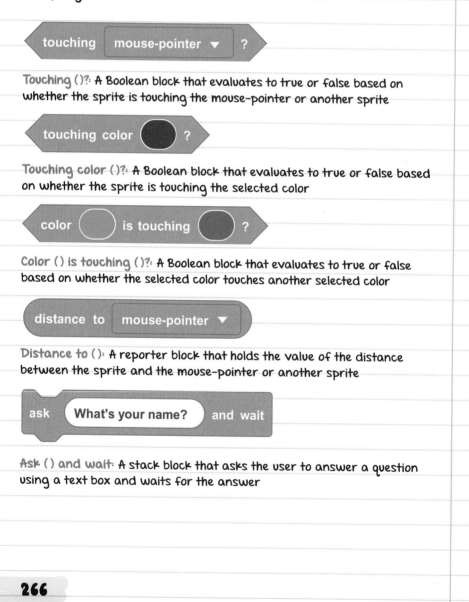

Touching ()?: A Boolean block that evaluates to true or false based on whether the sprite is touching the mouse-pointer or another sprite

Touching color ()?: A Boolean block that evaluates to true or false based on whether the sprite is touching the selected color

Color () is touching ()?: A Boolean block that evaluates to true or false based on whether the selected color touches another selected color

Distance to (): A reporter block that holds the value of the distance between the sprite and the mouse-pointer or another sprite

Ask () and wait: A stack block that asks the user to answer a question using a text box and waits for the answer

answer

Answer: A reporter block that holds the value of the user-given value from the ask block

key **space** ▼ **pressed?**

Key () pressed?: A Boolean block that evaluates to true or false based on whether the selected key is pressed

mouse down?

Mouse down?: A Boolean block that evaluates to true or false based on whether the mouse button is down

mouse x

Mouse x: A reporter block that holds the value of the mouse location on the x-axis

mouse y

Mouse y: A reporter block that holds the value of the mouse location on the y-axis

set drag mode **draggable** ▼

Set drag mode (): A stack block that makes a sprite draggable or not draggable by the user

loudness

Loudness: A reporter block that holds the value of the loudness from an attached microphone

timer

Timer: A reporter block that holds the value of the timer that automatically starts when a program is run

reset timer

Reset timer: A stack block that resets the timer to 0

backdrop # ▼ of Stage ▼

( ) of ( ): A reporter block that holds the value of the selected variable for the selected sprite or stage

current year ▼

Current ( ): A reporter block that holds the value of the current year, month, date, day of week, hour, minute, or second

days since 2000

Days since 2000: A reporter block that holds the value of the days since the year 2000

username

Username: A reporter block that holds the value of the Scratch username of the Scratcher using the program

CHECK YOUR KNOWLEDGE

1. Select all that are true. Reporter blocks can be placed:
   A. above other blocks
   B. below other blocks
   C. inside other blocks

2. What can you put inside an input field?

3. What are the two possible values a Boolean block can have?

4. Explain what reporter blocks do. Why are they useful?

5. What's the difference between the set () to () and change () by () blocks?

6. What is the value of the block below?

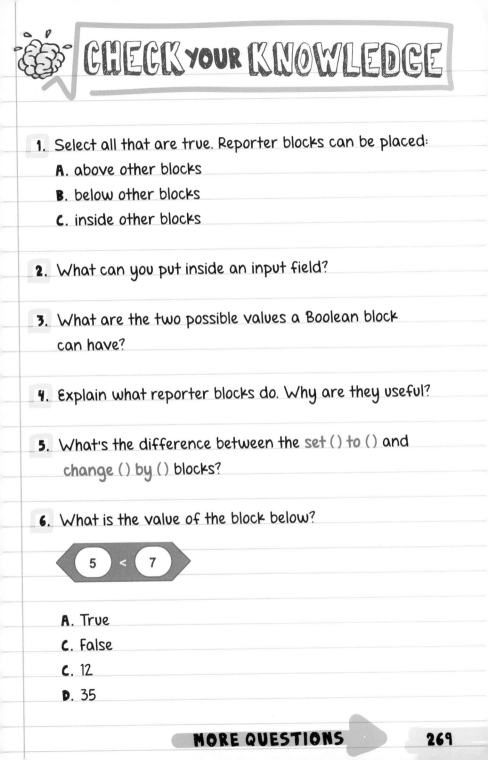

   A. True
   C. False
   C. 12
   D. 35

MORE QUESTIONS

7. What is the value of the block below?

5 * 7

A. True

B. False

C. 12

D. 35

8. Which Boolean block would you use to see if the W key is pressed on the keyboard?

9. What's the difference between a math block (*, /, +, -) and a comparison block (<, >, =)?

10. What's an advantage to using a variable multiple times in a program instead of typing out the values each time the variable is used as a parameter?

11. What's wrong with the following code?

12. Describe how to make a variable called "velocity" in Scratch.

CHECK YOUR ANSWERS

1. C

2. Text, numbers, and reporter blocks

3. True or false

4. Reporter blocks are variables. They store information. You can put them in the input field of other blocks.

5. The set () to () block assigns a variable a value, while the change () by () block adds a number to the variable value.

6. A

7. D

8. The key () pressed? block with the W selected

9. Math blocks store number values, but comparison operators are Boolean and store either true or false.

10. One advantage is that if you need to change the value, you can change it once by reassigning a new value to the variable instead of finding every place the value is and replacing it manually.

11. You cannot use the change () by () block on a variable value that is not a number. In the example, "speed" is set to "fast," which is not a number.

12. In the "Variables" Blocks palette, click on "Make a Variable." Then type in "velocity" in the "Variable name:" text field and press "OK."

Chapter 22

CONTROL BLOCKS AND EVENT BLOCKS

CONTROL BLOCKS

Blocks tell other blocks what to do. They tell scripts to run, pause, repeat, and stop. They are different from event handler hat blocks because they run based on internal conditions instead of external events (like the clicking of the green flag).

One type of control block is the repeat block, which will repeat the code inside it a set number of times.

REPEAT 20

YIKES, THAT BLOCK IS SOO CONTROLLING!

C BLOCKS AND CAP BLOCKS

The Control category also has two other types of blocks: the **C BLOCK** and the **CAP BLOCK**.

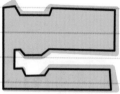

C blocks look like the letter C. Other blocks can be placed in the gap of the C so that the C block wraps around them. There are two main types of C blocks: **loops** and **conditionals**.

Loops repeat the code placed in the gap of the block.

Conditionals run the code placed in the gap only if their condition is met.

C blocks are found only in the Control category. There are different types of loops and conditional statements, but they all share the same basic C shape.

Cap blocks attach to the bottom of a script and are used to stop running the script.

Other blocks cannot be stacked below a cap block.

Cap blocks are found only in the Control category.

PUT A CAP ON IT. PARTY'S OVER.

EVENT BLOCKS

There are six event handler blocks. The hat-shaped blocks wait for things like a button press, mouse click, or message broadcast. When an event handler registers that their event happened, they run the script attached to it.

Event blocks can be used to make a soundboard that triggers different sounds to play when different number keys are pressed.

FOR EXAMPLE, the number keys 1, 2, 3, and 4 are each assigned a different sound.

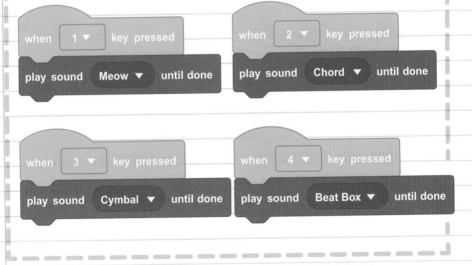

The when backdrop switches to () block listens for the backdrop to switch. For example, if you make a game that switches to a new backdrop for every level, you could set up an event to listen for the backdrop change and trigger new opponents to appear.

The broadcast block ![broadcast block] is used to send out messages. When this block is run, it broadcasts a message out to all of the sprites. Messages are sent without the user seeing anything, and only the when I receive () block responds when a message is broadcast.

FOR EXAMPLE, you could use a broadcast block in a script that sends a message called "Game Over." You could then add a when I receive (Game Over) block in another sprite or the backdrop to have it play a losing sound and bring up a new backdrop ending the game.

LOOPS

All loops are C-type blocks. At the top of the C is where the type of loop is shown (forever, repeat, or repeat until). The code that is repeated goes in the "mouth" of the C. Other blocks can stack above and below loops. You can also place a loop block inside another loop block, making a nested loop.

Basic Loops

Scratch uses three types of loops:

forever, repeat ( ), and repeat until ( ).

Forever loops will run forever, or until the program is stopped. You can animate a character to look like it is walking by using a forever block. You can tell the sprite to continually switch to the next costume. Loops run quickly, so you can also add the block wait ( ) secs to slow down the loop.

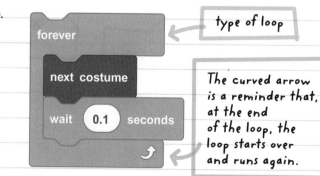

STILL WALKING.

type of loop

The curved arrow is a reminder that, at the end of the loop, the loop starts over and runs again.

Repeat () loops tell the sprite exactly how many times you want it to run when you type in a number in the text box.

FOR EXAMPLE, you can tell a sprite to change to the next costume and wait 0.1 seconds only 10 times instead of forever:

Repeat until () loops will continually repeat until the Boolean statement inside the loop becomes true.

FOR EXAMPLE, you can tell a sprite to continually change to the next costume and wait 0.1 seconds until the user presses the spacebar on the keyboard:

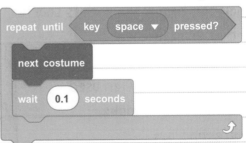

Loops can make programs more efficient. For example, if you wanted to draw a square, you could use a loop to make your script better. Instead of using all these blocks to draw a square . . .

you can look for a pattern of blocks that repeat themselves, put the repeated blocks inside a loop, and input the number of times you want the script to run.

Nested Loops

Nested loops are loops inserted within a loop. Nested loops are very helpful for repeating **SUBROUTINES** within a task. They can help make scripts shorter and more efficient.

Subroutines are often used in games and to make interesting art.

SUBROUTINE
A unit of code that performs a specific task and is used as part of a larger program

WE'RE NESTING DOLLS!

REPEAT 10
REPEAT 20
REPEAT 5

WE'RE NESTED LOOPS!

You can also use nested loops to make Spirograph-type art. The repeat (6) loop in a script draws a hexagon. The Scratch Cat uses the pen tool to draw a hexagon beneath it as it moves along the path set by the repeat (6) loop.

when ⚑ clicked
pen down
repeat 6
  move 70 steps
  turn 60 degrees

Then nest that loop inside the repeat (72) loop to redraw the hexagon 72 times.

when ⚑ clicked
pen down
repeat 72
  repeat 6
    move 70 steps
    turn 60 degrees
  change pen color ▼ by 10
  turn 5 degrees

You can rotate to the right by 5 degrees each time and change the color of each new hexagon as well.

Here's what the script run to completion looks like. There are 72 hexagons of different colors, each rotated 5 degrees to the right.

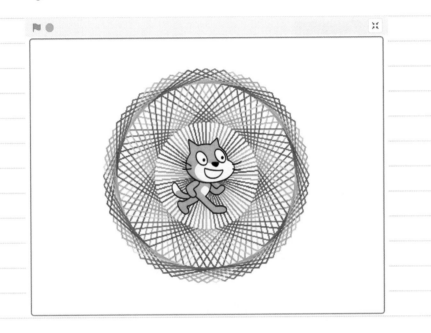

CONDITIONAL STATEMENTS

Scratch has two types of conditional blocks:

If ( ) then

If ( ) then else

Conditional statements use C-type blocks and are found only in the Control category of the Blocks menu.

Basic Conditional Statements

Basic conditional statements use only one Boolean block as a condition and aren't nested.

FOR EXAMPLE, you can use a basic conditional statement to allow a player to choose a path in a game:

when 🚩 clicked

ask **Which door do you choose? Door 1 or Door 2?** and wait

if (answer = Door 1) then

    say **You walk through Door 1 and receive a magic wand.**

else

    say **You walk through Door 2 and receive an enchanted hat.**

1. The script asks the user which door they choose.

2. A conditional block compares the user's answer to the term "Door 1" in a Boolean ( ) = ( ) block.

3. If the user answers "Door 1," then the block inside the first "mouth" will run.

4. If the user does not answer with "Door 1," then the code below "else" in the second "mouth" will run.

Compound and Nested Conditional Statements

Conditional blocks can nest inside each other just like loop blocks. Nested conditionals are built when you put one conditional inside of another conditional.

In a single "if else" statement, there are two consequences.

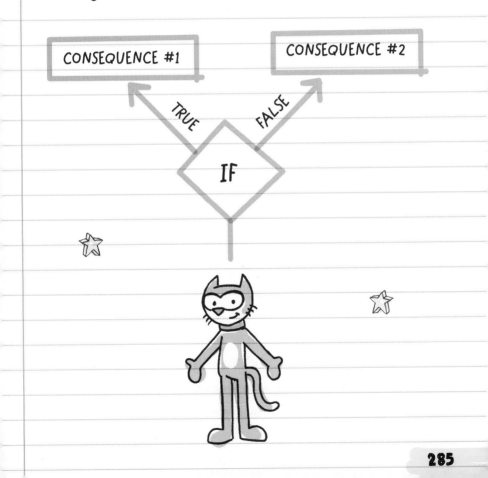

CONSEQUENCE #1

CONSEQUENCE #2

TRUE

FALSE

IF

Conditional blocks can be nested inside each other just like loop blocks. Nested conditional blocks create a more complex branching system, where many different results can occur.

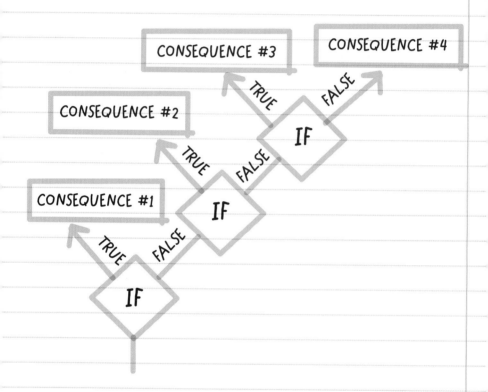

Multiple nested conditional blocks can be used to create a choose-your-own-adventure game. Start with the question asking which door the user chooses and the first condition with the Boolean block that is True if the user answers "Door 1." In the "else" (or FALSE) second "mouth" of the conditional block, we can add another condition checking for "Door 2." Continue to nest conditional blocks to add to the number of possible results.

FOR EXAMPLE, this game has four possible outcomes:

```
when 🏳 clicked

ask  Which door do you choose? Door 1 or Door 2?  and wait

if   answer = Door 1   then
                                                    outcome #1
   say   You walk through Door 1 and receive a magic wand.

else
   if   answer = Door 2   then
                                                    outcome #2
      say   You walk through Door 2 and receive an enchanted hat.

   else
      if   answer = Door 3   then
                                                 outcome #3
         say   You walk through the secret Door 3 and receive an extra life.

      else
         say   You have not chosen to walk through a door. You grow tired.

                                        outcome #4
```

Conditional statements can be combined to save space and simplify the script. The and Boolean block is used to combine two Boolean blocks.

FOR EXAMPLE, you can add a bonus round to a game by combining two conditions to entering the bonus round: having a score of over 100 points and playing on the "hard" difficulty level.

Nested, these conditions look like this:

You can simplify the script by combining the Boolean statements from both conditions with an "and" operators block:

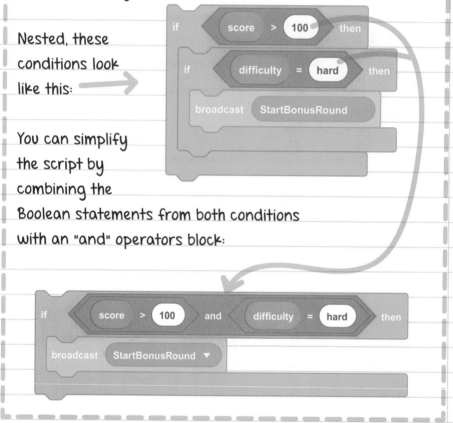

AND is True if both conditions are true;
OR is True if one or both conditions are true;
NOT turns True statements False and False statements True.

BLOCKS AND THEIR FUNCTIONS

Events

Blocks in the Events category are used to run scripts based on events that happen while the program is running.

```
when [flag] clicked
```

When green flag clicked: A hat block that runs the attached script when the green flag is clicked

```
when [ space ▼ ] key pressed
```

When () key pressed: A hat block that runs the attached script when the selected key is pressed

```
when this sprite clicked
```

When this sprite clicked: A hat block that runs the attached script when the sprite is clicked

```
when backdrop switches to [ backdrop1 ▼ ]
```

When backdrop switches to (): A hat block that runs the attached script when the backdrop switches to the selected backdrop when [loudness ▼] > (10)

When () > (): A hat block that runs the attached script when the video or timer value goes above the set amount

when I receive [message1 ▼]

When I receive (): A hat block that runs the attached script when the selected message is broadcast

broadcast (message1 ▼)

Broadcast (): A stack block that sends out the selected message to every sprite

broadcast (message1 ▼) and wait

Broadcast () and wait: A stack block that sends out the selected message to every sprite and waits to move on to the next block

Control

The Control category contains blocks that are used to control the flow of a program.

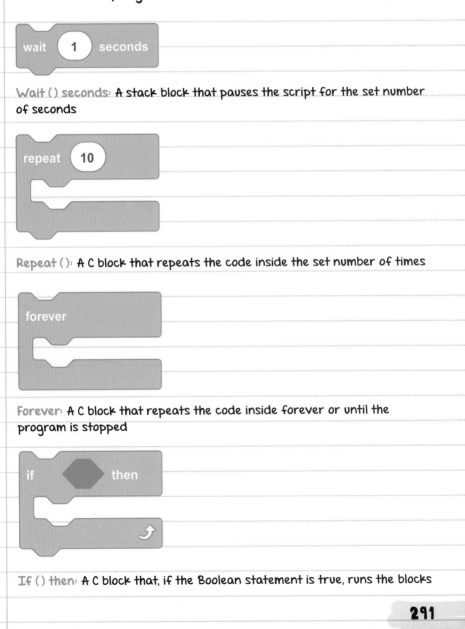

Wait () seconds: A stack block that pauses the script for the set number of seconds

Repeat (): A C block that repeats the code inside the set number of times

Forever: A C block that repeats the code inside forever or until the program is stopped

If () then: A C block that, if the Boolean statement is true, runs the blocks

If () then else: A C block that, if the Boolean statement is true, runs the blocks in the first part and otherwise runs the blocks in the second part

wait until

Wait until (): A stack block that pauses the script until the Boolean condition is true

repeat until

Repeat until (): A C block that repeats the blocks inside until the Boolean condition is true

stop all ▼

Stop (): A cap block that stops the selected script(s)

Clone Blocks: Cloning a sprite is when you make copies of it. Cloning is useful when you need several copies of the same sprite on the stage at once.

```
when I start as a clone
```

When I start as a clone: A hat block that runs attached script when a clone is made

```
create clone of ( myself )
```

Create clone of (): A stack block that creates a clone of the selected sprite

```
delete this clone
```

Delete this clone: A cap block that deletes the clone

1. What are loops? Why are they useful?

2. _____ loops are loops within other loops.

3. How is a repeat () loop different from a forever loop?

4. What does the broadcast () block do? After a program broadcasts a message, will the message appear on the stage?

5. Which kind of C block would you use to make a loop that keeps repeating until the user earns 10 points?

6. In the code below, what will be said first after the program is started?

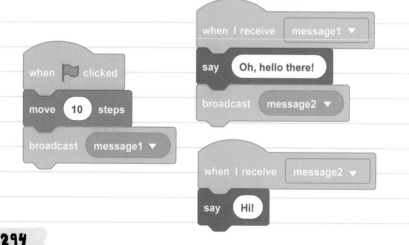

7. How many times will the word "hip" be said?

```
when 🏴 clicked
repeat  3
    repeat  2
        say  hip  for  1  seconds
        wait  0.1  seconds
    ↻
    say  hooray  for  2  seconds
↻
```

8. What does a cap block do? How does its shape affect how it connects to other blocks?

9. Use the code below to answer the following question. When will the sprite say, "Phew, I was growing too much!"?

```
when 🏴 clicked
repeat until  < key  space ▼  pressed? >
    change size by  10
↻
say  Phew, I was growing too much!  for  2  seconds
```

10. What does the following event block do? Why are event blocks important?

when this sprite clicked

11. What will happen in the code below if the variable "fruit" is set to "avocado"?

set fruit to avocado

if fruit = apples then

say Make apple juice.

else

if fruit = grapes then

say Make grape juice.

else

say You don't have the right fruit.

12. If you are trying to make multiple decisions that depend on each other, which type of conditionals should you use?

CHECK YOUR ANSWERS

1. A loop is a chunk of code that is repeated. They are useful because they can make your code more efficient and easier to write because you won't have to copy and paste the same script over and over again.

2. Nested

3. A repeat () loop will repeat the code inside it a set number of times, but a forever loop will go on forever or until the program stops running.

4. The broadcast () block sends out a message for its corresponding event block to run. No messages appear on the stage; the message is sent without the user seeing it.

5. repeat until ()

6. "Oh, hello there!"

7. 6 times—the inner loop repeats "hip" twice, and the outer loop repeats the inner loop 3 times. That's 2 x 3, which equals 6.

MORE ANSWERS

8. Cap blocks end a script; blocks cannot be connected below a cap block.

9. After the user presses the spacebar

10. The when this sprite clicked event block will run when the user clicks on the sprite. Event blocks make user interaction possible. They also allow programs to run different scripts at different times based on when events happen.

11. The sprite will say, "You don't have the right fruit."

12. Nested conditionals

REUSING SCRIPTS

MAKE YOUR OWN BLOCK

You can turn a repeating part of a script into a new block. This new block is called a **PROCEDURE BLOCK**. You can make a new procedure block with its own commands and behavior.

> Procedures are named chunks of code that you can use over and over again. In Scratch, you can make a procedure block by making a new **define ( )** block.

When you make a new
procedure, you click
"Make a Block," and
select the type of
block you would like
to make. Then you
define the procedure
with a definition

hat-type block (called define ()) and snap your code
blocks to it. After you make a new procedure block, a new
PROCEDURE CALL STACK BLOCK with the same name as the
new procedure is added to the My Blocks category of the
Blocks menu. You can **CALL THE PROCEDURE** (run it) with
the *new block name* stack block, which is named the same
as the new procedure.

For example, you can use a procedure block to make a game
where the object is to catch good items and avoid bad ones.
The game can give points to the player for catching good
items and take points away when they catch bad items. Your
game can have four items, each worth different points:

crystal = 10 points
potion = 5 points
bat = -10 points
lightning = -5 points

> For the game, minus (-)
> means that points
> will be taken away.

You can make a procedure block called **hit** and use the **define ()** hat-type block to define the procedure and add a parameter called "points":

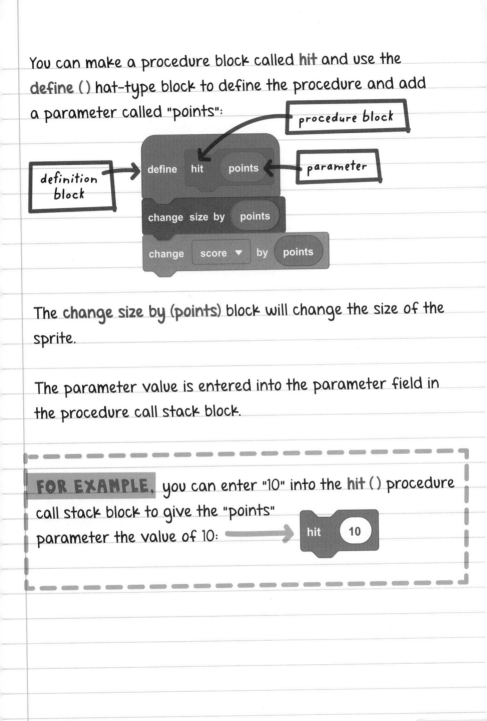

The **change size by (points)** block will change the size of the sprite.

The parameter value is entered into the parameter field in the procedure call stack block.

FOR EXAMPLE, you can enter "10" into the **hit ()** procedure call stack block to give the "points" parameter the value of 10:

If you run the **hit (10)** stack block with a value of 10 in the points parameter, then the sprite will get bigger on the stage by 10 percent. It will also add 10 points to your score variable.

You can add conditional statements that check to see if the sprite touches each of the four items and add a hit procedure stack block to each conditional statement.

You can enter a different parameter value in each of the hit procedure stack blocks based on the value of the item touched:

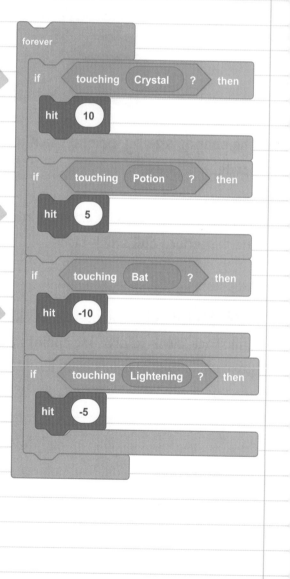

CLONING

CLONING a sprite is when you make copies of it. The clone blocks are found in the Control category of the Blocks menu.

CLONING MACHINE

FOR EXAMPLE, if you wanted to make it rain on the stage, instead of creating hundreds of individual raindrop sprites, you could clone a single raindrop sprite hundreds of times.

To do this, you need two scripts.

SCRIPT 1

Script 1 creates the clones of a sprite. You can use a loop to continually make new clones forever:

when ⚑ clicked

forever

create clone of [myself ▼]

wait (0.1) seconds

If you run Script 1 alone, it will create a bunch of clones of the sprite, but the clones won't be programmed to do anything.

Script 2 programs the sprites to act like raindrops, falling from the sky and disappearing when they hit the ground.

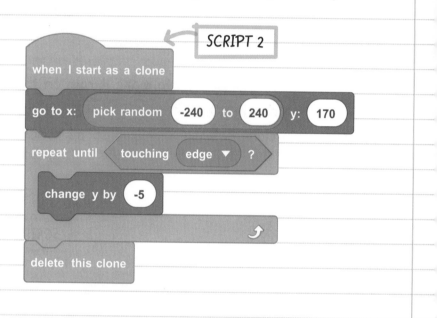

SCRIPT 2

```
when I start as a clone
go to x: pick random -240 to 240 y: 170
repeat until touching edge ▼ ?
    change y by -5
delete this clone
```

■ The when I start as a clone event hat block runs for each new clone that is created.

■ The pick random () to () block makes each raindrop start in a random location on the x-axis. You can also make the raindrop start at the top of the screen by setting the location on the y-axis. To set the location, add the go to x: () y: () block and add the pick random () to () block and all the parameters.

- Add a **repeat until** loop to animate the sprite to fall until it hits the ground.

- Use the **change y by** ( ) block and a -5 as its parameter value to make the raindrop move down the screen toward the ground.

- **Delete this clone** will delete the clone once it reaches the ground.

There is a 300-clone limit to Scratch programs. Once you reach the maximum on the screen, no new clones will be made. But because you are deleting your clones once they hit the ground you won't exceed the 300-clone limit.

OMG, IT'S RAINING CATS!

BLOCKS AND THEIR FUNCTIONS

My Blocks

The My Blocks category is different from all the other categories because you can create an unlimited number of new blocks. For each new block you create, a new define () hat block and *new block name* stack block appear in the category menu.

Note: Blocks in the My Blocks category appear only after a new procedure block has been made.

define | procedure | number or text | boolean

Define (): A hat block that defines a new procedure block along with specified parameters

New block name: A stack block that is used to call, or run, the corresponding procedure. When this block is run, the code underneath the corresponding define () block is run.

CHECK YOUR KNOWLEDGE

1. If you want to make a bunch of copies of a sprite, which blocks should you use?

2. How is making a new block different from just using a loop block?

3. Why should you delete a clone when you are done using it?

4. Why is making a new block better than copying and pasting code?

5. When a new clone is made, what script does it run?

ARE YOU A CLONE?

ANSWERS

CHECK YOUR ANSWERS

1. Clone blocks

2. Loop blocks repeat the same chunk of code multiple times in a row, while new blocks that you make can be used in different locations. You can also add different inputs to slightly change the way the block works.

3. There is a 300-clone limit, and once you reach the limit, no new clones will be made.

4. Good programmers don't copy and paste code. Efficient, concise code is better because it is easier to write, debug, and reuse.

5. Clones run whatever script is attached to the when I start as a clone block.

Unit 7

7

Programming in Python

Chapter 24

GETTING STARTED WITH PYTHON

INTRODUCING PYTHON

Python is one of the most widely used and easy-to-learn programming languages, which makes it popular for beginners. It can be used for many types of projects, ranging from designing websites to examining large amounts of data.

I'M SO POPULAR.

Python comes with many useful built-in FUNCTIONS, or tools, including:

- math functions like basic operations, square root, and choosing a random number

- options for drawing graphics

- user-friendly menus and buttons

IDLE

Python code is written in an **INTEGRATED DEVELOPMENT ENVIRONMENT PROGRAM (IDE)** like IDLE (Integrated Development and Learning Environment), the one that comes with Python when you install it.

The program IDLE is installed along with Python. It has two different windows: the **SHELL WINDOW** and the **EDITOR WINDOW**.

INTEGRATED DEVELOPMENT ENVIRONMENT (IDE)
A program that programmers use to type out and edit code and to create Python programs

The shell window is the window that appears when you open IDLE. On the screen you'll see ">>>," which shows you where to start typing.

> The >>> symbol is called the **prompt**.

To run code in the shell window, type it in next to the prompt and press enter. The **OUTPUT** of your code will appear on the line below. Or, if your code doesn't run properly, an error message will appear.

> **OUTPUT**
> The result of the code; what you see after the code has run

FOR EXAMPLE, you can type in the code print("Hello, World!") and your output will be "Hello, World!" like this:

```
>>> print("Hello, World!")
Hello, World!
>>> |
```

The shell window is great for running small pieces of code, but isn't good for writing whole programs because you can't save your work.

>>> TYPE HERE.

Shell window

The editor window is for writing out whole programs that are saved as files. The editor window starts out as a completely blank, untitled file. Python files end in **.py**, and you can save them anywhere on your computer. An example of a Python file name would be **firstproject.py**.

> This is a <u>file extension</u>. It names the format of a file.

When working in Python:

- name the file something that's related to your project

- save it somewhere that you'll remember

- save your work often

YOU CAN CALL ME .PY

SAVING FILES TIP

Create a new folder called "Python_Projects" inside your "My Documents" folder to save all your Python project files. This will help you stay organized and help you remember where to find your work.

CODE

Instructions must be written using code. All parts of the code have to be written according to the rules of the Python programming language.

> The rules for writing programs are called **syntax**.

Python comes with built-in functions (a section of code that performs a specific task). One of the functions is called **print**. The print function print() will display in the shell window the text that you add as a **PARAMETER VALUE**.

> **PARAMETER VALUE**
> The text put within the parentheses of a function

Hello, Python

"Hello, World!" is one of the most basic programs you can write in any computer language. The "Hello, World!" program can be made in Python by calling the print function and typing "Hello, World!" as the parameter value like this:

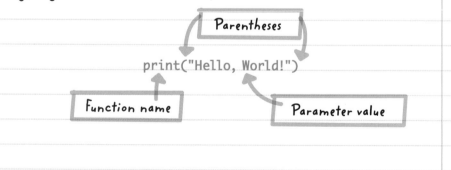

Parentheses

```
print("Hello, World!")
```

Function name

Parameter value

The **print()** function tells the computer to display the parameter value.

To **call a function** means to instruct the computer to use that specific tool.

Be very careful when typing out your code. If words are misspelled, your program may not run properly. Do not add extra spaces or symbols. Capitalization also matters. For example, entering "Print" instead of "print" won't work.

MY COMPUTER IS PICKIER ABOUT SPELLING THAN MY ENGLISH TEACHER!

BOOP!

KEEPING ORGANIZED

COMMENTS in your code are little notes to yourself and other programmers. Comments aren't run as part of the program but can be read by

BULLETIN BOARD

anyone reading your code. They act like sticky notes and can help organize your thoughts. Comments can be reminders, explanations about the code, and questions.

To make a comment in Python, use either the # symbol for a one-line comment or three quotation marks—single (''') or double (""")—for multiple lines.

```
# Comment on one line
'''Multiline
comment can take
many rows.'''
```

Single-line comments use the # only at the beginning, but multiline comments open and close with the quotation marks.

I'M HELPFUL AS WELL AS POPULAR.

Helpful Colors

Both the shell and editor windows automatically change the color of your text to help you read your code.

Purple is for built-in functions. For example, print() is a built-in function.

Orange is for key words that have special meaning, like "if" and "True."

Green is for all text that appears in quotation marks. Double or single quotation marks can be used as long as they match—in other words, don't start with single quotation marks and end with double quotation marks.

Blue is for the output text from when the program runs.

Red is for error messages that appear when the program doesn't run properly.

Black is for all the rest of the text in the program.

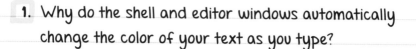

1. Why do the shell and editor windows automatically change the color of your text as you type?

2. What does the IDLE program do? Why is it helpful?

3. Write in the blank which window you should use for each of the following:

   A. _____ You want to write a large program in Python.

   B. _____ You want to save your work.

   C. _____ You want to quickly run a small piece of code.

4. Match each color in the left column with what it represents in IDLE in the right column.

A. Output	Purple
B. Text inside quotation marks	Orange
C. Key words	Green
D. Error	Blue
E. Built-in function	Red

5. Python (is/is not) a programming language used by professionals to create popular programs like YouTube and Google.

6. Why would you want to put comments in your code?

7. Which function should you use to display text in the shell window?

8. Draw the symbols around the text below to turn the sentences into a one-line or multiple-line comment.

Make this a one-line comment.

Make this a
multiple-line comment.

CHECK YOUR ANSWERS

1. The colors help you, the programmer, read your code more easily.

2. IDLE is used to write and run Python programs. It can be used to test short snippets of code or run .py program files.

3. **A.** Editor
   B. Editor
   C. Shell

4. purple: 5   green: 2   red: 4
   orange: 3   blue: 1

5. is

6. Comments help you organize your code, and they make it easier for you or other programmers to understand what each section of code does without having to read through the actual code.

7. print( )

8. #Make this a one-line comment.
'''Make this a
multiple-line comment.'''

Or, you can also use double quotation marks:

"""Make this a
multiple-line comment."""

Chapter 25

VARIABLES IN PYTHON

VARIABLES are used to store information. Storing information is useful when you want to reuse that information many times or use it at different times while running a program. They save you from entering the same block of code over and over.

In Python, the basic **DATA TYPES** that can be stored by variables include:

> **DATA TYPE**
> The kind of value the data is

- strings
- integers
- lists
- Boolean values

Variables can store values (content or data), like a **STRING**, number, **LIST**, or **BOOLEAN**.

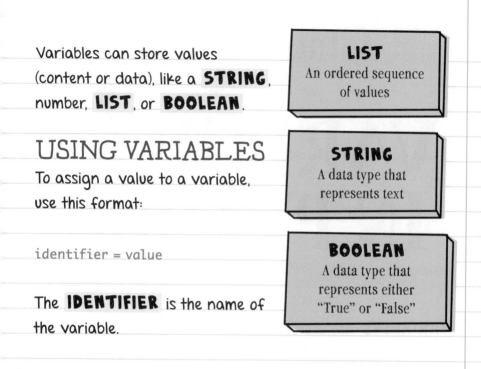

LIST
An ordered sequence of values

USING VARIABLES

To assign a value to a variable, use this format:

identifier = value

The **IDENTIFIER** is the name of the variable.

STRING
A data type that represents text

BOOLEAN
A data type that represents either "True" or "False"

FOR EXAMPLE, in a game where the player gets three lives, you could name a variable "lives" and assign it a value of 3:

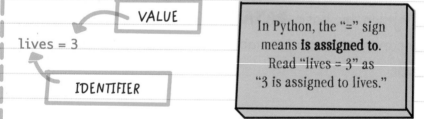

VALUE

lives = 3

IDENTIFIER

In Python, the "=" sign means **is assigned to.** Read "lives = 3" as "3 is assigned to lives."

After creating the variable and assigning it the value of 3, you can reuse the lives variable throughout the program.

Rules for Naming Python Variables

When coming up with the variable identifier, or name, you must follow these rules:

GOOD

* Use numbers, uppercase letters, lowercase letters, and underscores (_).

* Start the identifier with a letter.

* Keep your identifier short and simple, and have it describe the variable it's used for.

 Score

Mice_4

lives

When coming up with the variable identifier, or name, **do not do this**:

BAD

* Include spaces or symbols (like -, /, #, and @).

* Use key words that already mean something else in Python (like "print").

* Use the capital letters O or I or a lowercase l, because those can get confusing—a capital O looks like the number 0.

* Start your variable with a number or symbol.

key words in Python (not allowed as identifier names):

and	def	finally	in	pass	while
as	del	for	is	print	with
assert	elif	from	lambda	raise	yield
break	else	global	not	return	
class	except	if	or	try	
continue	exec	import			

When naming a variable, try to describe what it is.

FOR EXAMPLE, while you could name a variable for storing the number of lives a player has "j," you might forget what "j" means after you add in many more variables.

But if you name the variable "**lives**," you'll remember that the variable stores the number of lives for the player.

Also, keep variable names short; longer names lead to more typos and wasted time typing out the extra characters.

FOR EXAMPLE, although a variable called `the_number_of_lives_the_player_has_left` describes the data it stores, it's better to shorten it to just `lives`.

Formatting Variable Names

Programmers often use **NAMING CONVENTIONS** to make their code easier to read. A naming convention is a format for naming things like variables. Python will run correctly no matter which naming convention you pick. However, it's best to stick to one way in order to make your code easier to read.

Common naming conventions include:

DESCRIPTION	EXAMPLES
Single lowercase letter	x
Single uppercase letter	X
All lowercase	treasure
Lowercase and underscores	x_position
All uppercase	CAPTAIN

For Python, many people prefer to use **lowercase_and_underscores** when naming variables.

Uppercase and underscores	SHIP_NAME
Capitalized words (Pascal case) ← Capitalize the first letter of every word in the name.	JollyRoger
Mixed case (camel case) ↑ Capitalize only the first letter of the second word in a name. Think of it like a camel's hump in the middle of the name.	buriedTreasure
Capitalized words with underscores	Polly_Want_A _Cracker

1. Declare a variable called winning_number and give it a value of 1001.

2. Which of these are NOT allowed as Python variable names?
   A. @UserName
   B. handle
   C. Num_posts
   D. FriendCount

3. In Python, what does the "=" symbol mean?

4. Write a two-word variable using camel case.

5. Why might it be a good idea to stick with the same naming convention in a program you're making?

6. What's wrong with the following variable name?
date/Time

7. What's wrong with using the following variable name?
continue

8. What's wrong with the following variable name?
1001I1

CHECK YOUR ANSWERS

1. `winning_number = 1001`

2. **A**

3. It means "is assigned to."

4. One answer would be: exampleVariable

5. Using the same naming convention will help you stay organized and make your code easier to read because all your variables will follow the same format.

6. Python does not allow slashes in variable names.

7. "continue" is a key word in Python. Key words are reserved and cannot be used as variable names.

8. It's hard to read because the 1s, 0s, Os, Is, and ls look similar.

Chapter 26

STRINGS

STRINGS are a group of sequenced characters within either single or double quotation marks. You use strings to show messages or text on-screen in your program. When Python sees quotation marks around text, it reads it as a string.

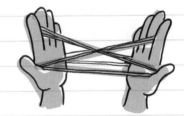

FOR EXAMPLE: These are all strings because they are surrounded by quotation marks:

"Game Over"

'time: 1:06'

"Lives left:"

"Welcome LOL. Can I tell you a joke?"

Don't mix single and double quotes. For example, 'board game night" doesn't work.

To assign a variable the value of a string, name the variable, add the assignment operator (the equal symbol), then add the string in quotation marks.

FOR EXAMPLE, for a joke-telling program, we can name a variable "welcome," add the assignment operator, then add the value "Welcome LOL. Can I tell you a joke?" like this:

```
welcome = "Welcome LOL. Can I tell you a joke?"
```

USING THE PRINT FUNCTION WITH A STRING

To display the value of a variable using the print function:

■ First assign the variable a value.

```
welcome = "Welcome LOL. Can I tell you a joke?"
```

- Then type the name of the variable inside the parentheses of the print function.

```
print(welcome)
```

VARIABLE

FUNCTION

This will make the shell window display the welcome message:

```
Welcome LOL. Can I tell you a joke?
```

IMPORTANT: if you used quotation marks around the variable name, like in the code below, the result would be different.

```
welcome = "Welcome LOL. Can I tell you a joke?"
print("welcome")
```

quotation marks included

This will make the shell window print: welcome

When you put text in quotation marks, Python recognizes it as a string instead of a variable. So instead of looking up the variable value, it just prints out the word "welcome" as a string.

Displaying Text on Multiple Lines

To make a string automatically display on multiple lines, use three single quotation marks (''') and type the text on new lines the way you want it to appear.

SMACK!

Changing the Value of a String Variable

You can change the value of a variable by adding another line of code that assigns the variable a new value in the same way you assigned the original value.

FOR EXAMPLE, to replace "LOL" with "meh":

reaction = "lol"
Value of reaction: lol

reaction = "meh"
Value of reaction: meh
"meh" replaces "lol" as the value of reaction.

print(reaction)
New value of reaction: meh

This will print: meh

The example prints "meh" because that was the latest value of reaction.

Once the value of a variable is changed, the old value is gone for good.

FORMATTING STRINGS

You can style strings so that they include the same type of punctuation and presentation as regular typed text.

Quotation Marks

All strings have quotation marks around them. So if you want to put quotation marks inside your string, you'll need to **ESCAPE** the interior quotation marks by placing a backslash (\) before each of them.

FOR EXAMPLE:

BACKSLASH

```
tornado_joke = "What do you get if you say \"tornado"\ ten
times backward and forward? . . . . A real tongue twister!"

print(tornado_joke)
```

This will print:

```
What do you get if you say "tornado" ten times backward and
forward? . . . . A real tongue twister!
```

When you **escape a character**, you are telling Python to treat that character as part of the string instead of as a special character.

EXCEPTION! If you use single quotation marks at the beginning and end of your string, then you can use double quotation marks as part of your string without needing to escape them. (Or, if you use double at the beginning and end, you can use single as part of the string.)

FOR EXAMPLE, you could assign the tornado_joke variable the following value and get the same result as before:

```
tornado_joke = "What do you get if you say "tornado" ten
times backward and forward? . . . A real tongue twister!"
```

But you should still know how to escape characters in case you need to use both single and double quotation marks or other characters in a string.

Line Breaks

To print on a new line, use an escaped "n" like this:

```
print("\n")
```

FOR EXAMPLE, you could break up the lines of a joke to emphasize the punch line:

```
print("I had a talking parrot.\n But it didn't say it was hungry,\n\n so it died.")
```

This will print:

```
I had a talking parrot. But it
didn't say it was hungry,

     so it died.
```

HEY,
NOT COOL!

OPERATORS

OPERATORS are symbols that represent actions that manipulate values. Many operators come from math.

HELLO, OPERATOR?

HELLO!

> ✱ is a mathematical operator that represents multiplying.
> ✚ is a mathematical operator that represents adding.

You can use operators with strings as well as numbers.

FOR EXAMPLE, to say "Hello!" 3 times, you could use:

```
print("Hello!" * 3)
```

MULTIPLICATION OPERATOR

"Hello!" ✱ 3 means "Hello!" × 3

This would print: Hello!Hello!Hello!

To add space between each "Hello!" add a space at the end of the string:

```
print("Hello! " * 3 )
```

SPACE

This will print: Hello! Hello! Hello!

String Addition

Operators can also be used to add strings together to make a sentence.

FOR EXAMPLE:

SPACE

```
part1 = "Why did the chicken cross the road? "
```

```
part2 = "To get to the other side."
```

```
print(part1 + part2)
```

This will display: Why did the chicken cross the road? To get to the other side.

Another way to add strings together is by creating a new variable that is the sum of two other variables.

```
part1 = "Why did the chicken cross the road? "
part2 = "To get to the other side."
whole_joke = part1 + part2
```

This would assign the variable whole_joke the value of Why did the chicken cross the road? To get to the other side.

Addition operators can combine both variables and strings into a new string variable value like this:

```
animal = "alligator"
joke = "Why did the " + animal + " cross the road?"
print(joke)
```

The spaces around the + signs make the code easier to read. Because they aren't part of a string, the computer ignores them. You could also correctly type this:

```
"Why did the "+animal+" cross the road?"
```

and it would display the same thing:

```
Why did the alligator cross the road?
```

Variables are helpful because they can change values, making programs more flexible.

Sometimes you want a user to input information.

The **input**() function displays the text you add between the parentheses and waits for the user to type something.

```
input("add your text here")
```

The shell window will display "add your text here" and wait for the user to type something in the window and press enter.

You can save the information the user types in the shell window to a variable.

To do this, before the input function, type the name of the variable you want to use and also add the assignment operator:

Variable that will store the user's answer

```
variable = input("add your text here")
```

Your text or question to display for the user

FOR EXAMPLE, you can use the input() function to ask the user to give a new value to the "animal" variable from the joke example:

```
animal = input("What's your favorite animal? ")
joke = "Why did the " + animal + " cross the road?"
print(joke)
```

> The program will ask the question, then wait for the user to type in their answer and press **ENTER**.

What's your favorite animal? **Alligator**

> After the user inputs their answer, this line will print using the information stored in the "animal" variable.

Why did the **Alligator** cross the road?

> This part is the answer the user entered.

String Functions

Python has built-in functions that change strings in helpful ways. There are functions to capitalize the first letter of a word or sentence, join multiple strings into a single string, convert a string to all lowercase letters, replace part of a string, format a string into a nicer-looking output, and more.

STRING FUNCTIONS help change data into a more usable format. For example, if you ask a user what their favorite animal is and they type "ALLIGATOR" in all caps, the lower() function can change all the capital letters to lowercase.

Use string functions by using this format:

```
variable.function()
```

If you have a variable called "animal" and you want to make sure the value is in lowercase, use the lower() function on the name variable:

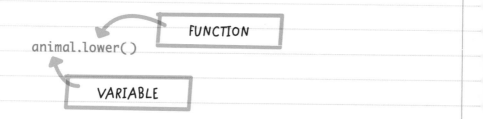

```
animal.lower()
```

FUNCTION

VARIABLE

You can use the string functions along with a string almost anywhere in a program.

Examples of different placements of the lower() function:

```
animal = input("What's your favorite animal? ").lower()
print("Why did the " + animal + " cross the road?")


animal = input("What's your favorite animal? ")
animal = animal.lower()
print("Why did the " + animal + " cross the road?")


animal = input("What's your favorite animal? ")
print("Why did the " + animal.lower() + " cross the road?")
```

All three examples will print the same output:

Why did the alligator cross the road?

SOME OF THE MOST COMMON STRING FUNCTIONS

capitalize(): Changes the first letter to uppercase and the rest to lowercase

lower(): Changes all uppercase letters to lowercase

swapcase(): Changes capital letters to lowercase and lowercase letters to capital

upper(): Converts lowercase letters to uppercase

CHECK YOUR KNOWLEDGE

1. Which of these is NOT a string:
   A. "string cheese"
   B. 'shoelace'
   C. "She said, \"keep pulling the thread\""
   D. 5 + 9

2. What will the Python code below print?
   ```
   art = "painting"
   print("my favorite kind of art is: " + art)
   ```

3. Explain how to make a string print on multiple lines.

4. If you want to ask a user their favorite color, what would be a good function to use? How would you write it?

5. What does it mean to escape a quotation mark in a string?

6. What code could you add as input to the print function below so that it prints on a new line?

   ```
   print(_____)
   ```

7. What will the following code print?

```
flavor1 = "chocolate"
flavor2 = "strawberry"
flavor3 = "vanilla"
print("My favorite sundae has these 3 flavors: " +
flavor1 + ", " + flavor2 + ", and " + flavor3 + ".")
```

8. Suppose you want to ask a user to input their dog's name, which you store in the variable "dog." You also want to capitalize the first letter of the dog's name. Which of the following will NOT capitalize the dog's name?

A. capitalize() = dog

B. dog = dog.capitalize()

C. dog = input("What's your dog's name?").capitalize()

D. print("Your dog's name is: " + dog.capitalize())

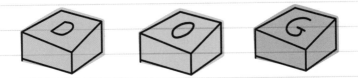

CHECK YOUR ANSWERS

1. D

2. my favorite kind of art is: painting

3. You can surround the string in three single quotation marks (''') and enter the text on new lines in the way you want it to appear. Or you can insert "\n" wherever you want a new line to start.

4. The input function, written like this: input("What's your favorite color?")

5. When you escape a quotation mark, you are making it part of the string instead of using it as a special character to mark the beginning or end of a string.

6. "\n"

7. My favorite sundae has these three flavors: chocolate, strawberry, and vanilla.

8. A

Chapter 27

NUMBERS AS VARIABLES

Variables can also be numbers. When assigning a number value to a variable, DO NOT surround the number with quotation marks.

```
number = 5
string = "five"
string = "5"
```

> A number can be a string if you surround it with quotation marks. But you can't do math with a string.

CALCULATIONS WITH NUMBER VARIABLES

In Python, you can use numbers to calculate math problems. For example, you can create a homework helper program where Python does the calculations.

You can make two number variables, add them together, and then print the sum like this:

> Remember to assign the values of "num1" and "num2" *before* you use them in a calculation for "sum." You can't use variables until *after* you assign them values.

```
num1 = 4
num2 = 5
sum = num1 + num2
print(sum)
```

This will print: 9

NUMBER TYPES

Python uses different types of numbers. Two of those types are **INTEGERS** and **FLOATS**.

Integers

In Python, **integers** are positive or negative whole numbers that don't use a decimal place.

You can create a variable called "num1" and assign it an integer value of 3:

```
num1 = 3
```
⟵ A whole number

String variables, even if they have whole numbers inside them, aren't recognized by Python as integers.

FOR EXAMPLE, when you add two strings together, they are combined as one string:

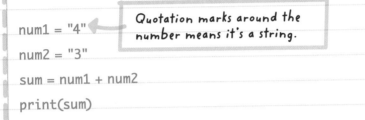

```
num1 = "4"
num2 = "3"
sum = num1 + num2
print(sum)
```

Quotation marks around the number means it's a string.

This will print 43, which is the string 4 and the string 3 combined into a single string.

Sometimes it's necessary to convert a variable to an **integer data type.**

FOR EXAMPLE, if you ask a user to enter a number using the **input()** function, Python stores their answer as a string.

```
width = input("Enter the rectangle's width. ")
height = input("Enter the rectangle's height. ")
```

In the program above, if the user entered 5 and 8, the numbers would be stored as strings—"5" and "8"—and not as integers.

Convert the user's answers from strings to integers using the int() function. You can then perform calculations with them.

Multiply the length and width of a rectangle to find the area like this:

> Width and height start out as strings.

```
width = input("Enter the rectangle's width. ")
height = input("Enter the rectangle's height. ")
width = int(width)
height = int(height)
print(width*height)
```

> Width and height are reassigned as integers.

The number values for width and height can now be used in calculations, such as finding the area.

Floats

Floats (or floating point numbers) are numbers that have a decimal point.

FOR EXAMPLE, the values to these variables are floats:

```
num1 = 3.3
num2 = 6.0
num3 = 2.9564576
```

FLOATS

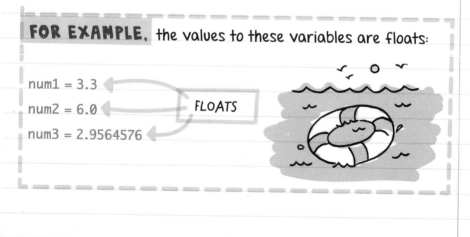

To convert a variable value from an integer or string to a float, use the **float()** function like this:

```
num1 = 6
```
num1 starts out as an integer.

```
num1 = float(num1)
```
num1 is reassigned as a float.

```
sum = num1 + 3.3
```
Calculations with a float keep the digits to the right of the decimal point.

```
print(sum)
```
Will display: 9.3 (the sum of 6.0 + 3.3)

NUMBER CONVERSION

int(): Converts a value to an integer. Useful for converting a user's input string into an integer to do math.

float(): Converts a value to a floating point number (number with a decimal point). Useful when you are using values that are not whole numbers.

MATHEMATICAL EXPRESSIONS

Numbers and math are used in programming to represent the location of a character in a game, calculate dates, set timers, display colors, calculate scores, and more. **VALUES** and **OPERATORS** combine to make **EXPRESSIONS**.

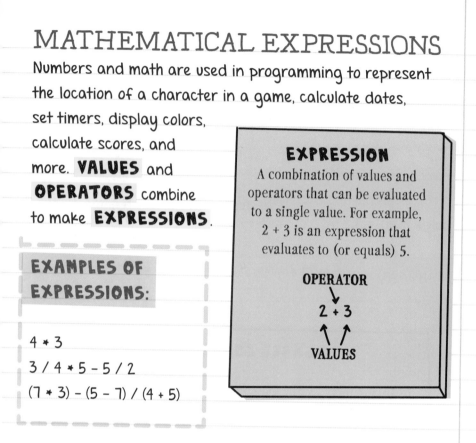

EXPRESSION
A combination of values and operators that can be evaluated to a single value. For example, 2 + 3 is an expression that evaluates to (or equals) 5.

OPERATOR
↓
2 + 3
↑ ↑
VALUES

EXAMPLES OF EXPRESSIONS:

4 * 3
3 / 4 * 5 - 5 / 2
(7 * 3) - (5 - 7) / (4 + 5)

Variables can also hold number values and be used in mathematical expressions. For example, if a variable called "x" holds the value of 4, it can be used in an expression:

VALUE
A piece of information. In mathematical expressions, values are numbers.

x + 6   Because x holds the value 4, this expression evaluates to 10.

There are seven common math operators:

NAME	SYMBOL	EXAMPLE
addition	+	5 + 2
subtraction	−	5 - 2
multiplication	*	5 * 2
division	/	5 / 2
modulus	%	5 % 2
exponent	**	5 ** 2
floor division	//	5 // 2

The remainder portion of a quotient. For example, 5 ÷ 2 = 2 with a remainder, or **modulus**, of 1.

Divides two numbers and ignores the remainder. For example, 5 ÷ 2 = 2 (the remainder, 1, is ignored).

The symbols "x" and "÷" are not used in Python.

ORDER OF OPERATIONS

Use the **ORDER OF OPERATIONS** when solving equations:

> **ORDER OF OPERATIONS**
> A set of rules for deciding the order that operations will be evaluated

1. Solve any parts of the equation that are inside brackets or parentheses. If there is more than one set of parentheses, solve the innermost equation first.

> Parentheses can be *nested*. This means that there can be one set of parentheses inside another set, like this: ((2 + 18) * 5) /10. The innermost equation is 2 + 18 and should be solved first.

2. Calculate exponents, absolute value, and square roots from left to right.

3. Solve all the multiplication and division from left to right.

4. Complete the addition and subtraction from left to right.

> To remember the order of operations, think "Please Excuse My Dear Aunt Sally," or **PEMDAS** (Parentheses, Exponents, Multiplication, Division, Addition, Subtraction). But be careful, because PEMDAS isn't foolproof. For example, you should do subtraction before addition if you're calculating from left to right—and the same goes for division and multiplication.

First, solve the equation in parentheses: 2 * (6 − 3)

$$6 - 3 = 3 \longrightarrow 2 * (3)$$

Then, multiply to get your answer: 2 * 3 = ⑥

If you have the same expression
without the parentheses . . . 2 * 6 − 3

First, multiply: 2 * 6 = 12 ⟶ 12 − 3

Then, subtract to get your answer: 12 − 3 = ⑨

Even though they contain the same numbers, the two
equations have different answers because of the order
of operations. Python will always follow the order of
operations when it returns a value.

Printing Mathematical Expressions

If an expression is inside the print function, then Python
will print the value of the expression to the shell window.

FOR EXAMPLE:

`print(5 * 3)`   This will print: 15

1. In Python, what does the ** operator do?

2. To find the remainder of a division, you would use the _____ operator.

3. What will each expression return?
   A. 5 // 4
   B. 3 * (5 + 2) – 6
   C. 2 * 5
   D. 4 / 2
   E. 6 % 2
   F. 6 / 3 + (2 – 1) + 2 * 3

4. Write out the code to print the answer to 5 times 2.

5. In the correct order of operations, which comes first: exponents or addition?

6. What is an expression?

7. In mathematical expressions, values are always (numbers / symbols).

8. If you want to find the whole-number value of a division operation **without** the remainder, you should use the _____ operator.

9. What will the following code print?

```
width = 4
height = 12
perimeter = width * 2 + height * 2
print(perimeter)
```

10. Where is the error in this program?

```
dog_years = human_years * 7
human_years = 3
print(dog_years)
```

11. What's the difference between an integer and a float variable?

MORE QUESTIONS

12. Will the following program print an integer or a float number?

```
d = 4.2
t = 3
speed = d / t
print(speed)
```

13. What function should you use to convert a variable to an integer?

CHECK YOUR ANSWERS

1. ** is used as the exponent operator.

2. Modulus or %

3. **A.** 1
   B. 15
   C. 10
   D. 2
   E. 0
   F. 9

4. print(5 * 2)

5. Exponents

6. An expression is the combination of values and operators that can be evaluated to a single value.

7. Numbers

8. Floor or //

9. 32

MORE ANSWERS

10. The problem is "human_years" is assigned the value of 3 after it is used in the first line (human_years * 7).

11. An integer is a whole number that does not have a decimal, and a float is a number that has a decimal.

12. Float, because "d" is a float and used to calculate "speed"

13. int( )

Chapter 28

LISTS AND BOOLEAN EXPRESSIONS

LISTS

A **LIST** is a variable that stores multiple values. This is useful when you have several pieces of information that you want to store in one place. Lists can store all types of values including numbers, strings, and other lists.

In Python, lists are formatted using square brackets (and sometimes quotation marks), with a comma between each item. For example, we can make a list called "fruits" and assign it the values apples, bananas, grapes, oranges, and pears:

LIST NAME   LIST ITEMS

```
fruits = ['apples', 'bananas', 'grapes', 'oranges', 'pears']
```

Think of a list as a row of boxes, where each box holds a value. Every box on the list gets a number, starting with 0. This number is called the **INDEX**.

list

index

The index is used to find or change specific values, or items, within the list. In the fruit example, apples is located at index location 0, and the index location of pears is 4.

A specific item in a list is located using the format list[#], where "list" is the name of the list and "#" is the index location of the item.

So, fruits[0] is apples and fruits[4] is pears.

To display the <u>second item</u> of the fruits list, use the print function, enter "fruits" as the name of the list, and "1" for the index location of the item:

```
print(fruits[1])
```

Because the index starts at 0, the second item has an index of 1.

This will print: bananas

You can also print out a section of the list by naming the range of indexes to print, like this:

ending index

```
print(fruits[1:4])
```

starting index

This will print: ['bananas', 'grapes', 'oranges']

The ending index (4: pears) is not included.

> When you use **print()** to display more than one item in a list, the output will include the brackets and quotation marks. That's because you're printing a list, not just items in a list.

There are lots of different ways to update a list.

> The last item isn't listed—only the items *up to* the ending index position are included in the list.

You can replace an item in a list after the list has been created.

▪ To replace a value of an item within a list,

    1. reference (name) the index location
    2. reassign the value

To replace grapes with kiwi: ['apples', 'bananas', 'grapes', 'oranges', 'pears']

The index location of grapes is 2. You can replace grapes by assigning index 2 of the fruits list to kiwi:

```
fruits[2] = "kiwi"
```

GET OUTTA HERE!

The list is now: ['apples', 'bananas', 'kiwi', 'oranges', 'pears']

To add an item to the end of
a list, use the **append()** function.

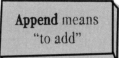

Append means
"to add"

If the list of fruits was a shopping list, the **append()**
function would add items to the end of it.

You can add "cherries" to the list by applying the append
function to the fruits list like this:

```
fruits.append("cherries")
```

The list is now: ['apples', 'bananas',
'kiwi', 'oranges', 'pears', 'cherries']

Commas are
added automatically
when you add new
items to a list.

To insert an item between two other
values in a list, use the **insert()** function.
Inside the parentheses, tell the
function where to insert the new
value and what the value should be.

Add "peaches" to index location 2 of the fruits list using
the **insert()** function like this:

```
fruits.insert(2, "peaches")
```

new item index location

value to insert

The list is now: ['apples', 'bananas', 'peaches', 'kiwi', 'oranges', 'pears', 'cherries']

■ To remove an item from a list, use the **remove()** function. Inside the parentheses, tell the function which item you want removed by entering the value (the name of the item, not the index number):

```
fruits.remove("kiwi")
```

The list is now:
['apples', 'bananas', 'peaches', 'oranges', 'pears', 'cherries']

MAKE ROOM!

I'M OUT!

■ To sort a list,

• use either the **sort()** function, which will put the list in numerical or alphabetical order (A-Z), or

• use the **reverse()** function, which will put the list in reverse order.

ME FIRST

```
fruits.sort()
```

orders the list to: ['apples', 'bananas', 'cherries', 'oranges', 'peaches', 'pears']

```
fruits.reverse()
```

orders the list to:
['pears', 'peaches',
'oranges', 'cherries',
'bananas', 'apples']

■ To get the number of items in a list, use the **len( )** function:

```
fruits = ['pears', 'peaches', 'oranges', 'cherries',
'bananas', 'apples']
fruit_length = len(fruits)    ← (Put the name of the list
print(fruit_length)               inside the parentheses.)
```

prints: 6

■ To add one list to the end of another list, use the "+"
operator:

```
fruits = ['apples', 'bananas', 'kiwi']
vegetables = ['carrots', 'peas', 'onions']
produce = fruits + vegetables    Give the new variable (the
print(produce)                    combined list) a name.
```

prints: ['apples', 'bananas', 'kiwi', 'carrots', 'peas',
'onions']

Lists Within Lists

A list can be set within another list. The second list is called the **INNER LIST**. You can use this list to show a subcategory—a more specialized group. The format for making a list within a list is a second set of brackets within the first:

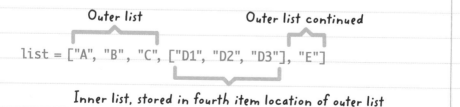

Outer list   Outer list continued

list = ["A", "B", "C", ["D1", "D2", "D3"], "E"]

Inner list, stored in fourth item location of outer list

1. enter the opening bracket

2. add the types of apples in quotation marks, and end with a closing bracket

3. continue with the rest of the list

Outer list   Inner list

```
fruits = ["bananas", ["Gala", "Empire", "McIntosh", "Golden
Delicious"], "kiwi", "oranges", "pears"]
```

Inner list   Outer list continued

The list of apples is stored as the second item of the fruits list.

To print just the favorite apples (the inner list) from the list of favorite fruits, use the print function with the second item (index location 1) of the favorite fruits list:

2nd item

```
print(fruits[1])
```

list name

prints: ["Gala", "Empire", "McIntosh", "Golden Delicious"]

373

You can print a single apple name by using the index location 1 to reference the list of apples and then adding the index location of the specific apple.

For example, to print "McIntosh" off the inner list of apples, use this code:

specific apple

```
print(fruits[1][2])
```

list of apples

prints: McIntosh

BOOLEAN EXPRESSIONS

In programming, it's very common to want to know if something is true or false. For example, in a game we want to know if the game is over, or if it is still going, or if a user got a question right or wrong.

Python automatically detects a Boolean-type variable when the value is set to "True" or "False," (a Boolean expression). When you're setting a variable to "True" or "False," make sure you capitalize the T in True and the F in False. For example: my_value = True.

Boolean variables are like light switches. There are only two options: on or off (True or False).

When you assign a Boolean expression to a variable, Python will set the value to "True" or "False" depending on whether the Boolean expression is true or false. For example:

height = 58 ← Assigns "height" the value of 58.

meet_limit = height > 50 ← Assigns "meet_limit" the value of "height > 50." This means that a height of greater than 50 will be considered true.

print(meet_limit)

This will print: True

The expression is True because the given height is 58, and 58 > 50, which means that **meet_limit** is **true**.

> Number variables store the answer to a calculation and not the mathematical expression. Boolean variables are similar because they store "True" or "False" as the answer to a comparison expression instead of the comparison itself.

This example shows assigning the variable of **test1** to the Boolean expression **2 is equal to** 4, which is false.

test1 = 2 == 4
print(test1)

This will print: False

COMPARISON OPERATORS evaluate information to be true or false. They compare two values to each other.

Comparison operators are:

SYMBOL	MEANING	SYMBOL	MEANING
==	is equal to	>	is greater than
!=	is not equal to	<=	is less than or equal to
<	is less than	>=	is greater than or equal to

Examples of expressions that evaluate to True:

EXPRESSION	MEANING	VALUE
2 == 2	2 is equal to 2	True
2 != 3	2 is not equal to 3	True
2 < 3	2 is less than 3	True
4 > 3	4 is greater than 3	True
2 <= 2	2 is less than or equal to 2	True
5 >= 3	5 is greater than or equal to 3	True

Examples of expressions that evaluate to False:

EXPRESSION	MEANING	VALUE
2 == 5	2 is equal to 5	False
2 != 2	2 is not equal to 2	False
3 < 3	3 is less than 3	False
2 > 3	2 is greater than 3	False
5 <= 3	5 is less than or equal to 3	False
2 >= 3	2 is greater than or equal to 3	False

1. _____ are used to store multiple values.

2. What function should you use to add an item to the end of a list?

3. How can you replace the second item in the list "cars" with "Porsche"?

4. What function should you use to add an item between two existing items in a list?

5. How do you store a list within a list?

6. Explain what the sort() function does.

7. Write the code that would print "bananas" given the list below:

```
fruits = ["apples", "bananas", "kiwi", "oranges", "pears"]
```

8. Which of the following does NOT evaluate to a Boolean value?

A. True

B. 3 ** 2

C. False

D. 3 > 2

9. What will the following program print?

```
score = 3
game_over = score > 5
print(game_over)
```

10. What will the following code print?

```
print(100 == 25)
```

11. How is "==" different from "=" in Python?

CHECK YOUR ANSWERS

1. Lists

2. append()

3. cars[1] = "Porsche"

4. insert()

5. Add a second set of brackets around the list inside another list. The inner list will take one item spot in the outer list.

6. The sort() function rearranges the list into numerical or alphabetical order.

7. print(fruits[1])

8. B

9. False

10. False

11. In Python, "==" is a comparison operator that checks if two values are exactly the same, but "=" is the assignment operator and assigns a value to a variable.

Chapter 29

FOR LOOPS

Python uses different types of **LOOPS** to perform different actions. *FOR* LOOPS repeat code a specified number of times.

> **LOOP**
> Code used to repeat a sequence of commands

FORMATTING *FOR* LOOPS

The *for* loop follows a very specific format; even the number of spaces you use on certain lines is important.

Steps for Creating a *For* Loop:

STEP 1: Enter the key word "for." *For* loops always start with "for" to show that the following code is a *for* loop.

STEP 2: Name the **COUNTER VARIABLE**. This variable's value increases each time the loop repeats. For example, if you are using a *for* loop that loops 10 times, starting with 0 and increasing by 1 each time the loop starts over, the counter variable will represent 0 in the first run, then 1 in the next run, then 2, then 3, and so on, increasing by 1 each time the loop starts over.

You can name the counter variable anything you want. Many programmers name their counter variable "i" out of tradition.

STEP 3: Add the key word "in" to show that you are about to specify how many times the loop should repeat.

STEP 4: Set the number of times the loop should repeat. Use the **range()** function to do this. The range function will count from zero up to, but not including, the number listed in the function's parentheses.

> **Range( )** defines where a counter starts, ends, and what number it should count by. The parameters include (start, stop, step). The **start** and **stop** parameters name the start and stop numbers for the counter. The **step** parameter tells how much the counter should count by. For example, range(4, 13, 4) will count from 4 to 12 (the number before the "stop" number) in increments of 4; the numbers counted in this range are: 4, 8, 12.

STEP 5: End the first line of the *for* loop with a colon (:).

Here's what a *for* loop, with a counter variable named *i*, counting by 1 from 0 up to 3, looks like:

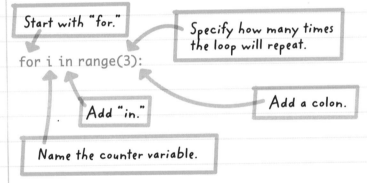

Start with "for."

Specify how many times the loop will repeat.

for i in range(3):

Add "in."

Add a colon.

Name the counter variable.

Below the first line of the *for* loop, add the code to be repeated.

Indent the code to be repeated by pressing the **TAB** key on the keyboard once or by using the space bar to add FOUR SPACES. In Python, the indent indicates that the code on that line is part of the code above it. You can add a print function to the loop by starting a new line and indenting it in the same way.

You can add code that runs after the loop has finished running.

To do that, start a new line that's not indented, like this:

```
for i in range(3):
    print("Hip hip hooray!")
print("Congratulations")
```

In the loop

Outside the loop

This will print:

Hip hip hooray!
Hip hip hooray!
Hip hip hooray!
Congratulations

Every time you create a *for* loop, you also create a new variable that counts the number of times the loop is repeated. That means the variable can be used within the repeated code.

In the previous example, the variable "i" was used in the *for* loop. Printing the value of "i" before "Hip hip hooray!" shows how the value increases each time the loop is run:

```
for i in range(3):
    print(i, "Hip hip hooray!")
```

This will print:

0 Hip hip hooray!
1 Hip hip hooray!
2 Hip hip hooray!

REMINDER: The range( ) function starts counting at 0 and stops counting before the number set in the parentheses.

In the display output, the "i" variable value in the first run of the loop is 0 and the last run shows "i" having the value of 2.

The counter variable can be used to count in other ways.

You could use the other parameters in the range() function to count by 2s between 2 and 10:

Start at this number.

```
for i in range(2, 10, 2):
    print(i)
```

Count (step) by this number.

This will print:

End before this number.

2, 4, 6, 8,
WHO DO WE
APPRECIATE?

2

4

6

8

To print every item in a list (like "fruits") use this code:

```
fruits = ['pears', 'oranges', 'mangos', 'cherries', 'bananas', 'apples']

for i in range(6):
    print(fruits[i])
```

item in list

list name

This would print:

pears

oranges

mangos

cherries

bananas

apples

There's an easier way to loop through an entire list without having to know the exact length of the list.

Instead of using the **range()** function, use the list itself, and the loop will run the same amount of times as the number of items in the list. Instead of being a number, the counter variable value will be set to each item of the list as it steps through the entire list.

To print every fruit in the "fruits" list, replace range() with the list name:

```python
fruits = ['pears', 'oranges', 'mangos', 'cherries', 'bananas', 'apples']

for i in fruits:
    print(i)
```

Use the list name instead of range().

The variable value of i is the list item, not a number.

CHECK YOUR KNOWLEDGE

1. Explain what the range() part of a for loop does.

2. Which part of a for loop's code should be indented?

3. What are two ways to print each item in the following list?

```
Seasons = ["Winter", "Spring", "Summer", "Fall"]
```

Turn the page for question #4 →

4. Write the output for each of the programs below:

PROGRAM NAME	PROGRAM	RESULT
A	```for i in range(4):``` ``` print(i)```	
B	```for i in range(10):``` ``` print(i * 5)```	
C	```for i in range(25, 101, 25):``` ``` print(i)```	

D	```colors = ["red", "blue",```
	 ```"yellow"]```
	 ```for i in colors:```
	 ``` print(i)```
	 ```print("Those are the primary```
	 ```colors")```	

E	```multiplier = 4```
	 ```for i in range(11):```
	 ``` print(i * multiplier)```	

F	```for i in range(7):``` ``` print(i)```	

CHECK YOUR ANSWERS

1. The range() function defines where the loop counter starts, ends, and what number it should count by.

2. The code that's four spaces in, or tabbed, is the part of the code that runs each time the *for* loop cycles.

3. One way:

```
for i in range(4):
    print(Seasons[i])
```

Another way:

```
for i in Seasons:
    print(i)
```

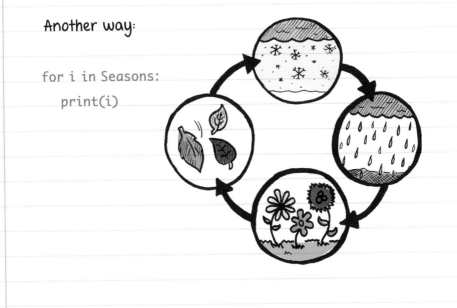

4. Code
results:

A: 0
1
2
3

B: 0
5
10
15
20
25
30
35
40
45

C: 25
50
75
100

D: red
green
blue
yellow
Those are the primary colors

E: 0
4
8
12
16
20
24
28
32
36
40

F: 0
1
2
3
4
5
6

Chapter 30

WHILE LOOPS AND NESTED LOOPS

WHILE LOOPS

WHILE LOOPS repeat as long as the conditional statements within them are True. A while loop looks similar to a *for* loop, but it replaces the counting portion with a CONDITIONAL STATEMENT.

> **REMINDER:**
> A conditional statement runs a chunk of code only when a certain condition is met.

While loops always start with the key word "while" followed by a Boolean expression and then a colon (:). The repeated code is indented below the first line.

You could make a password checker that will continue to loop until the user types in the correct password. The Boolean expression checks if the entered password is true. To do this:

Create the variable "password" and assign it the value **None**.

> "None" is a Python key word that means "empty."

> Create the variable "password" before you use it in the *while* loop.

```
password = None
while password != "myPassword1234":
    password = input("Enter the password: ")
    if password != "myPassword1234":
        print("Your password is incorrect.")
print("Correct password. Welcome.")
```

> This *while* loop will continually loop as long as the password entered is NOT the same as "myPassword1234".

> This condition will only run the print() function if the password variable value is not equal to "myPassword1234".

> The print() function will run after the password variable value DOES equal "myPassword1234".

Example output:

Enter the password: rememberMe
Your password is incorrect.
Enter the password: CantRemember
Your password is incorrect.
Enter the password: OhNowIDo
Your password is incorrect.
Enter the password: myPassword1234
Correct password. Welcome.

The program will continue the loop and prompt the user to enter the password until the user enters "myPassword1234". When that happens, the loop ends and the rest of the program (printing "Correct password. Welcome.") is allowed to run.

Infinite Loops

In Python, **INFINITE** loops (forever loops) are *while* loops that use a Boolean statement that can never become false.

These are all infinite loops because there is no way for the Boolean statements in each to become false:

```
while True:
    print("This is the song that never ends.")
```

```
while 4 > 3:
    print("This is the song that never ends.")
```

```
while "hello" == "hello":
    print("This is the song that never ends.")

while 5 <= 5:
    print("This is the song that never ends.")
```

None of these loops provide a way for the conditional statement to ever become false, so these loops will continue to loop forever (infinitely). The print() statement in each example will continuously loop and print over and over again, forever.

I'VE BEEN ON THIS THING FOREVER.

You can exit an infinite loop by pressing Ctrl + C on Windows, or command ⌘ + C on a Mac.

Sometimes you write an infinite loop as part of your program on purpose. For example, video games usually use an infinite loop to animate the characters, continually updating character movement and interaction as the player plays the game. But other times, an infinite loop may be written by accident, and it may crash your

I'M GONNA PASS OUT.

computer because the program is too large or tries to get the computer to process too much information.

NESTED LOOPS

A **NESTED LOOP** is when one loop is put inside another loop. They help create more complex repeating code. For example, you can use a password program as an outer while loop and nest an inner for loop to print out all the wrong guesses the user inputs before they guess the correct password:

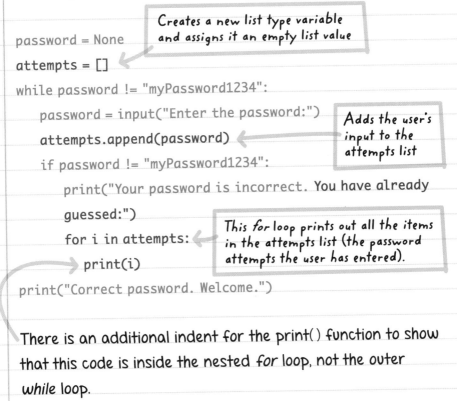

```
password = None          Creates a new list type variable
                         and assigns it an empty list value
attempts = []
while password != "myPassword1234":
    password = input("Enter the password:")
    attempts.append(password)          Adds the user's
                                       input to the
    if password != "myPassword1234":   attempts list
        print("Your password is incorrect. You have already
        guessed:")
        for i in attempts:          This for loop prints out all the items
            print(i)                in the attempts list (the password
                                    attempts the user has entered).
print("Correct password. Welcome.")
```

There is an additional indent for the print() function to show that this code is inside the nested for loop, not the outer while loop.

CHECK YOUR KNOWLEDGE

1. What's the difference between a *while* loop and a *for* loop?

2. A *while* loop that uses a conditional statement that will always be true is called _____.

3. What keys do you press to get out of an infinite loop?

4. Describe how a tab (or 4 spaces) is used in nested loops.

5. Write a loop that will give the following results.

PROGRAM NAME	PROGRAM	RESULT
A		The program will print: Go! Go! Go! as long as the variable "x" is more than 50.
B		The program will print: Good morning, Steve as long as the variable "name" is equal to "Steve".

PROGRAM NAME	PROGRAM	RESULT
C		The program will count from 7 to 11 by twos 3 times.
D		The program will count to 5 over and over again, forever.
E		The program will print: hip hip hooray hip hip hooray hip hip hooray
F		The program will print: 1 2 3 4 5
G		The program will print: hello, friend . . . forever, or until the program is stopped using Ctrl + C.

ANSWERS 399

CHECK YOUR ANSWERS

1. A *for* loop runs a set amount of times, and a *while* loop will run as long as its condition is True.

2. An infinite, or forever, loop

3. Ctrl + C on Windows or command ⌘ + C on a Mac

4. Tabs (or 4 spaces) are used to show which loop is inside the other. An additional tab or 4 spaces shows that the code is nested inside another inner loop.

5. Program answers:

A.
```python
while x > 50:
    print("Go! Go! Go!")
```
B.
```python
while name == "Steve":
    print("Good morning, Steve")
```
C.
```python
for i in range(3):
    for j in range(7, 12, 2):
        print(j)
```

Variable names may be different.

D.
```
count = True
while count:
    for i in range(1, 6, 1):
        print(i)
```

Variable names may be different.

E.
```
for i in range(3):
    for j in range(2):
        print("hip", end=" ")
    print("hooray")
```

Variable names may be different.

F.
```
num = 0
while num < 5:
    num = num + 1
    print(num)
```

Variable name may be different.

G.
```
while True:
    print("hello, friend")
```

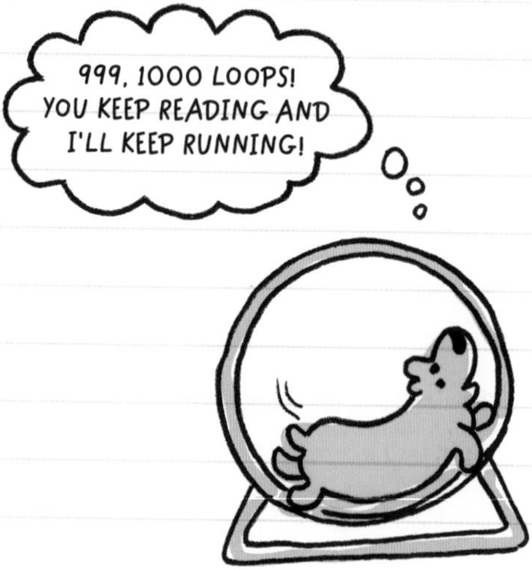
999, 1000 LOOPS!
YOU KEEP READING AND
I'LL KEEP RUNNING!

Chapter 31

CONDITIONAL STATEMENTS

CONDITIONAL STATEMENTS

CONDITIONAL STATEMENTS in Python always start with the key word "if," followed by the Boolean expression and a colon. The code that runs if the condition is true is added below the first line and indented one tab (or four spaces).

> Boolean expressions use ==, !=, <, >, <=, and >=.

FOR EXAMPLE, you can write a program that displays a message if a game player has reached the expert level. The code that prints "Skill Level: Expert" will run only if the xp (experience points) is greater than or equal to 90. If the xp is less than 90, nothing happens.

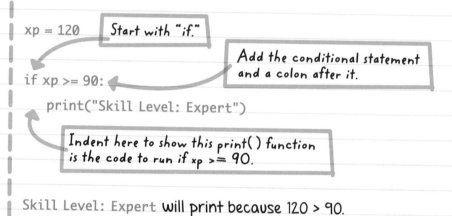

```
xp = 120
```
Start with "if."

```
if xp >= 90:
```
Add the conditional statement and a colon after it.

```
    print("Skill Level: Expert")
```
Indent here to show this print( ) function is the code to run if xp >= 90.

`Skill Level: Expert` **will print because 120 > 90.**

Else Statements

An **ELSE** statement is a statement that runs when the Boolean value is False. To use the *else* statement, type "else" on a new line. Then, on a new line, indent 1 tab (4 spaces) and add code that will run if the Boolean expression is false. For example, you could say: If xp is greater than or equal to 90, then display "Skill Level: Expert", but if the user's xp is less than 90, display "Skill Level: Novice."

```
xp = 50
if xp >= 90:
    print("Skill Level: Expert")
else:
    print("Skill Level: Novice")
```

tells what code should run when the Boolean expression is False

The example will display "Skill Level: Novice" because xp is 50, which is not greater than or equal to 90.

Elif

ELIF is used to combine an *else* statement with another conditional statement to check for additional information. *Elif* is used only after an "if" or another "elif" statement. Next to *elif*, add a Boolean expression and then a colon.

THE CELEBRITY COUPLE NAME FOR **IF** AND **ELSE** WOULD BE ELIF!

For example, you can add another experience level to the game by adding an *elif* statement to the code.

The first condition displays "Skill Level: Expert" if xp is greater than or equal to 90.

You can add an *elif* statement to display "Skill Level: Intermediate" if xp is greater than or equal to 50 and less than 90. If xp is less than 50, then the *else* statement will run the code to display "Skill Level: Novice."

```
xp = 50
if xp >= 90:
    print("Skill Level: Expert")
elif xp >= 50:
    print("Skill Level: Intermediate")
else:
    print("Skill Level: Novice")
```

A flowchart of the program shows the different branches for each condition:

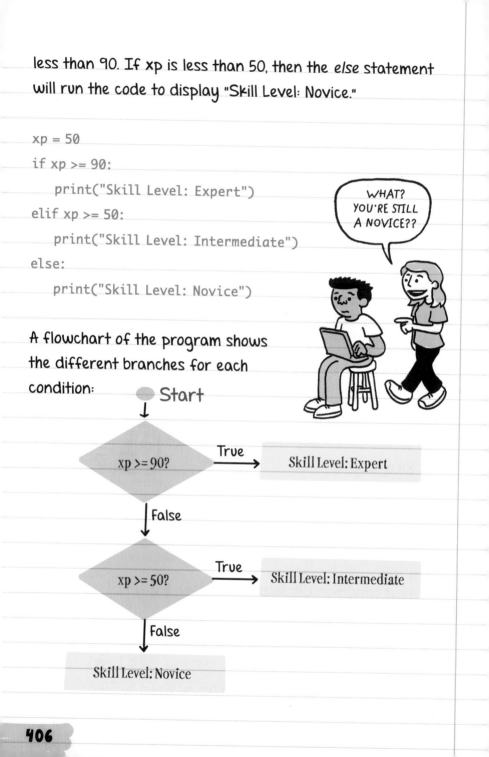

WHAT?
YOU'RE STILL
A NOVICE??

Start

xp >= 90? →True→ Skill Level: Expert

False

xp >= 50? →True→ Skill Level: Intermediate

False

Skill Level: Novice

Compound Conditional Statements

A **COMPOUND CONDITIONAL STATEMENT** is a conditional statement that contains two Boolean expressions. For example, you could make a game where the player gets bonus points if their score is greater than 50 AND their difficulty setting is set to "hard."

LOGICAL OPERATORS combine multiple Boolean expressions or values that evaluate to one Boolean value.

Python uses three logical operators:

AND: If both expressions are True, then the whole condition is True. If one or both of the expressions are False, then the whole condition is False.

OR: If one or both expressions are True, then the condition is True. It doesn't matter whether the other condition is True or False.

NOT: Switches the expression to its opposite (from True to False and False to True).

When we talk or write about AND, OR, and NOT, we use all caps; however, within Python programs, the words are written in all lowercase.

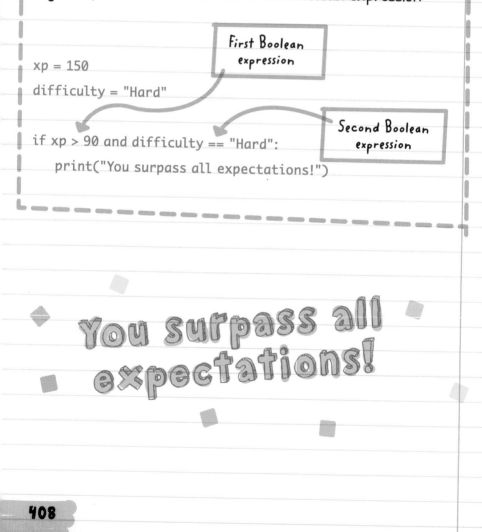

FOR EXAMPLE, we could display a special message if a player wins on the most difficult setting and their xp is greater than 90.

The compound conditional statement starts with "if", and then we can add a Boolean expression followed by the logical operator "AND" and the other Boolean expression:

First Boolean expression

```
xp = 150
difficulty = "Hard"

if xp > 90 and difficulty == "Hard":
    print("You surpass all expectations!")
```

Second Boolean expression

You surpass all expectations!

Examples of how logical operators work:

3 < 4 and 6 == 6

True AND **True** evaluates to **True**

4 != 4 and 6 > 2

False AND **True** evaluates to **False**

5 == 5 or 6 < 3

True OR **False** evaluates to **True**

4 > 12 or 7 != 7

False OR **False** evaluates to **False**

not(6 < 13)

True evaluates to **False**

TRUTH TABLES list all the possible outcomes of logical operators. Truth tables for AND, OR, and NOT:

AND TRUTH TABLE

Boolean 1	AND	Boolean 2	Evaluates to
True	AND	True	True
True	AND	False	False
False	AND	True	False
False	AND	False	False

OR TRUTH TABLE

Boolean 1	OR	Boolean 2	Evaluates to
True	OR	True	True
True	OR	False	True
False	OR	True	True
False	OR	False	False

NOT TRUTH TABLE

NOT	Boolean	Evaluates to
NOT	True	False
NOT	False	True

Nested Conditional Statements

NESTED CONDITIONAL STATEMENTS can be nested within loops.

NESTED CONDITIONALS

Loop

FOR EXAMPLE, you could make a game that loops until the game is over. The game play could be controlled using compound and nested conditionals.

Suppose you are creating a game where the user has to enter as many three-letter words as they can. If they repeat a word, the game is over. You can use a flowchart to map out the order and direction of actions.

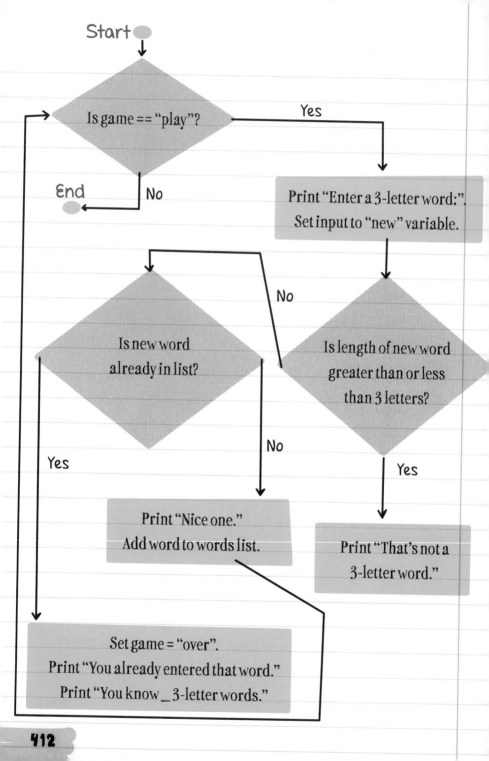

Start

Is game == "play"?

Yes

No

End

Print "Enter a 3-letter word:".
Set input to "new" variable.

Is new word already in list?

No

Is length of new word greater than or less than 3 letters?

No

Yes

Print "Nice one."
Add word to words list.

Print "That's not a 3-letter word."

Yes

Set game = "over".
Print "You already entered that word."
Print "You know _ 3-letter words."

Using the flowchart as a guide, you can create the program:

```python
words = []

game = "play"

while game == "play":

    new = input("Enter a 3-letter word: ")

    if len(new) > 3 or len(new) < 3:

        print("That's not a 3-letter word.")

    else:

        if new in words:

            game = "over"

            print("You already said that word. Game over.")

    print("You know", len(words), "3-letter words.")
```

Creates a blank list called "words"

Starts a while loop for game play

Sets the variable "new" to the user input

Checks if the word is 3 letters long

Prints if word is not 3 letters long

If the word is 3 letters, it moves on to the code below.

If the word is already in the list, it breaks out of the loop.

If the user enters a word they already used, it prints the game over message.

Tells how many words in the list

```
        else:
            print("Nice one.")
```

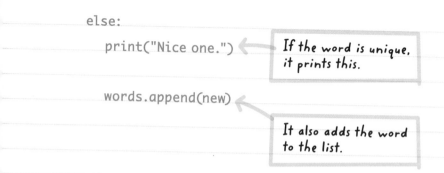

If the word is unique, it prints this.

```
        words.append(new)
```

It also adds the word to the list.

The nested conditional is:

If the word is three letters long <u>AND</u> unique, the game continues.

I KNOW SO MANY THREE-LETTER WORDS!

1. Label each of the following with the type of conditional statement it represents (if, if/else, if/elif/else):

A.
```
if at_dance == True:
    print("Dance the night away.")
elif busy != True:
    print("Go to the dance.")
else:
    print("Stay home.")
```

B.
```
if hands != "sweaty":
    print("hold")
else:
    print("wipe hands")
```

C.
```
if courage > 50:
    print("Say hello to your crush.")
elif courage < 10:
    print("Don't make eye contact.")
else:
    print("Smile at your crush.")
```

D.	if breath != "sweet" and crush_distance < 10: print("Go brush your teeth, now!")

E.	if crush == "at movies" or friends == "at movies":
	    print("Go to the movies.")
	else:
	    print("Stay home and chill.")

2. Write the output for each of the following programs:

A.	`num = 3`
	`if num >= 3:`
	`    print("Greater than 3")`	

B.	`shape = "square"`
	`if shape == "circle":`
	`    print("you win")`
	`else:`
	`    print("no such luck")`	

C.	`color1 = "red"`
	`color2 = "blue"`
	`if color1 == "red" and`
	`color2 == "yellow":`
	`    print("orange")`
	`elif color1 == "red" and`
	`color2 == "blue":`
	`    print("purple")`
	`else:`
	`    print("green")`	

D.	`fact = not(5 == 4)` `print(fact)`	

MORE QUESTIONS

3. What does the AND logical operator do?

4. Mark each compound conditional statement as True or False:
   A. You live on planet Earth AND the moon:
   B. You can breathe air OR breathe water:
   C. Not(You are human):
   D. Spider-Man is real OR Batman is real:

5. Draw a flowchart for each of the following descriptions.

   A. A program that first asks if the user wants to watch a Harry Potter movie. If they do, suggest which Harry Potter film they should watch based on if the user likes young Harry (movies 1 or 2) or older Harry (movies 3 to 7).

   B. A program that first asks if the user likes hats. If they don't like hats, tell the user to try out visors. If they do like hats, and if they like plain things, suggest baseball caps; otherwise, suggest top hats.

   C. A program that first asks if the user likes to be bored. If the user likes to be bored, suggest that they do nothing. If they don't like being bored, ask if they like to read. If they like to read, ask if they like to read a lot. If they like to read a lot, suggest that they read a novel; otherwise, tell them to read a magazine.

6. Write a program for the following flowchart.

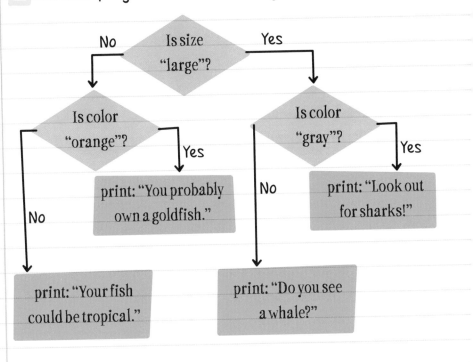

7. What would the program in question 6 print if the variable "color" had the value "orange" and the variable "size" had the value "small"?

CHECK YOUR ANSWERS

1.

A.	if/elif/else
B.	if/else
C.	if/elif/else
D.	if
E.	if/else

2.

A.	Greater than 3
B.	no such luck
C.	purple
D.	True

3. The AND operator combines two Boolean expressions to make a compound conditional statement. A compound conditional statement that uses AND is True only if both Boolean expressions within the statement are True.

4. A. False
   B. True
   C. False
   D. False

5. A.

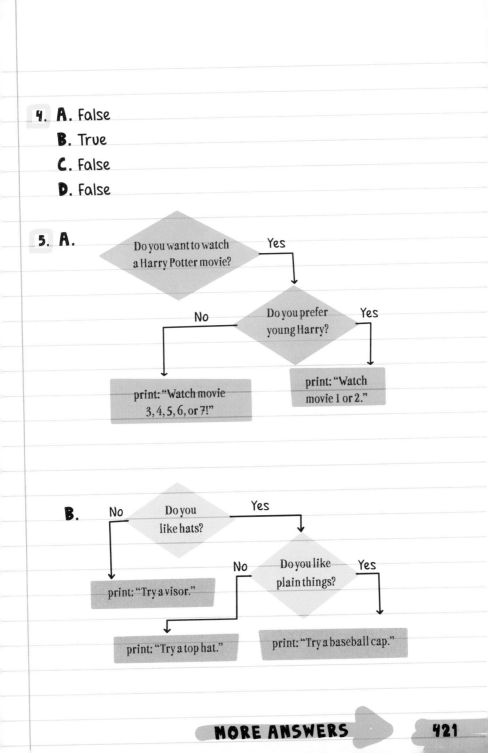

Do you want to watch a Harry Potter movie? — Yes

Do you prefer young Harry? — Yes

No → print: "Watch movie 3, 4, 5, 6, or 7!"

Yes → print: "Watch movie 1 or 2."

B.

No — Do you like hats? — Yes

No — Do you like plain things? — Yes

print: "Try a visor."

print: "Try a top hat."

print: "Try a baseball cap."

C.

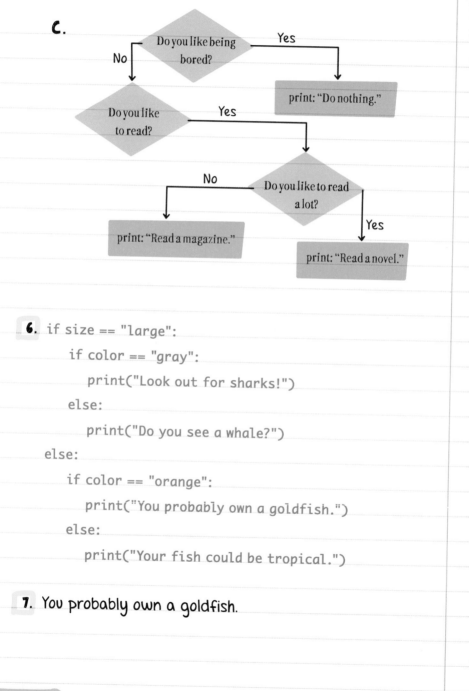

6.
```
if size == "large":
    if color == "gray":
        print("Look out for sharks!")
    else:
        print("Do you see a whale?")
else:
    if color == "orange":
        print("You probably own a goldfish.")
    else:
        print("Your fish could be tropical.")
```

7. You probably own a goldfish.

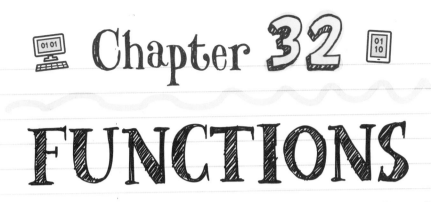

Chapter 32

FUNCTIONS

Functions are blocks of code that you can use to build a bigger program. You can add more premade functions by importing **modules**.

A kind of library

The words **function** and **procedure** mean almost the same thing. When talking about Python, we refer to function (some people might say "procedure").

TURTLE GRAPHICS

The TURTLE MODULE is filled with functions that allow you to treat the screen like a drawing board and use the turtle icon to draw on it.

A **library** is a collection of prewritten functions and code that can be imported into a project.

Importing the Module

You can import the turtle module using the **import** command. Start with the word "from," then enter the module name, and then enter "import," which means you want to import from the named module (in this case, "turtle").

You can name which specific functions you want to import from a module. To import all the functions, end the import command with "*".

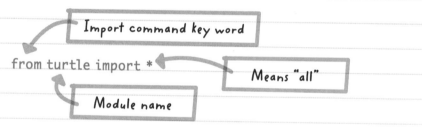

This means import all the functions from the turtle module.

Moving the Turtle

After importing the turtle module, you can use its functions to move the turtle around the screen. The turtle starts out facing to the right. You can make the turtle move using the forward and backward functions.

> The default "turtle" is actually just a triangle that points in the direction it's facing.

FOR EXAMPLE, you can make the turtle move forward 100 **PIXELS** on the screen with the command:

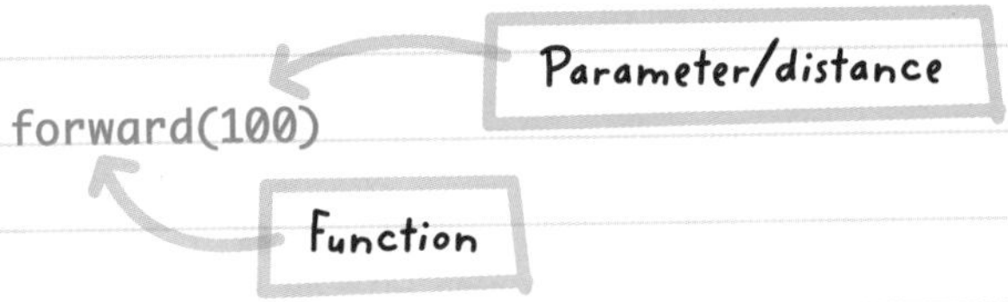

Parameter/distance

forward(100)

Function

This is what the code looks like:

```python
from turtle import *
forward(100)
```

The command will open a new window and draw a line from left to right that's 100 pixels long (the triangle at the end of the line is the turtle):

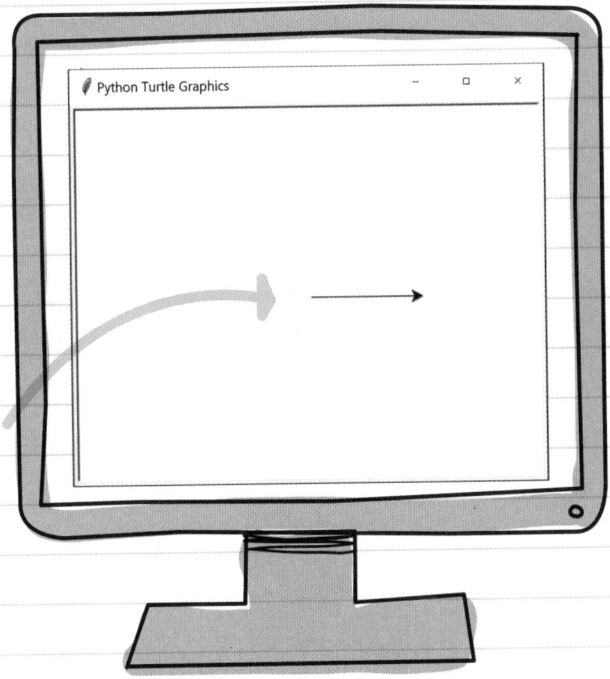

Python Turtle Graphics

> **PIXEL**
> A **pixel** (from **picture element**) is a point of light on a screen.
> The small points make up images on a computer display.

The **left( )** and **right( )** functions turn the turtle left or right based on the direction it is facing on the screen. Both of the functions require a parameter for the number of degrees they turn.

FOR EXAMPLE, to turn 90 degrees to the left, use:

```
left(90)
```

Parameter/degree

Function

You can use the turtle functions along with other parts of Python.

FOR EXAMPLE, you could use loops to make some interesting art. A *for* loop that repeats 6 times along with **forward** and **right** functions from the turtle module can be used to draw a hexagon:

```
from turtle import *
for j in range(6):
        forward(70)
        right(60)
```

> This directive tells the turtle to repeat the following code 6 times: move forward 70 pixels, then turn right 60 degrees.

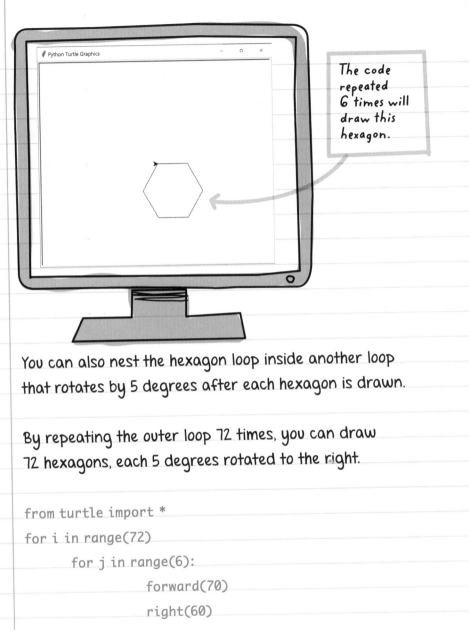

The code repeated 6 times will draw this hexagon.

You can also nest the hexagon loop inside another loop that rotates by 5 degrees after each hexagon is drawn.

By repeating the outer loop 72 times, you can draw 72 hexagons, each 5 degrees rotated to the right.

```
from turtle import *
for i in range(72)
        for j in range(6):
                forward(70)
                right(60)
        right(5)
```

Here's what the drawing looks like after running the program:

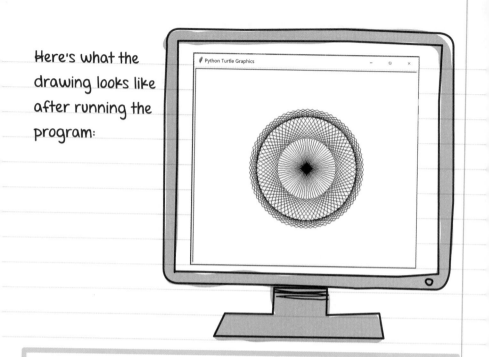

ADDITIONAL TURTLE ART FUNCTIONS

There are many more functions in the turtle module that can be used to create fun art.

FUNCTION	DESCRIPTION
forward()	Moves the turtle forward; parameter is number of pixels to move
backward()	Moves the turtle backward; parameter is number of pixels to move
right()	Turns the turtle clockwise; parameter is number of degrees to turn
left()	Turns the turtle counterclockwise; parameter is number of degrees to turn
penup()	Picks up the turtle's pen (ends tracing the movements of the turtle); no parameters

FUNCTION	DESCRIPTION
pendown()	Puts down the turtle's pen (begins to trace the movements of the turtle); no parameters
pencolor()	Changes the color of the turtle's pen; parameters are named colors
heading()	Returns the current heading—useful if you need to know which way the turtle is facing; no parameters
position()	Returns the current x and y position—useful if you need to know where on the screen the turtle is; no parameters
goto()	Moves the turtle to a specific position; parameters are x-axis and y-axis coordinates
fillcolor()	Changes the color the turtle will use to fill a polygon; parameter types are the same as pencolor()
begin_fill()	Remembers the starting point for a filled polygon—used before a shape you want to fill is drawn; no parameters
end_fill()	Closes the polygon and fills with the current fill color—used after a shape you want to fill has been drawn; no parameters
dot()	Draws a dot at the current position; no parameters
stamp()	Stamps the image of the turtle shape on the screen wherever the turtle is; no parameters
shape()	Changes the shape of the turtle; parameters are "arrow," "classic," "turtle," "circle," or "square"

Even though some functions don't use parameters, you still need to include the parentheses ().

FUNCTIONS

If you're using the same piece of code over and over in Python, then it's best to make your own function. When you make a new function, it's called **DEFINING A FUNCTION**.

To define a function, use this format:

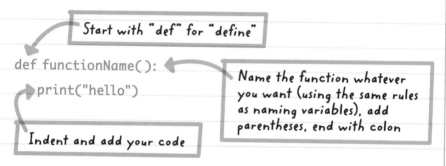

Start with "def" for "define"

```
def functionName():
    print("hello")
```

Name the function whatever you want (using the same rules as naming variables), add parentheses, end with colon

Indent and add your code

To **CALL A FUNCTION** is to use a function that is already defined. When you call a function, Python finds the function definition and runs the code found in the function body.

I'M GONNA CALL HIM.

YOU CAN'T. YOU DIDN'T GIVE HIM A NAME!

You can only call a
function after it has
been defined. To call a
function, use this format:

FUNCTION NAME

functionName()

PARENTHESES

Whenever you call a function,
the program jumps back to where
the function was defined, runs all the
code in the body of the function, then
goes back to where the program left
off when the function was called.

The **body** of the
function is the
indented part. The
body is the code that
will run when the
function is called.

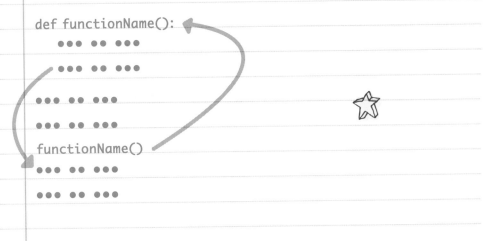

```
def functionName():
    ••• •• •••
    ••• •• •••
••• •• •••
••• •• •••
functionName()
••• •• •••
••• •• •••
```

Here's an example of a function that says "Hello, World!":

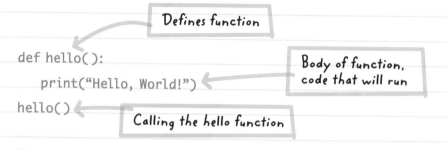

Defines function

```
def hello():
    print("Hello, World!")
hello()
```

Body of function, code that will run

Calling the hello function

This will print: Hello, World!

PARAMETERS AND RETURN VALUES

Parameters and variables are similar because they are both used to store information. However, a **PARAMETER** is different because it cannot be used outside a function. A parameter is data that is provided as input from a user. Functions can use parameters only within the body of the function. That's because a parameter in a function is only recognized within the function itself.

WHO ARE YOU?

FUNCTION

PARAMETER

FOR EXAMPLE, you can create a function that converts meters to feet. Inside the convert function, you can multiply the meters parameter by 3.281 (the number of feet in 1 meter) to get how many feet are in the specified number of meters.

Function definition

Parameter name

```
def convert(meters):
    feet = meters * 3.281
    return feet

convert(1)
```

Use the parameter like a variable.

Call the function and include the value of the parameter, in this case 1.

If you tried to use the meters parameter outside of the function definition, you'd get an error:

```
def convert(meters):
    feet = meters * 3.281
    print(feet)

convert(3)
print(meters)
```

Function definition ends here.

"Meters" used outside the function definition results in an error.

```
NameError: name "meters" is not defined
```

The **RETURN VALUE** of a function is the information that you can pass from the function back out to the main program. This is the function's output. To pass information out of the function, write "return" followed by the output data.

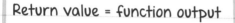

Return value = function output

```
def convert (meters):
    feet = meters * 3.281
    return feet
```

This will return the value of feet each time the function runs.

With the convert function defined, you could call the function many times and get a different return value each time.

convert(5)   returns 16.405 (5 * 3.281)
convert(234)   returns 767.754 (234 * 3.281)
convert(5,234)   returns 17,172.754 (5.234 * 3.281).

To print the return value, use the **print()** function with the function call inside it:

print(convert(1))

Function call

The program will print: 3.281

You can also add text around the function call to give an explanation of the code, like this:

```
print("3 meters = ", convert(3), "feet")
```

The program will print:

```
3 meters = 9.843 feet
```

HEY, I GOT A REQUEST TO RUN THE CONVERT FUNCTION AND THEY'RE GIVING ME 2 AS AN INPUT.

SURE THING. I'VE GOT THE FUNCTION DEFINITION RIGHT HERE.

You can repeat a small chunk of code while using a parameter to slightly change it for each use. For example, in a word game program, instead of typing "Please enter a noun" or "Please enter an adjective" repeatedly, you could make a function to do it for you:

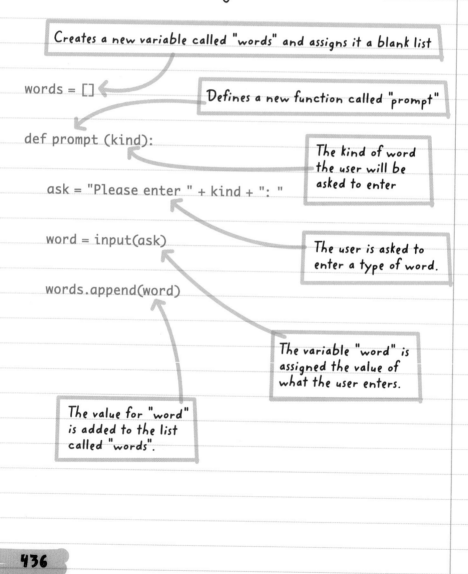

Creates a new variable called "words" and assigns it a blank list

```
words = []
```

Defines a new function called "prompt"

```
def prompt (kind):
```

The kind of word the user will be asked to enter

```
    ask = "Please enter " + kind + ": "
```

The user is asked to enter a type of word.

```
    word = input(ask)
```

The variable "word" is assigned the value of what the user enters.

```
    words.append(word)
```

The value for "word" is added to the list called "words".

```
prompt("an adjective")
prompt("a nationality")
prompt("a person")
prompt("a plural noun")
prompt("an adjective")
prompt("a plural noun")
```

> The type of word the user will enter

> The "prompt" function can be called many times, asking the user for different types of words by changing the parameters for each function call.

The word list, created by the user's input, is inserted into the word game:

```
print("Computers were invented by a", words[0], words[1],
"engineer named", words[2], ". To make a computer, you need
to take a lot of", words[3], ", melt them down, and make",
words[4], words[5], ".")
```

The output for this program is a completed story that uses the user's words to fill in key details.

1. How do you import all the functions in the turtle module into a Python program?

2. Write out the two lines of code you would need to move the turtle 45 pixels and turn right 30 degrees (assuming you've already imported the turtle module).

3. What does it mean to call a function? What code would you write to call a function called "BopIt" with no input information?

4. When you create a new function, you need to _____ it.

5. You can pass information into a function using _____.

6. You can pass information out of a function to the main program by using _____.

7. Explain what's wrong with the program below:

```
def distance (laps):
    meters = laps * 100
    return meters
print(laps)
```

8. In order to use a function after you've defined it, you need to _____ it. This is done with _____.

9. Write the return value for each of the following functions:

NAME	CODE	RETURNS

A.	```name = "Max"```
	```def hello_you(person):```
	    ```sentence = "Hello " + person```
	    ```return sentence```
	
	```hello_you("Max")```	

B.	```def plotter(x, y):```
	    ```instructions = "Plot a course```
	    ```through " + str(x) + " and " +```
	    ```str(y)```
	    ```return instructions```
	
	```plotter(3, 5)```	

MORE QUESTIONS

NAME	CODE	RETURNS
| C. | ```
def absolute_value(num):
    if num >= 0:
        return num
    else:
        return num * -1


absolute_value(-4)
``` | |
| D. | ```
def favorite(category, thing):
    sentence = "My favorite " +
    category + " is the " + thing
    return sentence


favorite("snake", "Python")
``` | |

CHECK YOUR ANSWERS

1. From turtle import *

2. forward(45)
   right(30)

3. When you call a function, you are using the name of the function to tell the program to run the code that corresponds to that function name.

   The code would look like: BopIt( )

4. Define

5. Parameters

6. Return

7. The "laps" parameter is used outside the function definition.

8. call, parentheses

9.

A.	Hello Max
B.	Plot a course through 3 and 5
C.	4
D.	My favorite snake is the Python

CHOOSE WISELY!

Unit

8

Web Development

Chapter 33

WHAT IS THE INTERNET?

COMPUTER NETWORKS

A **NETWORK** is a group of connected computers. For example, the computers, phones, and other devices that your family owns are all part of your home computer network. When you get a new tablet and enter in the Wi-Fi password, you're joining that tablet to your home computer network.

> **NETWORK**
> A group of connected computers that share information and resources

Devices in the same network can easily communicate and share resources with each other. For example, computers on a coffee shop's wireless network all share internet access, and a family's phones may be able to control their TV.

Local Area Networks

A **LOCAL AREA NETWORK (LAN)** is a type of network made up of nearby computers. A LAN can have anywhere from a few devices (like a home network) to hundreds of devices (like a school or hospital). Large organizations like colleges can have multiple LANs—maybe one per building.

> A **wide area network (WAN)** is made of connected LANs that are far from each other (like in different parts of the country or world). WANs connect thousands or even millions of devices.

Communicating on a LAN

Computers in a network communicate with **ETHERNET** (with wires) or **WIRELESS** (without wires).

Ethernet was developed in the 1970s. It's the **PROTOCOL**, or rules, for how devices communicate using cables to physically connect. Wireless was

PROTOCOL
A standardized set of rules

developed in the late 1990s. It's the protocol for using radio waves to send information through the air to connected devices.

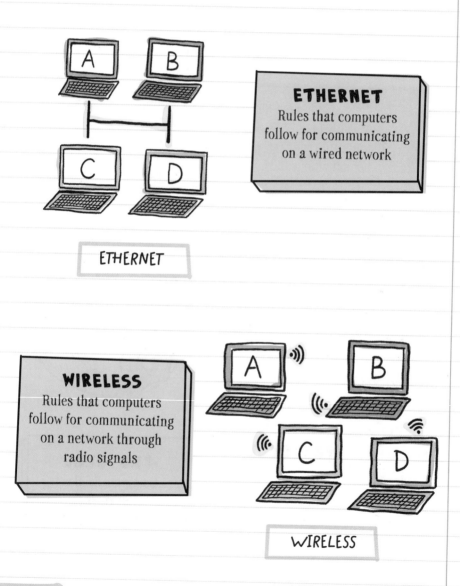

ETHERNET
Rules that computers follow for communicating on a wired network

ETHERNET

WIRELESS
Rules that computers follow for communicating on a network through radio signals

WIRELESS

WI-FI is a popular way to connect wirelessly to a network. "Wi-Fi" is believed to be short for "<u>wi</u>reless <u>fi</u>delity," which is taken from the term "high fidelity"—used to describe high-quality audio.

THE INTERNET

The **INTERNET** is a world-wide system of connected computer networks. It's a giant network of smaller networks. At home, your family's phones, computers, and other devices are all part of your home computer network sharing a connection to the internet.

Many places have their own networks. Schools, coffee shops, even malls almost always have their own networks to connect to the internet.

HOME NETWORK

THE INTERNET

HELLO

The Web Origin Story

The modern internet began in the early 1990s, when TIM BERNERS-LEE created the tools and framework for the World Wide Web. In a few months, he created:

- the first web browser, called WORLDWIDEWEB and later renamed NEXUS. (Now we can choose between Chrome, Safari, Microsoft Edge, and other browsers.)

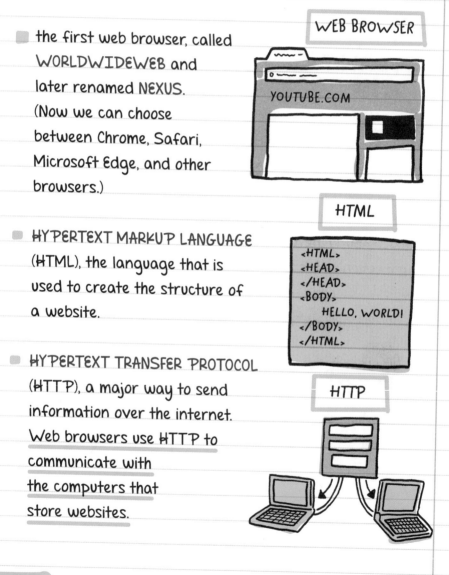

WEB BROWSER

YOUTUBE.COM

HTML

```
<HTML>
<HEAD>
</HEAD>
<BODY>
    HELLO, WORLD!
</BODY>
</HTML>
```

- HYPERTEXT MARKUP LANGUAGE (HTML), the language that is used to create the structure of a website.

- HYPERTEXT TRANSFER PROTOCOL (HTTP), a major way to send information over the internet. Web browsers use HTTP to communicate with the computers that store websites.

HTTP

The World Wide Web created a new era of communication. There are now many millions of devices and applications connected to the internet.

SENDING INFORMATION OVER THE INTERNET

When you download an item from the internet, such as music to your phone, the songs are too big to send all at once. Instead, each song is broken up into **PACKETS**, which are sent individually and then recombined on your phone.

> **PACKETS**
> Small units of data that are sent in binary code through a network

Each packet has a destination address and a packet number that tells the network where to send it and how to reassemble all the packets when they reach the final destination.

An **IP ADDRESS** is used to direct packets to the right network. IP addresses are unique addresses

> **IP (INTERNET PROTOCOL)**
> Rules for transferring information on the internet

> Every computer has its own MAC (Media Access Control) address made up of 16 digits and letters, which identifies the manufacturer and the specific model.

that label devices on a network and the internet. Every device has its own IP address. IP addresses can change and are assigned by an **internet service provider**.

IF COMPUTERS EACH HAVE THEIR OWN MAC ADDRESS, HOW COME THE INTERNET DIRECTS PACKAGES TO A NETWORK, NOT A DEVICE?

BECAUSE THAT'S HOW WE DO IT, OK?! THAT'S JUST THE PROTOCOL!

USING THE INTERNET TO SURF THE WEB

INTERNET ≠ **WORLD WIDE WEB**

The **INTERNET** is the connection and network between devices. You can use the internet to connect to and surf, or explore, websites.

The **WORLD WIDE WEB**, or web, is a collection of websites that are linked together through the internet. The web is the content you can view, read, listen to, stream, and download. Most websites have links that connect them to other websites. If you were to draw an image of all these links, it would look like a spiderweb made of websites around the globe. That's why it's called the World Wide Web.

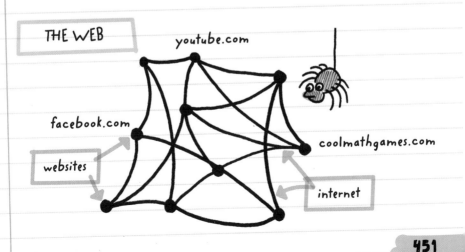

THE WEB

youtube.com

facebook.com

coolmathgames.com

websites

internet

When you open a website on your computer, you are opening a temporarily downloaded copy of the **HTML FILES** that make up that site.

HTML stands for "hypertext markup language" and is a language that is used to create websites. The "hypertext" part of the name means that the language is built for connecting websites together through links. Because websites are linked (by the internet), you are able to use HTML to jump from one site to another.

Every website is stored on a computer. When you open a web browser and type in a website, you are asking the computer on which the website is stored to send you a copy of the site. The computer where a website is stored is called a **HOST**.

"May I look at www.usa.gov?"

user's computer   Host

"Sure! Here's a copy."

A host can be an ordinary computer, but most of the time hosts are specialized computers called **SERVERS**. Servers have massive amounts of storage, have fast internet connections, and run specific software. This makes it easier for them to store all of a website's information.

452

Your computer downloads the website using a list of rules called **HYPERTEXT TRANSFER PROTOCOL (HTTP)**. Website addresses start with HTTP or HTTPS (a more secure version of transferring files). HTTP is a major way in which all websites are sent over the internet.

> **HYPERTEXT TRANSFER PROTOCOL (HTTP)**
> The rules for sharing web content. Web browsers use HTTP to communicate with servers.

> **HYPERTEXT TRANSFER PROTOCOL SECURE (HTTPS)**
> Shares the same function as HTTP but adds a layer of security by encrypting, or coding, all transferred data

FOR EXAMPLE, part of HTTP is a set of status codes that are sent from the server to the browser. These codes tell the browser what's going on with the server. An example of a status code is 404 NOT FOUND.

The 404 Not Found code lets the browser know that the server couldn't find the website that the browser asked for.

Finding Where a Website Lives

Every website on the internet has a **UNIFORM RESOURCE LOCATOR (URL)** or address.

Before you can access a website, your computer needs to find out which server stores the site you need. When you type a web address into your web browser, your computer

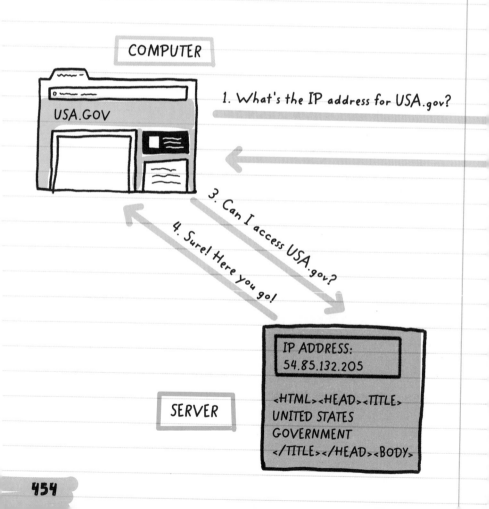

COMPUTER

USA.GOV

1. What's the IP address for USA.gov?

3. Can I access USA.gov?

4. Sure! Here you go!

SERVER

IP ADDRESS:
54.85.132.205

<HTML><HEAD><TITLE>
UNITED STATES
GOVERNMENT
</TITLE></HEAD><BODY>

first asks a **DOMAIN NAME SYSTEM SERVER** for the IP address of the server that is hosting the site. Your computer can then use that IP address to find the correct server and

DOMAIN NAME SYSTEM (DNS)
Databases that translate website URLs to IP addresses.

ask the server for access to the HTML files that make up a website. All of this happens in less than a second.

DNS SERVER

2. It's 54.85.132.205.

The **DNS server** works like the contact list on your phone. You select your friend's name from the list, and the phone calls the number linked to your friend. You don't have to memorize your friend's phone number, just like we don't have to memorize a website's IP address. But you could call your friend by entering their phone number, just like you could access a website by entering its IP address.

Popular websites are hosted on many servers throughout the world. This helps to keep the site running quickly when many requests to view the site are made at the same time. It also helps to prevent outages if one server goes down. Users are probably connected to the closest server.

Every minute, millions of people use the internet to view a wide variety of things. That's why the internet needs protocols to keep things organized.

The Transmission Control Protocol

Once your computer connects to the host server, the server follows **TRANSMISSION CONTROL PROTOCOL (TCP)**. Devices use TCP when all the requested information (website, picture, video) needs to be transferred.

TCP
A set of rules computers use when they are transferring information across the internet

FOR EXAMPLE, when you load a website, the server sends you the site information as small packets. If a packet gets lost along the way (usually due to a lost or weak connection), your web browser will send a new request for the missing packet. It will keep sending the request until it receives the packet and the entire site is loaded.

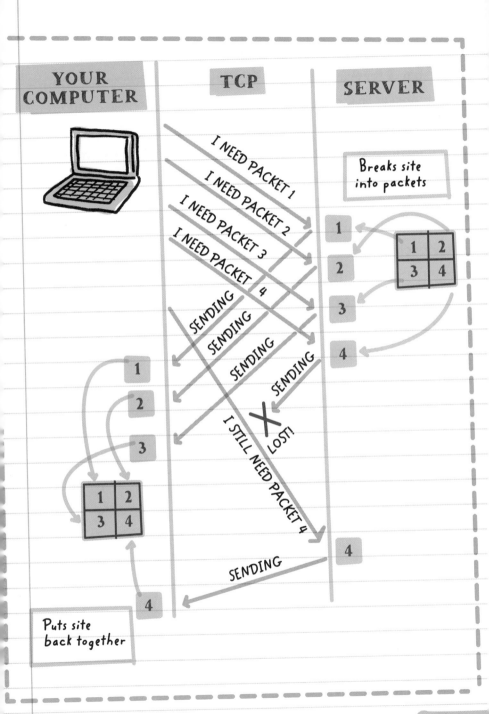

The User Datagram Protocol

USER DATAGRAM PROTOCOL (UDP) is another way to transfer information. It focuses more on speed than on getting every single packet to the final destination. This protocol is used when speed is more important than getting all the requested information.

FOR EXAMPLE, video conferencing services like Google Hangouts or Skype use UDP because users would rather keep the video call going, even if the image gets fuzzy, than pause the call and wait for every last pixel to load. A computer running a video conferencing service won't request the server to resend a packet that it didn't get.

WHO ARE YOU?

CHECK YOUR KNOWLEDGE

1. What's the difference between the internet and the World Wide Web?

2. What are packets?

3. Why are protocols necessary to transfer information and communicate on a network?

4. What is a DNS server?

5. How does a computer know if information sent over a network is meant for it?

6. Explain what a protocol is. Why is it useful to have a protocol for network communication?

7. What does a server do and how is it different from a personal computer?

8. What does "URL" stand for?

9. Why does a video service like Skype prefer to use UDP protocol?

10. Who created the tools used to surf the World Wide Web?

11. What does TCP stand for, and how is it different from UDP?

CHECK YOUR ANSWERS

1. The internet is the connection between devices, and the web is the content (including websites, videos, pictures, etc.).

2. In order to transfer files over a network, they need to be broken up into packets. Packets are small chunks of a file.

3. Without protocols, information would get jumbled up and lost. Protocols help make sure that information is delivered correctly and to the right location.

4. A DNS server is like a contact list on a phone. It's a system of databases that look up a URL and provide the IP address for the server that stores the site.

5. All information sent over a network has a destination address in the header, which is used to find the right computer.

6. A protocol is a set of standardized rules or procedures. Protocols make sure everyone follows the same set of guidelines. Ethernet and wireless are run by protocols so that information can be transferred in an organized manner.

MORE ANSWERS

7. Servers are computers that have a very fast internet connection and lots of storage space. They store websites, videos, pictures, and other information that users can access through the internet.

8. Uniform Resource Locator

9. UDP is a faster way to send information because it doesn't require that every single piece is transferred perfectly. People prefer a slightly spotty video call over a dropped call.

10. Tim Berners-Lee

11. Transmission control protocol. TCP is different from UDP because it checks to make sure all the requested information is delivered, and resends it if it isn't.

CYBERSECURITY

WHAT IS CYBERSECURITY?

CYBERSECURITY is needed to keep digital information safe. Cybersecurity is a set of techniques or ways used to keep information secret, available, and uncorrupted:

Secret: Information that shouldn't be shared with others needs to be kept private.

Available: Authorized people should be able to access their files and information stored on a computer. If someone puts a virus on your computer that prevents you from using it, they are making your information unavailable to you.

AUTHORIZED PERSON
Someone who has permission

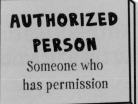

Uncorrupted: Files and information on a computer should not be

463

changed by an unauthorized person. If someone changes the password to one of your social media sites and logs on as you, they have corrupted your account.

CYBERSECURITY TECHNIQUES

Cybersecurity techniques can:

- prevent the wrong people from gaining access to information

- make it impossible to use the information, even if unauthorized people do get their hands on it

Usually multiple cybersecurity techniques are used to protect information.

Authentication

AUTHENTICATION is the process computers use to confirm someone's identity before giving them access to information. Computers can use different kinds of authentication:

- asking for a username and password
- scanning a fingerprint
- using a camera to recognize your face

TWO-FACTOR AUTHENTICATION combines two different kinds of authentication.

FOR EXAMPLE, to log on to your email account with two-factor authentication, you may need to enter your password and scan your finger on your phone. It's much harder for attackers to break through two-factor authentication.

Access Control

ACCESS CONTROL refers to authorized users having access to specific files. If you have a user account through your school, you can access your homework, grades, and other files that you need. But you can't access the teacher's account to change your grade, view another student's information, or download next week's exam. Access control uses authentication to prevent the wrong people from getting data they aren't authorized to view.

Sandboxing

SANDBOXING is putting an application in a secured part of the system with limited access to the rest of the computer system. This way, if an attack is made on the application, only that application will be affected, and the rest of the system will stay safe.

CRYPTOGRAPHY

CRYPTOGRAPHY is a strategy for keeping information secret. The goal of cryptography is to scramble information and messages so well that no one except authorized people can unscramble and read them. This adds another

I STOLE THE WORLD'S GREATEST CHILI CHEESE CORN DOG RECIPE...

...BUT I CAN'T UNDERSTAND A SINGLE WORD!

layer of security beyond access control, so that even if an unauthorized person gets the secret files, they still won't be able to read them.

The process of scrambling and unscrambling information is called encryption and decryption. **ENCRYPTION** is when readable information is transformed into a secret message, and **DECRYPTION** is the process of returning the secret message to readable information.

A **CIPHER** is the tool used to make information unreadable to people who don't have the **KEY**. The key is used with the cipher to decrypt an encrypted message. A cipher is also the tool that is used to translate a secret message back into its original, readable form. For example, a bank's website uses a cipher to translate customers' account information as it is sent between a computer and their server.

ENCRYPTION

CIPHER

SECRET

TERCES

Ciphers are much older than computers. The Roman dictator JULIUS CAESAR (100 BC–44 BC) used one of the earliest ciphers, which was named after him. The CAESAR CIPHER shifts each letter forward a fixed number of positions, for example, three spots on the alphabet.

> The key to the Caesar cipher is to move each letter forward a certain number of spots.

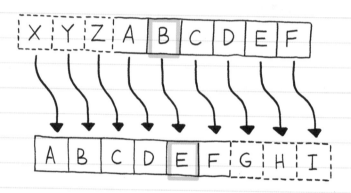

For example, using the Caesar cipher, "Hello, World" would be encrypted to "Khoor Zruog."

You could decrypt the message "Khoor Zruog" by using the key in reverse and shifting each letter backward three spots.

The Caesar cipher is easy for some people to crack and even easier for computers to crack.

CRACKING A CODE OR CIPHER
When someone finds a way to decrypt encrypted messages without being told the key

During World War II (1939–1945), the German military improved the Caesar cipher with a machine called ENIGMA. It used a complicated combination of different ciphers. Every letter that was typed in went through multiple layers of encryption, and then the key shifted for the next letter. So two of the same letters in the original message would be set to different letters in the encrypted version.

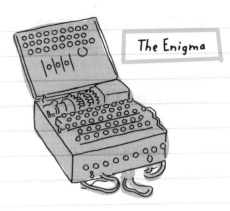

The Enigma

Alan Turing (England, 1912–1954): During World War II, Turing worked on a team tasked with breaking the German encryption machine, Enigma. His creation, the **BOMBE**, was an early computer that succeeded in decrypting messages coded by Enigma.

HACKERS

HACKERS are people who break into computers and large computerized systems. There are many types of hackers, and not all of them are bad.

Companies and governments hire white hat hackers to help protect systems and information.

BLACK HAT HACKERS break into a system to steal information or do damage.

WHITE HAT HACKERS hunt for bugs and other faults to fix them before black hat hackers can use those faults to break in.

HACKTIVISTS break into systems to accomplish social or political goals.

The term "hacker" also means someone who uses objects in creative new ways. For example, using your sunglasses to prop up your phone is a hack, because sunglasses aren't meant to be used that way. This definition builds on the concept of the computer hacker, who gains access to a system using code, bugs, and other digital features in creative ways.

ATTACKS

Hackers can use different attacks to break into a system.

A **BRUTE FORCE** attack is when a hacker uses a computer to guess every authentication possibility. For example, guessing every possible password combination is a brute force attack.

If you set your password to a 4-digit number, a computer could guess every number between 0 and 9999 to find your password within seconds. This is why websites and apps usually require you to use at least eight characters that include numbers, symbols, and some capital letters. There are over 600 trillion combinations you could use to make one of these passwords, which is why longer, more complicated passwords are much harder to crack with brute force attacks.

ARE YOU STILL TRYING TO FIGURE OUT MY PASSWORD? I TOLD YOU IT'S TOO LONG TO CRACK.

DO THE MATH

Personal identification numbers (PINs) that are 4 digits long and use 10 numbers (0–9) have 10*10*10*10 or $10^4 = 10,000$ possible combinations. But a password that is 8 characters long and uses 10 numbers, 26 lowercase letters, 26 uppercase letters, and 10 characters has $72^8 = 722$ million combinations.

Another way that hackers can access systems is by using **MALWARE**. Malware includes any type of harmful software installed on a computer.

Malware includes:

Ransomware: keeps a user from accessing a computer until they pay the hacker money.

Spyware: spies on the user to steal information like usernames and passwords.

Trojan horse (or Trojan): Any type of harmful software that is disguised as a normal file.

Virus: software that spreads like a disease to other computers. Viruses are especially dangerous within networks since they can spread to all computers connected within that network.

Worm: harmful software that can make copies of itself and spread on its own. Worms often spread by sending themselves through mass emails.

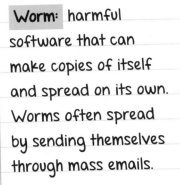

No Coding Required

SOCIAL ENGINEERING is the most popular type of attack, and it doesn't use coding at all. Social engineering is when a person pretends to be someone else to get what they want. **PHISHING** is one type of social engineering, where an attacker pretends to have a legitimate email address or website in order to get your username and password.

FOR EXAMPLE, an attacker could send out an email that asks you to log on to one of your social media accounts. But instead of linking to your actual account, they send you to a site they set up to look exactly like the real thing. When you log on to their fake site, you are giving the attacker your username and password, which they can then use to log on as you on the real social media site.

Distributed denial-of-service (DDoS) attacks are when a hacker uses lots of computers (probably infected by a virus) to send so many messages to a server at the same time that the system is overloaded and crashes. Usually, a hacker uses a DDoS attack to collect a ransom or to accomplish a political goal, like shutting down a website they don't agree with.

CHECK YOUR KNOWLEDGE

1. What is cybersecurity?

2. Which cybersecurity technique confirms the user's identity?

3. Which cybersecurity technique isolates an application so that if it is attacked, other applications are not?

4. Which type of hacker breaks into systems legally?

5. What is a brute force attack?

6. Match the description to the type of malware.

Ransomware   can copy itself and spread on its own

Spyware   is disguised as a normal file

Trojan   spreads like a disease

Virus   keeps users from using their computers
                until they pay up

Worm   spies on the user to steal information

7. What is a cipher used for?

8. This message was encrypted using the Caesar cipher
   and shifting each letter forward three spots. Decrypt it:
   gdb

9. What is encryption?

10. What is phishing?

11. What is the name of the German machine used to
    encrypt the messages of German soldiers during
    World War II?

ANSWERS

CHECK YOUR ANSWERS

1. The set of techniques used to keep information safe

2. Authentication

3. Sandboxing

4. White hat (Although hacktivists' intentions may be good, what they do is still illegal.)

5. Using a computer to guess every authentication possibility

6. Match the description to the type of malware.

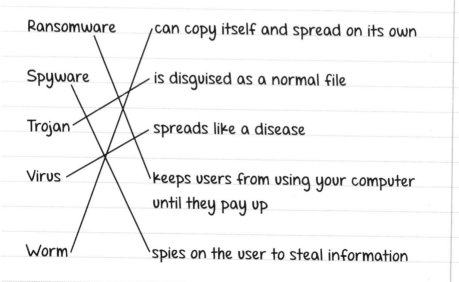

Ransomware — keeps users from using your computer until they pay up

Spyware — spies on the user to steal information

Trojan — is disguised as a normal file

Virus — spreads like a disease

Worm — can copy itself and spread on its own

7. To encrypt and decrypt messages, making information unreadable to people who don't have the key

8. day

9. Encryption is the process of scrambling information so that only someone with the key can decrypt and understand it.

10. Phishing is a type of social engineering where someone pretends to be an authoritative figure to get you to share personal information like your username and password.

11. Enigma

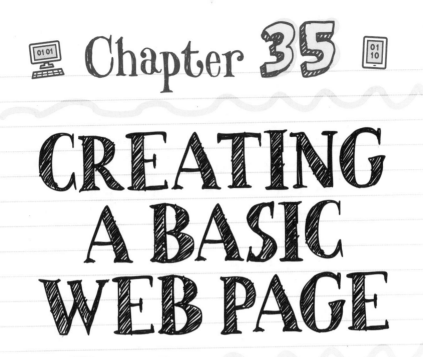

Chapter 35

CREATING A BASIC WEB PAGE

BUILDING BLOCKS OF WEBSITES

All websites are created using **HTML CODE**. HTML is what professional web developers (people who make websites for their job) use to organize and display text, images, videos, etc. in a web browser. HTML is used to tell a web browser *what* to display.

> **HTML**
> Stands for **Hypertext Markup Language**. The "hypertext" part means that it connects websites together, so you're able to go from one site to the next.

CASCADING STYLE SHEETS (CSS) is used by websites to tell the browser *how* the site should be displayed. You can use CSS to change the color of text, insert a background image, and more.

Early websites were made using only the language HTML and early versions of CSS, which means they didn't have much styling, interactivity, or animation. Now there are many languages used in addition to HTML and CSS to create lively and interactive websites. HTML and CSS are used to create the layout and look of a website, while other languages like JavaScript and PHP are used to run programs that make sites more interactive.

OH, YOU'RE LEARNING SPANISH? THAT'S NICE. I'M LEARNING FOUR LANGUAGES: SCRATCH, PYTHON, HTML, AND CSS.

¿QUÉ?

BEST FRIENDS FOREVER

TOOLS FOR WRITING A WEBSITE

Professional web developers sometimes pay to use special code editor programs where they write the code that makes up websites. However, the TEXT EDITOR that comes preinstalled on computers (Notepad or TextEdit) can be used as well.

HTML website files are saved as an ".html" file type. For example, a website called "index" should be saved as "index.html."

File name

Tells the browser this is an HTML file

You can name your HTML files whatever you want. "Index" is usually what the main page of a website is named. Be sure to include ".html" after the name of your file; otherwise web browsers won't read it correctly.

VIEWING A WEBSITE

To view a website, you need a **WEB BROWSER**. Web browsers are programs that can read HTML files and display them as websites on your computer. Examples of web browsers are Chrome, Safari, Microsoft Edge, and Firefox.

Go to the folder where your .html file is saved, right-click (or command click on a Mac), and under the "Open with" menu, select a browser. When you open your file, the browser displays the website.

WEB PAGE BASICS

All websites contain **CONTENT**. Content is the text, images, or other parts of a website that the viewer sees when they look at the site in their web browser. **WEB BROWSERS** are programs that can read HTML files and display them as websites on a computer.

You can read the HTML code from any site by right-clicking on the page in a web browser and selecting "view page source." A new window will open, revealing all the code for that page.

https://www.usa.gov

USA.GOV
Welcome to the United States

WOW. CHECK OUT ALL THAT CODE!

.dtd">
</html>

Tags and Elements

ELEMENTS are the parts of the webpage; they are like building blocks. Each type adds a different detail, or layer, to what you want to build.

TAGS are like quotation marks. The opening quotation mark tells you when a quote begins, and the closing quotation mark tells you when the quote ends. Start and end tags work in the same way. They surround each piece of content in the code for a website.

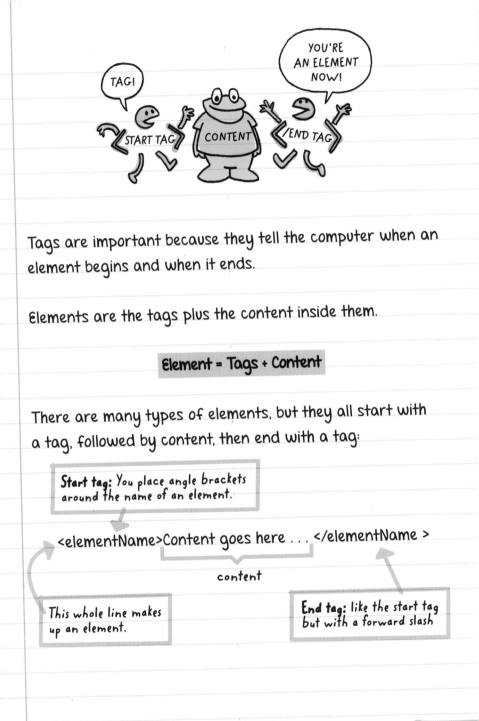

Tags are important because they tell the computer when an element begins and when it ends.

Elements are the tags plus the content inside them.

Element = Tags + Content

There are many types of elements, but they all start with a tag, followed by content, then end with a tag:

Start tag: You place angle brackets around the name of an element.

`<elementName>Content goes here . . . </elementName >`

content

This whole line makes up an element.

End tag: like the start tag but with a forward slash

Elements are used to format text and divide the website into sections. For example:

ELEMENT	DISPLAYS AS
This text is bold	This text is bold
<h1>This is a heading</h1>	This is a heading
This text is emphasized	This text is emphasized
<button>This is a Button</button>	This is a Button

WEBSITE ELEMENTS

Every website should include the <html>, <head>, and <body> elements.

The **<HTML> ELEMENT** holds all other elements between its opening and closing tags. This element marks where the HTML document starts and ends.

The **<HEAD> ELEMENT** holds elements that give additional information about the website. Most of the elements in the <head> element do not display content on the website for the viewer to see. These elements give information to the web browser, including additional CSS code, the site's title, or key words for search engines to look for.

The **<BODY> ELEMENT** is where all the website content that you see goes. The text, images, videos, animations, and anything else you want displayed on your site go here.

The head and body of a website can look like this:

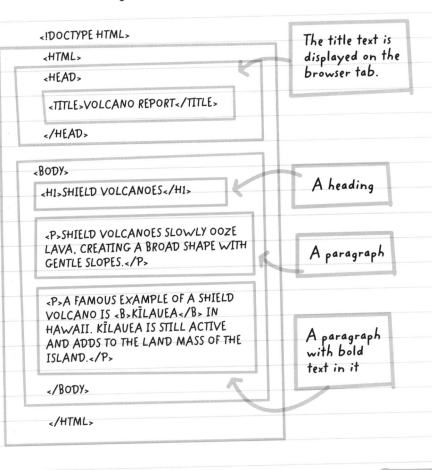

```
<!DOCTYPE HTML>
<HTML>
  <HEAD>
    <TITLE>VOLCANO REPORT</TITLE>
  </HEAD>

  <BODY>
    <H1>SHIELD VOLCANOES</H1>

    <P>SHIELD VOLCANOES SLOWLY OOZE
    LAVA, CREATING A BROAD SHAPE WITH
    GENTLE SLOPES.</P>

    <P>A FAMOUS EXAMPLE OF A SHIELD
    VOLCANO IS <B>KĪLAUEA</B> IN
    HAWAII. KĪLAUEA IS STILL ACTIVE
    AND ADDS TO THE LAND MASS OF THE
    ISLAND.</P>

  </BODY>

</HTML>
```

The title text is displayed on the browser tab.

A heading

A paragraph

A paragraph with bold text in it

FORMATTING HTML

Indentation and white space don't matter in HTML. Indenting nested elements makes it easier to keep everything organized. Indenting the <h1> element in the text below shows that it's nested inside the <body> element.

```
<body>
    <h1> Shield Volcanoes</h1>
</body>
```

It's important to put the close tags in the right place. This code has a bold element nested inside a paragraph element:

```
<p>A famous example of a shield volcano is <b>Kīlauea</b>
in Hawaii. Kīlauea is still active and adds to the land mass
of the island.</p>
```

This displays:

A famous example of a shield volcano is **Kīlauea** in Hawaii. Kīlauea is still active and adds to the land mass of the island.

The <b> tag is used to make "Kīlauea" bold. The elements are properly nested because the <b> start and </b> end tags are inside the <p> start and </p> end tags.

If your tags are nested incorrectly, content may show up wrong, it would be harder to keep code organized, and it would make finding errors more difficult.

Incorrect nesting:

```
<p>A famous example of a shield volcano is <b>Kīlauea in Hawaii. Kīlauea is still active and adds to the land mass of the island.</p></b>
```

The </b> end tag comes after the </p> end tag, which confuses the nesting order and will not show the text correctly.

HTML is not case sensitive. This means that all these examples work the same:

```
<BODY>          All uppercase
<body>          All lowercase
<Body>          Mixed capitalization
```

But most web developers type their tags in lowercase, mostly because it used to be required and has become a habit.

Comments

You can add comments to your HTML code that won't be read by the browser. Comments are notes to yourself about the program. They look like this:

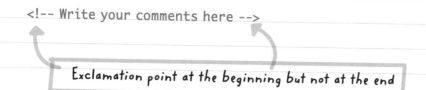

```
<!-- Write your comments here -->
```

Exclamation point at the beginning but not at the end

Opening and closing tags need to be different so that the programmer and the computer don't get confused about where tagged content starts and stops.

FOR EXAMPLE, the opening <!-- tag looks different from the closing --> tag, and the opening tag has an exclamation point while the closing tag does not.

1. What are the two most commonly used website languages? What part of the website does each language control?

2. What does HTML stand for?

3. Fill in the blanks below to label each part

   _____   _____
        ↓   ↓
   <elementName>_____</elementName>

                _____

4. To code an HTML file, you can buy a professional program, or you can use one of these built-in programs: _____ or _____.

5. When you're saving an HTML file, what should be at the end of your file name?

6. What program do you need to use to view a website?

7. What is the common file name used for the main page of a website?

8. What is the name of the text, images, or other parts of a website that the viewer sees?

9. The beginning and end of an element are marked with _____ .

10. Write out a comment in HTML.

11. Which three HTML elements should you use in every website you make?

12. Explain what it means that HTML tags are not case sensitive.

13. In which element do you place the most visible content you want viewers to see?

14. Which statement is true about spacing?
    A. Spacing in HTML is required as part of how the code runs.
    B. Spacing in HTML, like indenting elements, helps the programmer read their code, but doesn't impact how the code is run.

15. What kind of elements go inside the <head> element?

16. All website content code should be added between the _____ start and end tags.

17. The structure of a website is made up of _____.

CHECK YOUR ANSWERS

1. HTML—controls layout
   CSS—controls design

2. Hypertext markup language

3.
   <u>start tag</u>   <u>end tag</u>
      ↓   ↓
   <elementName>___content___</elementName>

   ___element___

4. TextEdit for Mac, or Notepad for PC

5. .html

6. A web browser like Chrome, Microsoft Edge, Firefox, or Safari

7. index.html

8. Content

9. Tags

MORE ANSWERS

10. <!-- This is a comment -->

11. <html>, <head>, and <body>

12. You can capitalize tags however you want, and it won't affect the code.

13. The <body> element

14. B

15. Elements that give extra information about the website to the browser. For example, the site title or key words are stored in the <head> element.

16. <body>

17. HTML elements

Chapter 36

HTML TEXT ELEMENTS

HEADING ELEMENTS

Websites use headings to divide the text and act as titles for each section. **HEADING ELEMENTS** make text bigger and bolder.

← darker

There are 6 heading tags: **<h1>**, **<h2>**, **<h3>**, **<h4>**, **<h5>**, and **<h6>**. The <h1> tag is the highest level—that means it's the biggest and boldest.

FOR EXAMPLE, an <h1> heading can be used for a top-level heading like "Types of Volcanoes", and an <h2> subheading can be used for the types of volcanoes like "Shield," "Cinder Cone," and "Composite."

```
<h1>Types of Volcanoes</h1>
<h2>Shield</h2>
<h2>Cinder Cone</h2>
<h2>Composite</h2>
```

That code would look like this in a browser:

Types of Volcanoes
Shield

Cinder Cone

Composite

PARAGRAPH AND FORMATTING ELEMENTS

The **PARAGRAPH ELEMENT**, <p>, is used to make paragraphs. HTML ignores all spaces and new lines in code, so if you want text to appear as its own paragraph, use the <p> element.

You can also use the <b> element to make text **bold** or the <i> element to make text *italic*.

FOR EXAMPLE, you can surround some content with <p> tags, specific text with <b> tags to make it bold, and <i> tags to make it italic:

PARAGRAPH

BOLD

<p>A famous example of a <b>shield volcano</b> is Kīlauea in Hawaii. <i>Kīlauea is still active</i> and adds to the land mass of the island.</p>

ITALIC

The paragraph would look like this:

A famous example of a **shield volcano** is Kīlauea in Hawaii. *Kīlauea is still active* and adds to the land mass of the island.

HORIZONTAL RULES AND LINE BREAKS

The **HORIZONTAL RULE** (or horizontal line) **<hr>** element breaks up content by displaying a thin line across the web page. It's like drawing a line across the page for a new topic.

You can add an <hr> element right after an <h1> heading to show a separation between the sections:

```
<h1>Types of Volcanoes</h1>
<hr>
<h2>Shield</h2>
<p>A famous example of a <b>shield volcano</b> is Kīlauea
in Hawaii. <i>Kīlauea is still active</i> and adds to the
land mass of the island.</p>
<h2>Cinder Cone</h2>
<h2>Composite</h2>
```

Horizontal line between the <h1> and <h2> headings

The **LINE BREAK ELEMENT**, <br>, displays a blank line between elements. It can be used to separate sections or provide blanks spaces on a website.

BREAK IT UP!

```
<h1>Types of Volcanoes</h1>
<hr>
<h2>Shield</h2>
<p>A famous example of a <b>shield volcano</b> is Kīlauea
in Hawaii. <i>Kīlauea is still active</i> and adds to the
land mass of the island.</p>
<br>
<h2>Cinder Cone</h2>
<h2>Composite</h2>
```

Line break element between
<p> and <h2> elements

With the horizontal rule and line break elements, the web
page would look like this:

Types of Volcanoes

Shield

A famous example of a **shield volcano**
is Kīlauea in Hawaii. *Kīlauea is still active*
and adds to the land mass of the island.

Cinder Cone

Composite

EMPTY ELEMENTS

Most HTML elements have a start and end tag with content between them. Some elements have no content and no end tag. These are called **EMPTY ELEMENTS**.

The **<hr>** and **
** elements are called **empty elements** because they have no end tags.

LIST ELEMENTS

LIST ELEMENTS format text as a bulleted or numbered list. Lists use a combination of elements.

The **UNORDERED LIST ELEMENT** <ul> is used to display a bullet list of items. For example, you can use an unordered list to make a list of your friends or foods you like to eat.

MY FAVORITE FOODS

- AVOCADO
- PIZZA
- BANANA
- RICE
- BBQ CHICKEN

To make each item separate (on a separate line), you also need to use the **LIST ITEM ELEMENT** <li> for each bullet point item in your list. Always use <li> list item elements inside a <ul> unordered list element.

I LOVE BEING ALL TOGETHER!

FOR EXAMPLE, to create an unordered list of famous volcanoes using the <ul> and <li> elements:

```
<h1>Volcanoes</h1>
<hr>
<h2>Famous Volcanoes:</h2>
<ul>
    <li>Mount Vesuvius</li>
    <li>Mount St. Helens</li>
    <li>Kīlauea</li>
</ul>
```

List items each get their own <li></li>

The entire list is wrapped in <ul> tags

The web page will look like this:

Volcanoes

Famous Volcanoes:

- Mount Vesuvius
- Mount St. Helens
- Kilauea

An **ORDERED LIST** uses the tag **<ol>** and displays a numbered list of items. Ordered lists can be used to show top-ten favorite dance moves or for giving a list of sequential steps. Each item also needs the list item <li> element.

FOR EXAMPLE, you can create a list of the largest volcanoes on Earth:

```
<h2>Largest Volcanoes on Earth:</h2>
<ol>
    <li>Tamu Massif</li>
    <li>Kilimanjaro</li>
    <li>Mauna Loa</li>
</ol>
```

List items each get their own <li> and </li> tags

Entire list wrapped in <ol> tags

Here's what the web page would look like:

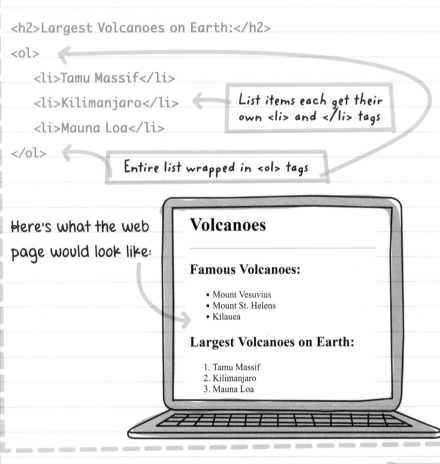

Volcanoes

Famous Volcanoes:

- Mount Vesuvius
- Mount St. Helens
- Kīlauea

Largest Volcanoes on Earth:

1. Tamu Massif
2. Kilimanjaro
3. Mauna Loa

CHECK YOUR KNOWLEDGE

1. What is wrong with the code below?

   `<p>This is a paragraph</b>`

2. What is wrong with the code below?

   `<p>I like to <b>Move it, Move it</p></b>`

3. Rank the website heading elements from biggest to smallest.

4. What tag should you use to make text bold?

5. What tag should you use to make text italic?

6. What's the difference between these two list elements: `<ul>` and `<ol>`?

7. Individual items on a list are identified using which tag?

8. How is the `<p>` element used?

9. If an element doesn't have any content or an end tag, it's called an _____.

10. What does the \<br\> element do?

11. Which of the following is an empty element?
  A. \<br\>
  B. \<ol\>
  C. \<p\>
  D. \<h3\>

12. What does the \<hr\> element do?

CHECK YOUR ANSWERS

1. The start tag and end tag must have the same name.

2. This code isn't nested properly. The </p> and end tags should be switched.

3. <h1>, <h2>, <h3>, <h4>, <h5>, <h6>

4.

5. <i>

6. <ul> is used for unordered lists (bullets), while <ol> is used for ordered lists (numbered)

7. <li> or list item

8. The <p> element is used to set off a chunk of text as its own paragraph.

9. Empty element

10. The <br> element creates a line break or a blank line between elements.

11. **A**

12. The <hr> element draws a horizontal line between elements on a web page.

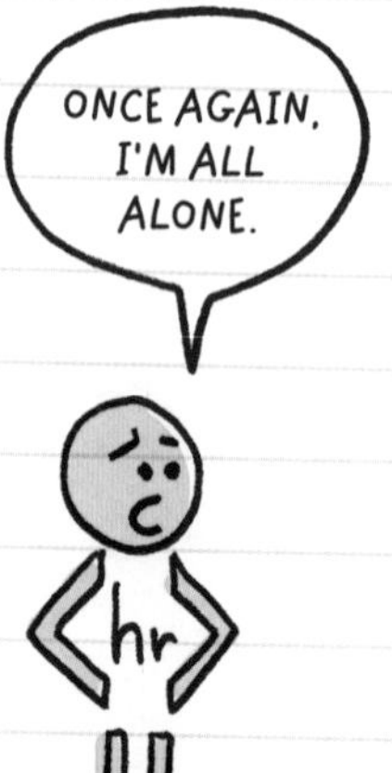
ONCE AGAIN, I'M ALL ALONE.
hr

Chapter 37

LINK ELEMENTS

In HTML, the "hypertext" part of the name means that links can be used to connect to other pages, websites, or files.

A **HYPERLINK** is a connection between websites. A link turns an HTML element into a button that takes users to a new website.

Links are what make websites useful. Users are able to instantly jump to related information on other web pages. For example, when you search for "volcanoes" on a search engine, you will be given a list of websites that mention volcanoes. You can click on any of the search results and jump to the website, because the search engine has added the links for each site listed.

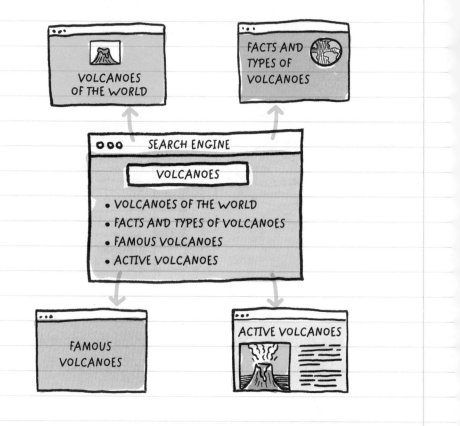

Links also power the **NAVIGATION MENU** on a website. A navigation menu is a collection of links, each of which leads to a specific location on a website. Links are what make it possible to visit each page within the site with a click of a button.

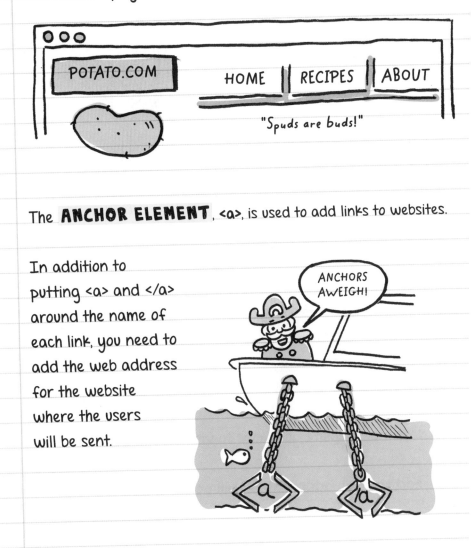

The **ANCHOR ELEMENT**, <a>, is used to add links to websites.

In addition to putting <a> and </a> around the name of each link, you need to add the web address for the website where the users will be sent.

ATTRIBUTES add additional information about elements. For example, you can use an attribute to add the website address to a link, the width and height you want an image to be, or other style information.

ATTRIBUTE
Extra information within an element

ATTRIBUTES

HEIGHT

WIDTH

Attributes are included inside the start tag and follow this pattern:

attribute name="information"

the website you want to go to

To create a link to another website, use the href attribute.

Use an anchor element <a> with an href attribute to add a link to the volcano-related website "www.EruptingVolcanoes.com":

1. Name the website you want to visit using <a href="   ">.

2. Add the web address that will act as the link.

3. Add the </a> tag to show where the link ends.

`<a href="www.EruptingVolcanoes.com">Visit Erupting Volcanoes Site</a>`

Anchor tags will turn "Visit Erupting Volcanoes Site" into a clickable link.

Additional information (the website we are linking to)

IMAGE ELEMENTS

Images make websites more interesting and engaging.

The **IMAGE ELEMENT** **<img>** is used to add images to websites. The <img> element is an empty element, so there is no end tag.

The **SRC** (source) attribute is used to specify the file name and where an image file is located so that the browser can find the file and display it on the website. Image files need to be stored with your website file or referenced from another website.

For example, you can use the web address of a volcano picture from another website to add it to the volcano web page. When viewing a website, right-click on the image in Windows (command click on a Mac)

Don't worry if the picture looks too big or too small—it can always be resized using CSS later.

and select "copy image address" from the menu. This copies the address where the image is stored. You can use this address as the value for your src attribute.

The copied image address from another website would be formatted like this:

"www.eruptingvolcanoes.com/images/volcano1.jpg"

A   B   C

Images stored with a website are usually kept in files. Their location is specified in the web address, where the first part is the website (A). Then a forward slash and the name of the folder the image is kept in (B). Then another slash and the name of the image with the file extension (C).

To link to an image, you'll first add an <img> element and then paste the image's web address into the src attribute value like this:

Type this in.

Paste the image address you copied here.

<img src="www.eruptingvolcanoes.com/images/volcano1.jpg">

Link only to pictures you own or that you have been given permission to use with proper attribution.

IT'S ALWAYS A GOOD IDEA TO GET PERMISSION FIRST BEFORE USING AN IMAGE.

1. What do the elements <hr> and <img> have in common?

2. What is a link?

3. Why are links useful for websites?

4. Which part of the element below is the attribute?
<a href="www.myfavoritewebsite.com">Click Here</a>

5. Look at the lines of code below. Which element would you use to add a link to your website?
A. <link src="www.website.com">click here</link>
B. <link href="www.website.com">click here</link>
C. <a src="www.website.com">click here</a>
D. <a href="www.website.com">click here</a>

6. What type of attribute is shown in the element below?
<a href="www.allthelinks.com">All The Links</a>

7. What element should you use to add a picture to your site?

8. What type of attribute do you need to add the image file name to your image elements?

9. What is wrong with the following code?
`<a href="">click here</a>`

10. Circle the unnecessary code in the following line:
`<img src="catapalooza.jpg"></img>`

CHECK YOUR ANSWERS

1. <hr> and <img> are both empty elements.

2. A link is a connection to another website or other content on the internet.

3. Links allow you to easily and instantly jump to other sites, information, videos, pictures, or pages.

4. <a href="www.myfavoritewebsite.com" >Click Here</a>

5. D

6. href

7. <img>

8. src

9. It's missing the web address between the quotation marks for the href attribute.

10. `<img src="catapalooza.jpg"></img>`
Because the `<img>` element is an empty element, a closing tag is unnecessary.

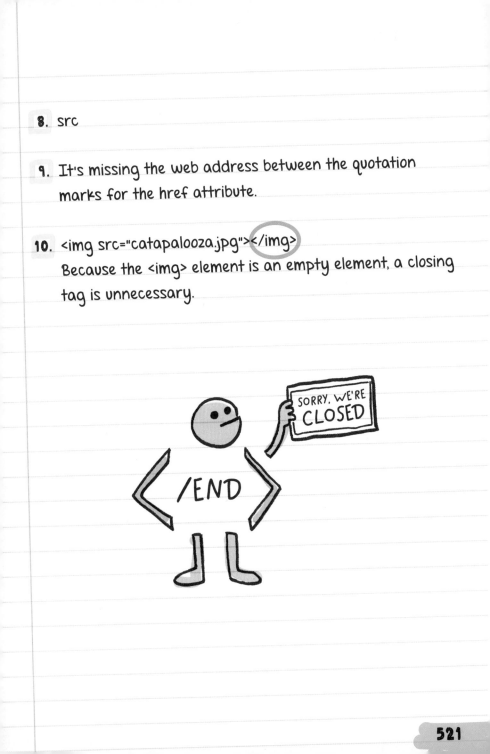

SORRY, WE'RE CLOSED

‹ /END ›

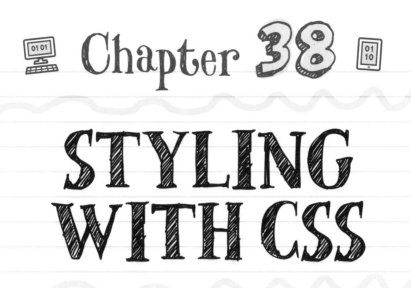

Chapter 38

STYLING WITH CSS

CASCADING STYLE SHEETS (CSS)

By itself, HTML makes useful websites, but it isn't great for making good-looking websites. **CASCADING STYLE SHEETS** (CSS) is the language used to add style to HTML files. CSS describes the color, size, layout, backgrounds, fonts, and other design features for websites. It also allows you to style your web page differently for different environments (like handheld devices, laptops, and desktops) while keeping the HTML content the same.

YOU'RE SO STYLISH.

There are different ways to add CSS to a website:

- You can add CSS directly to an HTML file in the head or as an attribute within each HTML element.

- You can make a separate CSS file to store the information. This makes your code easier to read and to organize.

MAKING A CSS FILE

This is the better way!

To make a new CSS file, use the same editor that you used to make an HTML file (TextEdit or Notepad). You can name a CSS file anything, but many programmers save a website's CSS file as **style.css**. For simplicity, save your CSS file in the same folder as your HTML file.

Creating a CSS Style

STYLES are made by pairing a **SELECTOR** with **DECLARATIONS**.

A selector assigns the style to a particular element in the HTML file. The selector is the name of the element without the <> brackets.

> **STYLE**
> A specific change to how HTML content looks

A declaration is the change in appearance. For example, you can make text purple or put borders around images.

Selector = elements to be styled
Declaration = what the new style should look like

Add curly brackets around the declaration(s). Add an indent for each declaration to keep the code clean. Like HTML, CSS doesn't pay attention to white space. If you deleted all the spaces and indents, the code would run the same.

FOR EXAMPLE, you could type this code into a .css file to change all the <h1> heading elements in a website to appear blue:

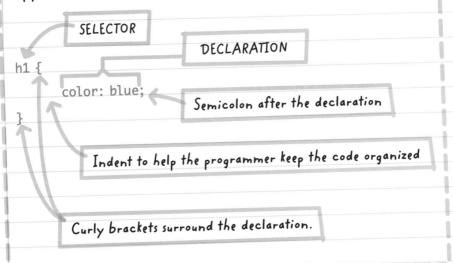

SELECTOR

DECLARATION

```
h1 {
    color: blue;
}
```

Semicolon after the declaration

Indent to help the programmer keep the code organized

Curly brackets surround the declaration.

Formatting the style with the declaration indented on a separate line and with the closing curly bracket on the bottom line is only a suggestion to help the programmer read the text more easily. The programmer could write all the code on a single line like this **h1{color:blue;}** and the computer would read it the same.

Linking Your CSS and HTML Files

Before the new styles from a CSS file can be applied to a website, the files need to be linked. You can apply the styles in a CSS file to an HTML website by adding an element to the head of the HTML. The link element needs three attributes:

1. The **REL ATTRIBUTE** stands for "relationship" and tells what the relationship is to the file you are linking in the <link> element. When the value is "stylesheet," you're telling the browser that you want the referenced file to be used as the CSS style sheet for the website.

a template that shows style and layout settings

2. The **TYPE ATTRIBUTE** says what type of file it is—for example a text/CSS file.

3. The **HREF ATTRIBUTE** identifies the name and location of the CSS file. If the CSS file is in the same location as the HTML file, then you just need to add the file name.

This is the format to link "style.css" to an HTML file using the link element:

```
<head>

    <link rel="stylesheet" type="text/css" href="style.css">

</head>
```

rel attribute

type attribute: Specifies this as a CSS file

href attribute: Name of the CSS file

Sometimes programmers store their CSS files in a separate folder (usually called "css") on their website's server. If you do this, add the folder name and a forward slash to the href value like this:

folder name

```
<head>
    <link rel="stylesheet" type="text/css" href="css/style
    .css">
</head>
```

This <link> element, with all its attributes, tells the web browser to find the file "style.css" and apply the styles from that file to this HTML document.

After linking a CSS file to an HTML file, any changes made to the CSS will change how the website is displayed when the browser is refreshed.

CSS COLOR ATTRIBUTES

There are three properties that you can use in a style to change the color of a web page.

Color changes the color of the text within an element.

Background changes the background color of the space that the element takes up. For example, setting the background color of the <body> element to gray will turn the entire page gray, but turning the background of a <p> element pink will only turn the background of the paragraph pink.

Border color changes the color of the border if an element has a border. If there is no border, this style will do nothing.

border = color

There are a few different ways to specify a color using CSS:
color names
HEX
RGB

Color Names

COLOR NAMES is a set of 147 colors that have been given specific names and can be used in CSS.

Using named colors is convenient because you don't have to memorize or look up color codes. But it can be limiting because there are only 147 colors.

FOR EXAMPLE, you can use the named color "red" as a value for a color property to represent pure red.

Format color references like this: **property: value;**

PROPERTY

color: red;

VALUE (THE NAMED COLOR: RED)

Examples of color names:

Tomato Orange DodgerBlue Medium SeaGreen

Gray SlateBlue Violet LightGray

FOR EXAMPLE, you can make an <h1> header element text tomato red using the value "tomato" with the color property:

```
h1 {
    color: tomato;
}
```

Hexadecimal (HEX)

HEXADECIMAL, or HEX, is a type of code used to represent over 16 million colors. The code uses 6 characters and combines the numbers 0-9 and letters A-F.

In CSS, every HEX color code begins with "#". For example, the HEX value for the color pure red is: #FF0000. There are many shades of red, each with a different value. For example, #700000 is a much darker shade of red than pure red.

RGB

RGB stands for "red, green, blue" and is another type of code for representing the same colors that HEX does. RGB code uses three values (numbers 0-255) to say how much red, green, or blue is in the color. The number 0 means there is no color, and the number 255 means there is the highest amount of that color.

The first value in the code represents the amount of red, the second value is for green, and the third value represents blue: (red, green, blue).

FOR EXAMPLE, the code below represents pure red:

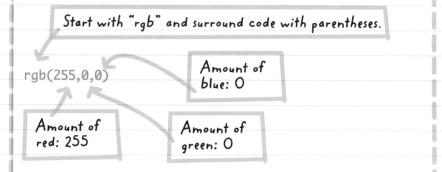

Start with "rgb" and surround code with parentheses.

rgb(255,0,0)

Amount of blue: 0

Amount of red: 255

Amount of green: 0

The value shows that the highest amount of red is present in the color, with zero amounts of green or blue.

Here's what it would look like to set the background color to the same shade of light gray using the color name, HEX, and RGB values (all these styles would produce the same results):

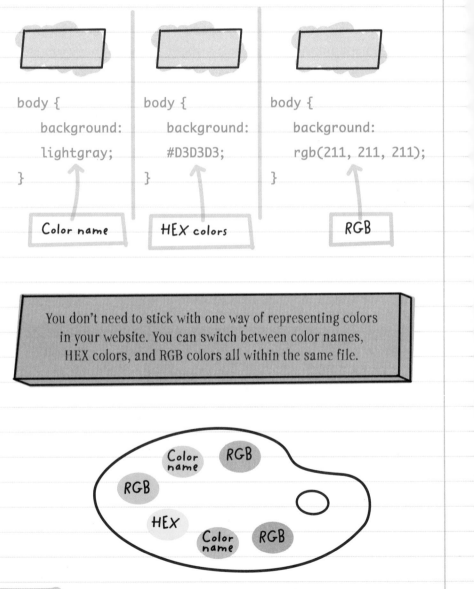

```
body {
    background:
    lightgray;
}
```
↑ Color name

```
body {
    background:
    #D3D3D3;
}
```
↑ HEX colors

```
body {
    background:
    rgb(211, 211, 211);
}
```
↑ RGB

You don't need to stick with one way of representing colors in your website. You can switch between color names, HEX colors, and RGB colors all within the same file.

ELEMENT-SPECIFIC PROPERTIES

Some elements, like tables and lists, have properties that are used only for their element (unlike general color properties).

FOR EXAMPLE, you can change the bullet style of an unordered list using the list-style-type property along with one of the specified values shown below:

This is the default

disc ●   square ■

circle ○   none   (no bullet point is displayed, just the text)

If you wanted to display an unordered list using squares instead of the discs, you could insert the CSS code into your style sheet that selects the <ul> element and use the description shown below:

```
ul {
    list-style-type: square;
}
```

Most programmers don't memorize all the properties and values associated with every element available in HTML. You can look up CSS properties and values on the internet.

COMMENTS

Comments keep your styles organized so that when the CSS document becomes longer, it's easy to locate different pieces of code.

Comments in CSS are ignored by computers.

In CSS, comments start with /* and end with */.

FOR EXAMPLE, you can add a comment in a CSS file labeling "Heading styles" like this:

```
/* Heading styles */   ←   comment
h1 {
        color: tomato;
}

h2 {
        color: #D3D3D3;
}
```

---

1. What does CSS stand for?

2. What are two ways that you can use CSS with your HTML code?

3. What is CSS used for?

4. Comments in CSS start and end with _____.

5. What CSS code would you write to make an entire website's background violet?

6. The code below has a bug in it. What needs to be added to fix it?

```
h1
    color: gray;
}
```

7. Label the property and value in the declaration shown below.

color: orange;

_____ _____

8. What does the selector do in a CSS style?

9. Which property do you need to use to change the color of the line in an <hr> element?

10. Which property do you need to use to change the color of the text in an <h1> heading element?

CHECK YOUR ANSWERS

1. Cascading style sheets

2. CSS can be placed directly into an HTML file, or you can create a separate CSS file and link it to the HTML file.

3. Styles like colors, sizes, fonts, and other designs for websites

4. /* and */

5. body {
        background: violet;
    }

6. The opening curly bracket needs to be added.
    h1 {
        color: gray;
    }

7.   color: orange;
         ↓   ↓
    ___property___   ___value___

8. The selector is used to specify which elements the style should apply to. For example, a style with the "p" selector will apply to all <p> elements.

9. border-color

10. color

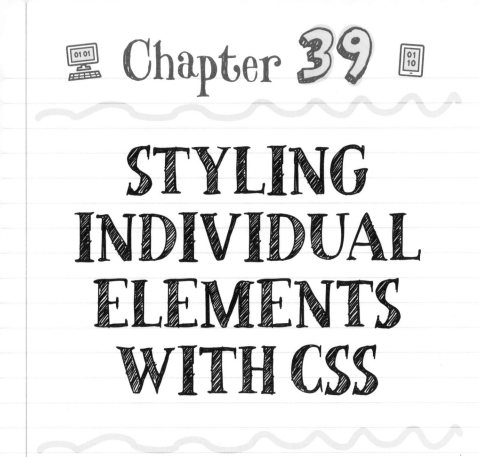

Chapter 39

STYLING INDIVIDUAL ELEMENTS WITH CSS

IDENTIFYING AN ELEMENT

ID (IDENTIFIER) SELECTORS are like name tags—they identify a specific element and apply CSS styling to it. An id name within a CSS document says, "This style applies only to the element with this id."

When using id attributes, you must work in both the CSS and the HTML documents.

CSS Id Selector

You can create an id selector for a CSS style that will be applied to a specific element in an HTML file. Instead of using the element name, like "p," as the selector for the new style, type "#" and an id name. The id name can be anything you want, but no spaces are allowed. You can make an id selector called "introduction" and assign it a style that has a font size of 18 **PIXELS** like this:

> **px** stands for **pixel** and is one of the ways of measuring font (type) size. The standard font size on websites is 16 px, which is the same size as the 12-point font in Microsoft Word.

```
#introduction {
    font-size: 18px;
}
```

A **pixel (px)** is also the smallest point of light on a screen. If you look very closely at a screen, you can see tiny dots. Each one of those dots is a pixel. Step back from the screen and all the dots blend together to make a clear image.

HTML Id Attribute

Attributes are added to tags to give the computer more information about the element. Use the id attribute to identify the element you want to style with the CSS code you added to the CSS file. For example, you can insert an id attribute called "introduction" to identify a <p> element within the web page:

Add this code here to the opening <p> tag.

```
<p id="introduction">Oh, hello there! . . .</p>
```

With the addition of the id attribute, this <p> element will now be styled according to the #introduction style created in CSS, and the font size for "Oh, hello there! . . ." will be set to 18 px when displayed on the website.

THE CLASS SELECTOR

The **CLASS SELECTOR** is used to style a group of elements. The class selector identifies multiple elements and applies the same style to all of them.

When using the class selector, you must work in both the CSS and the HTML documents. For example, you can use the class selector to make the text blue in two of the three paragraphs in a website.

CSS Class Selector

To create a class selector for a CSS style, type a period (.) and a class name. The class name can be anything you want, but no spaces are allowed. You can make a class selector called "overview" and assign it a style where the text color is blue:

```
.overview {
    color: blue;
}
```

HTML Class Attribute

You can add a class attribute to specific <p> elements by typing **class=** and the class name.

FOR EXAMPLE, you can insert a class called "overview" to identify two <p> elements within the page:

Add this code to the opening <p> tag.

```
<p class="overview">Oh, hello there! . . .</p>
<p class="overview">On this site we . . .</p>
<p>To learn more about . . .</p>
```

These two paragraphs will display in blue text on the website.

Classes can be added to multiple elements, even if the elements are not the same type. You could also add the class to headings and it would turn the heading blue:

Add the class attribute and "overview" value.

```
<h1 class="overview" >Introducing . . .</h1>
```

IMPORTANT: Be very careful with spelling and capitalization. If you spell or capitalize the id or class in the HTML file differently than the way you spell and capitalize it in the CSS file, the style won't be applied correctly. If the text isn't showing up the way you intended, the first thing you should check is spelling and capitalization.

WIDTH AND HEIGHT

The CSS properties **width** and **height** allow you to resize elements like images, lists, and paragraphs.

When it's describing the width or height of an image, px represents how many pixels wide or tall the object should be.

When resizing images, if you resize just the width, the height will automatically scale to match the width.

and 200 px tall,
and you set the
width to 200 px
wide, the height
will automatically
scale to 400 px
tall because the
width of this
image is half
of its height.

LOOKS LIKE WHAT I LEARNED IN MATH CLASS ABOUT RATIOS MAY COME IN HANDY.

To set an image on a website to 175 px wide, add this code to the CSS file:

```
img {
     width: 175px;
}
```

You can also size an image by percentage in relation to the size of the element block it is displayed in.

BORDERS, MARGINS, AND PADDING

You can use CSS to add space around images.

Borders add a colored frame around all elements including images, paragraphs, headings, and lists.

Margins and **padding** add blank space around an element. Padding is the space between the element's content and its border. The margin is the space between the border and the rest of the website.

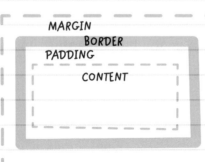

MARGIN
BORDER
PADDING
CONTENT

You can add a margin to an <img> element using the margin property in CSS.

Some properties, like the border property, are special because you can add more than one value in the same declaration.

For example, add "6px solid orange" as the values to make the borders 6 px thick, solid lines, and orange:

```
img {
        border: 6px solid orange;
}
```

Insert a semicolon at the end of each declaration.

To create a style that includes the margin, border, padding, and width of an image, you can combine all the declarations using a single img selector, with each new declaration on a new line:

```
img {
    margin: 10px;
    border: 6px solid orange;
    padding: 20px;
    width: 50%;
}
```

The style will set all <img> elements to have a margin of 10 px, a solid border that's 6 px wide and orange, a padding of 20 px, and a width of 50 percent of the width of the browser window.

> The declaration could also be written as **img {margin: 10px; border: 6px solid orange; padding: 20px; width: 50%;}**. The indents and separate lines make it easier for the programmer to read.

☆

CHECK YOUR KNOWLEDGE

1. What's the difference between the id selector and the class selector in CSS?

2. Px stands for _____.

3. Id selectors in CSS always begin with what symbol?

4. In CSS, class selectors have a _____ before the class name.

5. If you want to change the size of a picture, which CSS properties should you use?

6. Which provides space between the element content and the border: margin or padding?

7. Refer to the table on the next page to answer questions 7A-D.

   A. What code should you add to make the <p> element with the content "Good Luck!" display in tomato red text? Where should you add it and in which file?

HTML FILE: "INDEX.HTML"	CSS FILE: "STYLE.CSS"

``html
<!DOCTYPE html>
 	
<html>
<head>
    <title>Test Prep</title>
    <link rel="stylesheet"
type="text/css"
    href="style.css">
</head>
<body>
<h1>This is a test</h1>
<p>Things to remember:</p>
<ul>
    <li>Don't stress out</li>
    <li>Keep Calm and Test On<//li>
    <li>Do your best!</li>
</ul>
<p>Good Luck!</p>
</body>
</html>
``
	``css
	#redText {
	        color: tomato;
	}
	li {
	        font-size: 24px;
	}
	.border {
	        border: 2px solid
	        gray;
	}
	``

B. What code should you use to add a 2 px solid gray border to both the <h1> heading and the second list element? Where should you add it and in which file?

C. What code should you modify to change the list item font size from 24 px to 16 px? Which file should you modify?

D. What code should you add to make all the listed items appear gray? Where should you add the code?

CHECK YOUR ANSWERS

1. The id selector is used to select a single element with the corresponding id, while the class selector is used to select multiple elements in the same class.

2. Pixel

3. #

4. Period

5. Width and height

6. Padding

7. **A.** You should add id="redText" to the last <p> element of the HTML file like this:

`<p id="redText">Good Luck!</p>`

B. You should add class="border" to the <h1> element and the second <li> element to the HTML file like this:

```
<body>
<h1 class="border">This is a test</h1>
<p>Things to remember:</p>
<ul>
    <li>Don't stress out</li>
    <li class="border">Keep Calm and Test On</li>
    <li>Do your best!</li>
</ul>
<p>Good Luck!</p>
</body>
```

C. You should modify the "font-size: 24px;" declaration in style with the "li" selector to say "font-size: 16px;" in the CSS file like this:

```
li {
    font-size: 16px;
}
```

D. You should add this new declaration to the style with the "li" selector in the CSS file:

```
li {
    font-size: 16px;
    color: gray;
}
```

Index

SYMBOLS

=	assignment operator, 151	
+	addition operator, 342-343, 357	
-	subtraction operator, 357	
*	multiplication operator, 357	
\	division operator, 357	
==	is equal to operator, 168, 170, 376-377, 403	
>	is greater than operator, 168, 376-377, 403	
>=	is greater than or equal to operator, 168, 376-377, 403	
#	hashtag, 50, 316, 530, 540	
<	is less than operator, 168, 376-377, 403	
<=	is less than or equal to operator, 168, 376-377, 403	
!+	is not equal to, 168, 376-377, 403	
%	modulus, 357	
**	exponential, 357	
//	floor division, 357	

INDEX

A

abacus, 13
abstraction, 141, 143
access, authorized, 463–466
access control, 465
accessibility, 90
"Accessibility" settings, 30
adding lists, 371
addition, string, 342–345
age-appropriate content, 90
algebraic expressions, 155
algorithm design, 141, 143
algorithms
    about, 110–111
    basic, 223–246
    creating, 133–135
    definition of, 6
    description of, 6–7
    studying, 111–112
    using, 110–120
alpha testing, 91
American Standard Code for Information
    Interchange (ASCII), 130
analysis, description of, 8
Analytical Engine, 115–116
anchor elements, 513–515
AND statements, 171–174, 288, 407, 409–410
animating a cat, 225–232
append function, 369, 372
Apple II, 15
application/application software (apps), 17,
    21. See also programs; software
Arduinos, 72
arrays, 157, 247
artificial intelligence (AI) programs, 42,
    140–141
assigning values, 324–325
assignment operators, 151
attacks, 470–475
attributes
    about, 514–515
    color, 528–532
    href, 514–515, 527
    id, 541
    rel, 526
    src, 515–517
    type, 527

attributions, 101–103
authentication, 464–465
authorized access, 463–466

B

Babbage, Charles, 115
backdrops, 216, 276
back-end languages, 122–123
background, 528
backpack area, 206–207
bar graphs, 62
base 2, 126
base 10, 126
basic algorithms, 223–246
basic conditional statements, 284
basic loops, 278–280
Berners-Lee, Tim, 448
beta testing, 91–92
binary code
    about, 123–125
    description of, 48
    representing letters using, 130
    representing numbers using, 126–129
bitmap mode, 211
bits, 131
black hat hackers, 470
blank lines, printing, 340
blind users, 30–31
blocks
    about, 200–207
    for animating a cat, 225–232
    Boolean, 254, 256–259, 279, 284, 287–288
    broadcast, 276–277
    C blocks, 274, 278–283
    cap blocks, 274
    clone, 293
    control, 273–274, 291–293
    event, 224, 275–277, 289–290
    extensions for, 217–218
    glide, 230–232
    go to, 231
    hat, 224–225
    looks, 237–239
    making your own, 299–302
    math, 254–255
    motion, 215, 234–236
    My Blocks, 306

nesting, 258, 278
operators, 254–259, 263–265
pen, 229, 242–243
procedure, 299–302
procedure call stack, 300
repeat, 273
reporter, 247–251, 254, 263–265
running, 223–224
sensing, 266–268
sound, 240–241
stack, 224
turn, 228–229
types of, 224–225
variables in, 247–253, 260–263
blocks menu, 202–203
body of function, 431
<body> element, 486–487
BOMBE, 469
Boolean, George, 157
Boolean blocks, 254, 256–259, 279, 284, 287–288
Boolean values/expressions
    about, 156–157, 247
    comparison operators in, 168–171
    in compound conditional statements, 407–411
    in conditional statements, 403
    in Python, 323–324, 374–377
border color, 529
borders, 546–548
broadcast blocks, 276–277
brute force attacks, 470–471
build step, as part of engineering design process, 71
built-in variables, 250–251
bytes, 131–132

C blocks, 274, 278–283
C++, uses for, 122–123
Caesar cipher, 468–469
calculations
    with number variables, 351–352
    operators for, 254–259
calling a function, 315, 430–431
calling procedures, 193–194, 300
camel case (mixed case), 329
cap blocks, 274
capitalization, 315
capitalize function, 347
cascading style sheets (CSS), 523–538

about, 481–482, 523–524
class selector in, 543
color attributes in, 528–532
colors in, 50
comments in, 534
element-specific properties in, 533–534
id selector in, 540–541
linking HTML files and, 526–528
making file for, 524–528
styling individual elements with, 539–553
cat, animating, 225–232
CDs (compact discs), 13, 18
census data, 61
central processing unit (CPU), 18–19
charts, 61, 63
ciphers, 467–469
citations, 103
class selector, 541–544
clone blocks, 293
cloning, 303–305
code
    definition of, 46
    how computers read, 123–132
    HTML, 481–483, 484, 488–490
    machine, 124–125
    in Python, 314–315
    reusing, 191–196
coding, early days of, 115–116
collaborating, 97–108
color attributes, CSS, 528–532
color coding, in Python, 317
color names, CSS, 529–532
colors
    encoding, 48–51
    representing, 51
Colossus Mark 1, 14
command-line interface (CLI), 30
commenting out, 82
comments
    about, 81–83
    attributions in, 101–102
    in CSS, 534
    in HTML code, 490
    in Python, 315–316
    in Scratch, 205
community, getting help from, 101–102
comparison operators, 168–170, 256–259, 376–377
compilers, 125

compiling, definition of, 124
compound conditional statements, 171–174, 285–288, 407–411
computable responses, 58
computational thinking, 139–146
computer, definition of, 2
computer networks, 444–447
computer science
    concept areas of, 6–9
    description of, 2–12
computer scientists, work of, 4
computer systems, designing, 68–72
computer technology, uses of, 3
computers
    description of, 13–27
    human-computer interaction, 29–37
    impacts of, 9
    as information processors, 41
    interacting with, 29–37
    parts of, 16–23
    reading code and, 123–132
    through time, 14–15
computing systems
    definition of, 2
    description of, 6
conditional statements, 163–178
    about, 163–167
    basic, 284
    comparison operators in, 168–170
    compound, 171–174, 285–288, 407–411
    elif statements, 405–406
    else if statements, 165–166, 174
    else statements, 165, 404–405
    nested, 174–175, 285–288, 411–414
    in procedures, 302
    in Python, 403–422
    in Scratch, 283–288
    while loops, 181, 393–397
conditionals (C blocks), 274
consumers, 4
content
    age-appropriate, 90
    of websites, 484
control blocks, 273–274, 291–293
convert function, 433–435
costume list, 210
costumes, 209–210, 237–239
countdowns, 386
counter variables, 381–386
cracking a code or cipher, 468
creating a web page, 481–496

creators, 4
credit, 101–102
cryptography, 466–469
CSS. See cascading style sheets (CSS)
cybersecurity, 463–479

D

data
    about, 43–46
    definition of, 8
    description of, 8
    encoding, 47–51
    information flow and, 19–20
    types of, 323–324
    using, 61–63
data encoding schemes, 47–48
deaf users, 30–31
debugging programs
    commenting out and, 82
    description of, 31, 32
    in Scratch, 233
declarations, 524–526
declaring procedures, 191–193
declaring variables, 150
decoding information, 47
decomposition, 141–142
decryption, 467–469
defensive programming, 73–76
defining a function, 430
diagrams for troubleshooting, 32
distributed denial-of-service (DDoS) attacks, 475
documenting, 81–88
domain name system (DNS) servers, 455–456
double quotation marks, 316
downloading information, 449–450
drivers, 100

E

editor window, 311, 313
efficiency, algorithms and, 111–112
efficient, definition of, 57
electrical circuits, 123
elements
    about, 484–486
    anchor, 513–515
    <body>, 486–487
    in cascading style sheets (CSS), 533–534, 539–553
    empty, 502
    formatting, 498–499

\<head\>, 486–487
heading, 497–498
height of, 544–546
HTML text, 497–509
\<html\>, 486
identifying, 539–541
image, 515–517
link, 511–521
list, 503–505
list item, 503–504
paragraph, 498–499
unordered list, 503–504
website, 486–487
of websites, 486–487
width of, 544–546
elif statements, 405–406
else if statements, 165–166, 174
else statements, 165, 404–405
empty elements, 502
encoding colors, 48–51
encoding data, 47–51
encryption, 467–469
engineering
    definition of, 68
    everyday, 72
engineering design process, 68–71
ENIAC, 14–15
Enigma, 469
equal signs, 151
escaping a character, 338–339
ethernet, 445–446
event blocks, 224, 275–277, 289–290
event handlers, 188
events, 187–190
expectations, setting clear, 98
expressions, mathematical, 356–357
extension
    .html, 482–483
    .py, 313
extensions, 217
external actions, 188

F
Facebook, programming languages for, 122
feedback, incorporating, 89–96
files, saving, 313
float function, 355
floats, 352, 354–355
flowcharts
    comparison operators in, 169–170
    for conditional statements, 406

creating algorithms and, 133–135
else if statements in, 167
else statements in, 165
if . . . then statements in, 164
logical operators in, 172–173
nested conditionals in, 175
for three-letter word game, 412
for loops, 180, 381–392
forever loops, 278, 281
formatting elements, 498–499
formatting for loops, 381
formatting HTML, 488–490
formatting strings, 338–340
formatting variable names, 328–329
404 Not Found code (status code), 453
front-end languages, 122
functions
    append, 369, 372
    body of, 431
    calling, 315, 430–431
    capitalize, 347
    convert, 433–435
    defining, 430
    definition of, 192
    float, 355
    input, 344–345
    insert, 369–370, 372
    int, 354
    len, 371, 372
    lists and, 367–372
    lower, 346–347
    premade, 103
    print, 314–315, 334–337, 367–368
    procedures and, 423
    in Python, 311, 314–315, 423–442
    range, 382–388
    remove, 370, 372
    reverse, 370–371, 372
    sort, 370, 372
    string, 345–347
    swapcase, 347
    turtle art, 428–429
    turtle graphics, 423–429
    upper, 347

G
game developers, 21
gigabytes, 132
glide block, 230–232
go to block, 231
graphical user interface (GUI), 30

graphics processing unit (GPU), 19
graphs, 61-62
grid system, 214-215

H
hackers, 469-470
hacktivists, 470
hardware
  closer look at, 17-20
  description of, 16
  as part of computing systems, 23
hat blocks, 224-225
<head> element, 486-487
heading elements, 497-498
height of elements, 544-546
hexadecimal (HEX) color notation, 48, 49-50, 51, 530, 532
Hollerith Tabulating Machine, 61
Hopper, Grace, 125
horizontal rules, 499-501
hosts, 452
href attribute, 514-515, 527
HTML code, 481-483, 484, 488-490
.html extension, 482-483
HTML files, 452, 526-528
HTML text elements, 497-509
<html> element, 486
Hubble Space Telescope, 132
human-computer interaction, 29-37
hyperlinks, 511-512
hypertext markup language (HTML)
  basic web pages and, 481-483
  class selector in, 543-544
  definition of, 448, 481
  description of, 452
  extension for, 482
  formatting, 488-490
  id attribute, 541
  web browsers and, 484
hypertext transfer protocol (HTTP), 448, 453
hypertext transfer protocol secure (HTTPS), 453

I
id (identifier) selectors, 539-541
identifiers, 148-149, 152-153, 324
identifying an element, 539-541
IDLE (integrated development environment program), 311
if . . . then statements, 163-167

if then statements, 283
if then else statements, 283
image editor, 211
image elements, 515-517
images
  borders, margins, and padding for, 546-548
  resizing, 544-546
impacts of computing, description of, 9
improve the solution, 71
incorporating feedback, 89-96
indentation, 383, 488
index, 366
infinite loops, 395-397
information
  collecting and using, 57-66
  data and, 44-45
  decoding, 47
  definition of, 45
  downloading, 449-450
Information Age, 40-41
information processors, 41
inner lists, 372-373
input
  description of, 17
  information flow and, 19-20
  user, 250-251, 344-345, 432-437
input data, 44, 46
input function, 344-345
insert function, 369-370, 372
int function, 354
integers, 352-354
internal actions, 188
internet, 444-462
  about, 447-449
  description of, 8-9
  sending information over, 449-450
  surfing web and, 451-458
  web versus, 451
internet service providers, 450
interviews, 58
iOS, 22
IP address, 449-450, 455
IP-internet protocol, 449

J
JavaScript
  interactivity and, 482
  uses for, 122
Julius Caesar, 468

K

key words in Python, 326
keys, 467
kilobytes, 132

L

languages
    back-end, 122–123
    front-end, 122
    JavaScript, 122, 482
    natural, 140
    PHP, 122, 482
    See also hypertext markup language
        (HTML); programming languages
len function, 371, 372
libraries, 103, 423
lidar, 42
line breaks, 499–501
line graphs, 62
linear scale questions, 60
link elements, 511–521
list elements, 503–505
list item element, 503–504
lists
    about, 365
    adding, 371
    changing properties of, 533
    functions and, 367–372
    HTML text and, 503–505
    inner, 372–373
    list elements, 503–505
    list item element, 503–504
    for loops and, 387–388
    operators and, 371
    ordered, 505
    punctuation for, 365–366
    in Python, 323–324, 365–374
    replacing values in, 368
    in Scratch, 251–253
    sorting, 370–371
    sound, 212
    sprite, 208–209
    symbols for, 365
    symbols for inner, 372–373
    variables and, 157, 247
    within lists, 372–374
local area networks (LANs), 445
logical operators, 171–174, 258, 407–411
looks blocks, 237–239
loop statements, 179–186
loops

basic, 278–280
forever loops, 278, 281
infinite, 395–397
for loops, 180, 381–392
nested, 182–183, 280–283, 397
in Python, 381–401
repeat loops, 278–279, 281–283
repeat until loops, 278–279
in Scratch, 274, 278–283
while loops, 181, 393–397
Lovelace, Ada, 115–117
lower function, 346–347
lowercase_and_underscores, 328

M

MAC (Media Access Control), 449
machine code, 124–125
Makey Makeys, 72
making your own blocks, 299–302
malware, 472
map apps, 41
margins, 546–548
math blocks, 254–255
mathematical expressions, 356–357
megabytes, 132
micro:bits, 72
mixed case (camel case), 329
mobile applications, programming
    languages for, 121
mobile developers, 21
modules, 423–424
Morse code, 47
motion blocks, 215, 234–236
moving the turtle, 424–427
multiple-choice questions, 59–60
My Blocks, 306

N

naming conventions, 328–329
naming variables in Python, 325–327
natural language, 140
navigation menus, 513
navigators, 100
negative integers, 77
nested conditional statements, 174–175,
    285–288, 411–414
nested loops, 182–183, 280–283, 397
nesting blocks, 258, 278
networks, description of, 8–9
Nexus, 448
NOT statements, 173–174, 288, 407, 411

number conversions, 355
number types, 352–355
numbers
  representing using binary, 126–129
  as variables, 323, 351–364
numeric values, 155–156

O ⌇⌇⌇⌇⌇⌇⌇⌇⌇⌇⌇⌇
observations, 60
open-ended questions, 59
operating systems, 22
operations, order of, 358–359
operators
  in expressions, 356
  lists and, 371
  logical, 171–174, 258, 407–411
  in Scratch, 254–259, 263–265
  string, 341–347
OR statements, 172–173, 288, 407, 409–410
order of operations, 358–359
ordered lists, 505
organization, in Python, 315–317
output
  description of, 20
  information flow and, 20
  in Python, 312
  return values, 434–437
output data, 44

P ⌇⌇⌇⌇⌇⌇⌇⌇⌇⌇⌇⌇
packets, 449, 456
padding, 546–548
pair programming, 100
paragraph elements, 498–499
parameter values, 314
parameters, 194–196, 226–227, 383, 432–437
paraphrasing, 103
parentheses, 227, 358–359
Pascal case, 329
password checker, 394–395, 397
passwords, cyberattacks and, 470–471
pattern recognition, 141, 142
PEMDAS (Please Excuse My Dear Aunt
  Sally), 358
pen blocks, 229, 242–243
personal identification numbers (PINs), 471
phishing, 474–475
PHP
  interactivity and, 482
  uses for, 122
pie charts, 63

pixels (picture element), 426, 540–541
place values, binary, 127–128
plain text files, for README files, 83
plan, as part of engineering design process,
  70
positive integers, 77
premade functions, 103
print function, 314–315, 334–337, 367–368
printing mathematical expressions, 359
problem, identifying, 69–70
procedure blocks, 299–302
procedure call stack block, 300
procedures, 191–198
  calling, 193–194, 300
  conditional statements in, 302
  declaring, 191–193
  functions and, 423
processing, description of, 18–19
programming
  defensive, 73–76
  description of, 6–7
  early days of, 115–116
  pair, 100
  See also Python; Scratch
programming languages, 121–138
  about, 121
  creating algorithms and, 133–135
  description of, 113
  how computers read code, 123–132
  using, 122–123
programs
  algorithms and, 112–114
  applications versus, 17
  definition of, 6
  as part of computing systems, 6
  See also application/application
    software (apps); software
prompt, in Python, 311
protocols, 445–446
pseudocode, 133, 182
punch cards, 116
punctuation
  being careful with, 315
  for lists, 365–366
  See also symbols; individual punctuation
    marks
.py extension, 313
Python
  algorithms and, 113–114
  code in, 314–315
  color coding in, 317

conditional statements in, 403–422
functions in, 311, 314–315, 423–442
getting started in, 310–321
key words in, 326
lists and Boolean expressions in, 365–380
for loops in, 381–392
loops in, 381–401
numbers as variables in, 351–364
organization in, 315–317
prompt in, 311
reserved words in, 153
strings in, 333–350
uses for, 122–123
variables in, 323–332, 351–364
while loops and nested loops in, 393–401

Q

quotation marks
    for comments, 316
    in print function, 335
    in strings, 333–334, 338–339

R

radar, 42
raindrops, 303–305
RAM, 18
range function, 382–388
ransomware, 472
rational numbers, 77
README files, 83–84, 101–102
rel attribute, 526
remove function, 370, 372
repeat blocks, 273
repeat loops, 278–279, 281–283
repeat until loops, 278–279
reporter blocks, 247–251, 254, 263–265
reserved words, 153
return values, 196, 434–437
reusing scripts, 299–308
reverse function, 370–371, 372
RGB color notation, 48, 49, 51, 131, 531–532
roles, creating clear, 99
Ruby, uses for, 122
running blocks, 223–224

S

sandboxing, 466
say block, 227
scanners, 48–49
Scratch
    about, 200

basic algorithms in, 223–246
blocks in, 200–207, 215, 217–218
blocks types in, 234–243, 260–268,
    289–293
cloning in, 303–305
conditional statements in, 283–288
control blocks in, 273–274
data and operators in, 247–272
debugging strategies for, 233
event blocks in, 275–277
getting started in, 200–222
loops in, 278–283
making your own blocks in, 299–302, 306
operators in, 254–259, 263–265
reusing scripts in, 299–308
sharing projects in, 217
sprites in, 208–216
Scratch cat, 225–232
screen readers, 31
scripts, 223–246
    about, 223–224
    animating a cat with, 225–232
    debugging strategies for, 233
    description of, 203–204
    reusing, 299–308
    storing, 206–207
    walk, 226–230
    See also blocks
scripts area, 204
selectors, 524–526
self-driving cars, 42
sensing blocks, 266–268
servers, 452
shell window, 311–312
single quotation marks, 316, 336
slide rules, 14
smartphones, 13, 15
social engineering, 474–475
social media apps, 41–42, 474–475
software
    closer look at, 21–23
    description of, 16
    as part of computing systems, 23
    system, 22
    troubleshooting strategies and, 33
    See also application/application
        software (apps); programs
sort function, 370, 372
sorting lists, 370–371
sound blocks, 240–241
sound editor, 212

sound list, 212
sounds, for sprites, 212
sprite lists, 208–209
sprites, 200, 208–216, 225–232
spyware, 472
src attribute, 515–517
stack blocks, 224
stage, 213–216
start parameter, 383
status code (404 Not Found code), 453
step parameter, 383
stop parameter, 383
storage, description of, 18
storing information, 40–55
storing scripts, 206–207
strengths, focusing on, 98
string addition, 342–345
string functions, 345–347
string operators, 341–347
string values, 263
strings
    description of, 154
    formatting, 338–340
    in Python, 323–324, 333–350
styles, 524–526
styling with CSS, 523–538
subroutines, 280–283
surveys, 58–60
swapcase function, 347
symbols
    #, 316
    =, 151
    >>>, 311
    backslash, 338
    for Boolean expressions, 403
    comparison operators, 168–170, 376
    for CSS comments, 534
    double quotation marks, 316
    for HTML comments, 490
    for inner lists, 372–373
    for mathematical operations, 357
    parentheses, 227, 358–359
    quotation marks, 316, 333–334, 335,
        338–339
    single quotation marks, 316, 336
    underscore (_), 152
syntax, 314, 315
system software, 22
systematic approach to troubleshooting,
    31–32

tags, 484–486, 488–489, 497–498
team, working on a, 97–99
terabytes, 132
test cases, 74, 75–76
testing, 71, 73–80, 82
text displays, on multiple lines, 336
text editors, 482
three-letter word game, 411–414
thumbnail images, 208–209
timelines, setting realistic, 98
touch screens, 20
Transmission Control Protocol (TCP), 456–457
Traveling Salesperson Problem, 112
Trojan horse, 472
troubleshooting
    definition of, 31
    strategies for, 32–33
    See also debugging programs
truth tables, 410–411
Turing, Alan, 469
turn block, 228–229
turtle graphics, 423–429
Twitter, programming languages for, 122
two-factor authentication, 465
type attribute, 527

underscore symbol, 152
Uniform Resource Locator (URL), 454
unordered list elements, 503–504
upper function, 347
usability, 90
USB flash drives, 18
use cases, 74–75
User Datagram Protocol (UDP), 458
user input, 250–251, 344–345, 432–437
user interface (UI), 29–31
user-centered design, 89–91

values
    assigning, 324–325
    in expressions, 356
    numeric, 155–156
    replacing in lists, 368
    return, 196, 434–437
    returning, 196
    variable, 148–151
variables, 148–162
    about, 148–149

assigning and naming, 150–153
built-in, 250–251
calculations with number, 351–352
changing value of string, 337
counter, 381–386
declaring, 150
formatting names of, 328–329
naming, 325–327
naming with strings, 334
numbers as, 323, 351–364
parameters, 194–196
in Python, 323–332, 351–364
in Scratch, 247–253, 260–263
types of information stored by, 154–157
See also conditional statements
vector mode, 211
video conference services, 458
viruses, 464, 473

W 〰〰〰〰〰〰〰
walk script, 226–230
web. See World Wide Web
web browsers, 483, 484
web developers, 21
web pages
    creating basic, 492–496
    programming languages for, 121
websites
    accessing, 451–453
    building blocks of, 481–482

content of, 484
definition of, 121
elements of, 486–487
finding, 454–456
programming languages for, 122
tools for writing, 482–483
viewing, 483
while loops, 181, 393–397
white hat hackers, 469–470
wide area networks (WANs), 445
width of elements, 544–546
wi-fi, 446
Windows, 22
wireless, 445–446
workloads, equal, 99
World Wide Web
    origin of, 448–449
    surfing, 451–458
    using internet to surf, 451–458
    See also web pages; websites
worms, 473

X 〰〰〰〰〰〰〰
x- and y-coordinates, 214–215
xp (experience points), 154

Y 〰〰〰〰〰〰〰
YouTube, programming languages for, 122